W. A. Baille-Grohman

Sport in the Alps

In the Past and Present

W. A. Baille-Grohman

Sport in the Alps
In the Past and Present

ISBN/EAN: 9783743427662

Manufactured in Europe, USA, Canada, Australia, Japa

Cover: Foto ©Andreas Hilbeck / pixelio.de

Manufactured and distributed by brebook publishing software (www.brebook.com)

W. A. Baille-Grohman

Sport in the Alps

SPORT IN THE ALPS

IN THE PAST AND PRESENT

AN ACCOUNT OF THE CHASE OF THE CHAMOIS, RED-DEER,
BOUQUETIN, ROE-DEER, CAPERCAILLIE, AND BLACK-
COCK, WITH PERSONAL ADVENTURES
AND HISTORICAL NOTES

AND

SOME SPORTING REMINISCENCES OF
H.R.H. THE LATE DUKE OF SAXE-COBURG-GOTHA

BY

W. A. BAILLIE-GROHMAN

AUTHOR OF 'TYROL AND THE TYROLESE,' 'CAMPS IN THE ROCKIES,' ETC.;
CONTRIBUTOR TO THE BADMINTON LIBRARY

MEMBER OF THE ALPINE CLUB

WITH NUMEROUS ILLUSTRATIONS AND PHOTOGRAPHS FROM LIFE

LONDON
ADAM AND CHARLES BLACK
1896

In Pleasant Memory

OF .

EARLY LESSONS IN STALKING

THESE PAGES ARE DEDICATED TO

LIEUT.-COLONEL L. SCHNORR VON CAROLSFELDT

CONTENTS

ILLUSTRATIONS

PRINTED SEPARATELY FROM THE TEXT

ILLUSTRATIONS

PRINTED IN THE TEXT

INTRODUCTION

HUNDREDS of books upon climbing and adventure in the Alps have appeared in the course of the last five-and-thirty years; dozens of Alpine Clubs have been established in all the hilly countries of Europe, thousands annually spend their holidays clambering about on the slopes of the Alps, while tens of thousands go sight-seeing to the same region. Is it not strange that during this period of great, not to say excessive, activity in connection with "Alpinism," not a single attempt has been made by English writers to describe the Alps from the standpoint of the sportsman?

To go back even to the days preceding the formation of the first Alpine Club—the English Alpine Club being the one that enjoys that honour—there existed only one book in the English language which deals with sport in the Alps. This is Charles Boner's *Chamois Shooting in the Bavarian Mountains*, published almost half a century ago. This classic treats, however, of only a small district of what the "climber" of to-day would describe as the foothills of the real Alps. A little book, *Tyrol and the Tyrolese*, which the writer published more than twenty years ago, though it contains

some chapters on sport of the rough kind, such as the hardy
natives enjoy, has, I fear, proved of little use to English
fellow-sportsmen desirous of reading up the subject with a
view of visiting the Alps for sport. Most of the great
mountain systems of the world were first visited by pioneer
British sportsmen, the climber following at a much later
period. That the contrary should be the case with that
great mountain system that is nearest to the British Isles,
of which many parts can, in fact, be reached in less time
than some of the more isolated forests north of the Tweed,
is, to say the least, a singular circumstance.

To the wish to fill in some measure this void in sporting
literature, must be ascribed the present attempt to do justice
to a subject with which a life-long acquaintance has made
me familiar.

This attempt of mine, as I may at once confess, leaves
almost unnoticed the very country which to the climbing
fraternity, as well as to the sight-seer, possesses the greatest
attraction, *i.e.* Switzerland. There are two reasons why I
have confined myself to the Central and Eastern Alps, dealing with the Western only in so far as is concerned that
minute portion situated on the Southern or Italian face,
which is the only remaining refuge of the Bouquetin.

The first and best reason is, that the Swiss Alps harbour
comparatively but few chamois, and no red-deer whatever.
Since the day when the battle of Sempach, 500 years
and more ago, decided the future republican rule of the
Northern cantons, the holding of large landed properties
became unconstitutional, and the chase was thrown open to
every adult native. Republican equality of civil rights and

game-preserving cannot, we know, exist side by side. For a modern illustration of this fatal effect of democratic rule upon *ferae naturae* we need but glance at those once choice hunting-grounds in the Western portion of the great Transatlantic republic. What has happened there of late years is but a repetition, on a large scale, of what occurred in Switzerland during the first century or two after that country's emancipation from monarchical government. There, even that most shy of all mountain game, the Bouquetin, which then, as now, inhabited only the most remote and inaccessible recesses of the snowy Alps, became practically extinct within that period. If this could happen, it need not be pointed out that the chamois and the red-deer had much less chance of escaping extermination.

It is true that within the last twenty years the Federal Swiss Government, by creating in 1876 three sanctuaries, have made praiseworthy efforts to re-stock certain Swiss mountain ranges with chamois, and that the local governments of certain cantons, by extending the close season to eleven months of the year, have shown a similar desire. But for obvious reasons no great head of game, enduring for more than one, or at the most two, seasons, is ever likely to result from these measures. A further difficulty obstructing the path of the stranger, is the regulation prohibiting non-residents to shoot chamois. Though in some districts this law, one is told, is often broken, it is not pleasant to place oneself at the mercy of informers.

The second and perhaps rather personal reason is that Switzerland, since fashion has made it the goal of ever-increasing crowds of holiday-makers, often of an objectionable

type, has lost its charm to one admirer of Alpine solitude
and unsophisticated mountain life. To view nature amid
surroundings to which one is condemned by this invasion,
is not an unalloyed pleasure. Fortunately there are wide and
beautiful districts left in the Alps which are as yet uninvaded
by fashionable crowds, and to these byeways the reader will
be invited to accompany the writer.

Two of the chapters will be found to relate to what, I
fear, may prove dry reading, viz. an account of the chase
of mountain game in old times. A fine day is supposed to
inspire the Englishman with an irresistible desire to go out
and kill something. But there are many days in the year
when this longing cannot be satisfied, and what better use
can be made of them, than to devote them to research in
library and archive, for is not the pleasure of reading how
somebody else went forth and slew the noble beast next to
going out and killing the great stag oneself?

If at the risk of being considered egotistical I have added
a chapter containing some personal reminiscences of my boyhood in the Alps, I have at least safeguarded the reader by
placing it at the end of the book, so that by thus reversing the usual order of things he may not be taken unawares. He has now received fair warning that the last
few pages are but a recital of the writer's apprenticeship
to Alpine venery, in those years of early youth that leave
their impress for life.

With the exception of three drawings by Mr. Caton-
Woodville, and those illustrations which are reproductions
from photographs or old prints, I am indebted to my wife
and Colonel von Schnorr for the pictorial matter in this book.

In conclusion, my thanks are due to the proprietors of the *Field* and the *English Illustrated Magazine* for their permission to republish some of the substance of articles that have appeared in the columns of these journals. ·

THE AUTHOR.

Schloss Matzen, Tyrol,
June 1896.

CHAPTER I

CHAMOIS-HUNTING IN THE OLD DAYS

FOUR hundred years ago sporting scribes, when instructing "princes and other high-born readers" in the ways of sport, admonished them to provide themselves with their barber-surgeon when they went to the forest to track the fierce wild boar, so that gashes inflicted by the quarry to man and beast might be at once dressed. When, however, they went in pursuit of the great hart or of the bear, their chaplain, rather than their barber-surgeon, should accompany them, for, said they, all that man can do when a hunter is gored by the one or mauled by the other, is to administer the last rites of the church, so that the door of heaven may be found at least on the latch. But if princes and highnesses would foolishly and rashly go into the snowy mountains in pursuit of a beast some call the chamois, over which gnomes and pixies hold watchful guard, the priest had best be left at home to read masses for the salvation of the sportsman's soul, while the barber-surgeon had best take with him a sack wherein to collect the bones when the eagles and wolves have picked them clean. For to return safe and sound from those weird wildernesses of ice and rock is only to be achieved by very special intercession of divine providence.

That the men who held such opinions were also devout believers in all kinds of nasty nostrums to "proof" oneself against evil spirits, vertigo and breathlessness, need hardly be mentioned. More interesting than a recital of their superstitions, will be a glance at the conditions which made the hunting of big game in the Alps in those days a far more riskful undertaking than it is to-day. In the first place, the arms then in use were of a most primitive kind. To tackle a wounded bear in his lair, or receive the charge of a cornered boar of the immense size then attained by these beasts, or to finish off a hart of great head when at last brought to bay by the hounds, the hunter only armed with a short spear or with the even less formidable sword-like *hanger*, was a feat calling for very different sporting attributes than does the shooting down, with repeating rifles at long ranges, of the much-degenerated modern progeny of these monarchs of medieval woods.

At the time to which we are referring, chamois-stalking was considered a very perilous sport, even if a good conscience and an ardently praying chaplain secured one against the machinations of the gnomes and pixies, whose mode of attack, we are told, was to overcome the daring hunter at the moment of greatest danger with an irresistible longing to throw himself down the giddy abyss at his side, or to loosen with invisible hand the rock on which he had gained a precarious foothold, and thus hurl him where eagles and wolves could perform their part of the obsequies. The chamois-hunter of those days set about his sport in a manner, it is safe to say, no modern brother craftsman would dream of imitating. He went into the mountains armed only with a spear-like javelin 9 or 10 feet in length, which he threw at his quarry. To get to such close quarters, as would enable men of even such giant's biceps as seem to have been possessed by these tough old Nimrods, called for sporting qualities of no mean order, for to corner chamois needs not only a perfect knowledge of the ground, but climbing powers such as would be the boast of any candidate for membership in the Alpine Club. Indeed, I can speak for one old Alpine Club man, who would consider such a task a hopeless one for him to attempt unaided. That this cornering of chamois was really performed in the days preceding the adaptation of firearms for hunting purposes, there is but little doubt, though we may safely assume that success in this particular feat was not attained without the assistance of others, who prevented the escape of the game from places where the hunter could get near enough to throw his javelin. With such assistance it is possible, though by no means easy, to spear the nimble mountain antelope. On several occasions the writer could have transfixed driven chamois when, utterly fagged by a long uphill flight in very hot weather, they passed his stand within a few yards, their mouths open and their tongues hanging out. But to spear chamois under other conditions, and without the assistance of beaters and stoppers, is, it is safe to say, impossible.

Another factor that made chamois-hunting appear such dangerous sport to our forefathers has already been touched upon, viz. the superstition that goblins and fairies were for ever guarding their favourites, and were only too ready to lure the daring intruder to destruction. Every phenomenon of Alpine life was connected with some occult power; the avalanches were the playthings of the snow-fairies, and when the heat of the summer's sun bared the lower slopes, the fairies bombarded the intruder with showers of stones. To sleep on a mountain was, until the middle of last century, considered a most reckless proceeding. While the enhanced violence with which thunder and lightning visit elevated

mountain regions, has to this day not lost in the minds of the
unsophisticated inhabitants a supernatural significance, as is
betokened in the more secluded glens by the ringing of all
the church bells and the sprinkling of holy water during the
outburst of the elements. It was this fear of unknown evil
consequences, which contributed so largely in delaying Alpine
exploration until comparatively modern days, and gave the
feat of Balmat's first ascent of Mont Blanc, little more than a
century ago (1786), the world-wide celebrity it did.

Under these circumstances the paucity of the literature
relating to chamois-hunting in olden days need not surprise
one. Two early black-letter works named *Weisskunig* and
Theuerdank,[1] and two manuscripts, constitute the principal
literary remains concerning chamois-hunting in the age that
witnessed the discovery of America. All four emanated
either directly from the pen, or, at any rate, must be considered as the creation of that famous old sportsman, Emperor
Maximilian (1459-1519), acknowledged by all his contemporaries as the Master of the Masters of the Chase, and
who was one of the few foreigners who proved himself
equal to British archers in the handling of the long-bow,
in the management of which the English, since the time
of Edward III., were acknowledged by all nations to have
been far and away the most skilled. Such strength had he
in his arms, that, as he himself relates in the first-named
work, he once shot a wooden arrow, on which there was no
iron whatever, through a plank of very hard larch wood
3 inches thick.[2]

The woodcuts, 354 in number, that adorn the printed
works, however primitive in their perspective and in their
artistic qualities, were drawn by the first artists of the time.

---

[1] In the Appendix will be found a more ample description of these works.
[2] The account says "3 Zwerch Finger breit," rather more than three
English inches. Seasoned larch wood is an exceedingly hard wood.

They form an exceedingly interesting and, in fact, unique series, treating the adventures of various kinds that befell Maximilian not only when hunting the chamois, the stag, the bear, and the wild boar, but when travelling in the many foreign lands he visited, and when engaged in the numberless battles, sieges, and skirmishes, in which he took a leading part, in his wars against the French, Hungarians, Turks, Italians, Swiss, and Venetians.

There are few figures, even in modern history, that appeal to such an extent to the sport and adventure-loving, as does that of the Last Knight, as Maximilian is often called ; and as for the subject of the present chapter, there would be very little to write, had not Maximilian left us the accounts to which I have alluded. The two manuscripts, though less known than the two printed works, are of as great interest to us, for they contain minute instructions concerning the chase of the chamois and the hart, the former, it is very evident, being the one to which the Emperor was most partial. They may be briefly described as, firstly, the Secret Hunting Book or Hunting Instructions, which is preserved in the Imperial Library in Vienna ; and secondly, a treatise on the same subject written at the Emperor's dictation by his Master of the Game, Charles von Spaur. It consists of 244 folio pages, embellished with several interesting miniatures, and is preserved in the Royal Library in Brussels.

These four works give one a fairly accurate idea of the manner in which the chase of the chamois was conducted by Maximilian, while some additional notes found in the archives at Innsbruck, the capital of the country, in which lay his favourite hunting-grounds, no less than some of his arms preserved in the Imperial Museums in Vienna, enable one to picture to oneself the personality of this bold climber and explorer of the mountain wilds. The goblins of the mountains seem to have inspired him with little dread, for the only

specific reference to supernatural powers one finds in his
Secret Instructions, is where he admonishes the Hapsburg
prince, who may be his successor on the throne, and for whose
benefit the little treatise is written, "to rise at three of the
clock so as to hear mass read" before starting on the
chamois chase, where death in various forms ever hovers on
the sportsman's tracks. Such sound advice, as to wear a stout
leathern cap to cover the skull, so as to protect the latter
against falling stones, and to have good care that the six
spikes of the crampons for one's feet are of the stoutest
make, show the practical turn of Maximilian's mind, and that
he knew perfectly well what he was about. Another proof
of this is afforded by the fact that, notwithstanding he was
probably one of the last sportsmen of great position who
ordinarily used the cross-bow (Charles V. being probably the
very last one), he yet found that this arm could be improved
and rendered safer to the bearer and his surroundings, when
carried on horseback or through thick woods, than it had
hitherto been. An accident, described in *Theuerdank*, which
nearly ended fatally for him, probably led him to invent the
trigger-catch, which prevented the arm going off while in any
other than a horizontal position.[1] For big game short arrows
with massive iron points were used, while for small game
lead bullets were preferred. Though, as a rule, different
cross-bows were used for arrows and bullets, there were such
that could be converted so as to use either. Maximilian
must have been an excellent shot with this arm, for he shot

---

[1] Cross-bows were furnished with such formidable bows of steel that to
bend them a portable hand windlass was employed, and as this took some
time, the sportsman, during the chase, carried the cross-bow bent ready to
be fired. One of Maximilian's cross-bows is in Vienna ; it was one of his
"light stalking bows"; his heavy arms must have been indeed most formidable
weapons. The steel bow is very nearly 4 inches wide, and half an inch
thick, and the bow string is 27 inches long. On the shaft is inscribed
in Gothic lettering, "Si Deus pro nobis quis contra nos." Maximilian
evinced a great partiality for cross-bows manufactured in the Low Countries.
The bow-strings came invariably from Antwerp.

ducks as they rose from the water, killing on one occasion 100 ducks with 104 shots. Once he killed 26 hares, without missing once, with one and the same arrow, though his biography does not mention how many of them were running

FIG. 1.—Steel Cross-bow of Maximilian's time, showing the attachment for the use of Balls.

(Preserved in the Royal Museum in Munich.)

shots. In winter, on account of great cold rendering steel dangerously brittle, Maximilian tells his successor he is to use in the chase of the chamois a cross-bow with a bow made of horn.[1] The "hand-gonne" or fire-tube, as the first exceed-

[1] The use of the English bow is only mentioned in connection with flying game in Maximilian's writings.

iugly primitive firearm used in the chase was called, was never used by the Emperor for chamois-hunting. Considering the smallness of the stock, unwieldy shape and great weight, which made it necessary to rest the long barrel on a forked prop, while applying a slow match to the touch-hole, this can hardly surprise us. In *Weisskunig* there is narrated the following incident, proving the superiority of the cross-bow, when in such skilled hands as those of Maximilian, over the hand-gonne of his day. Maximilian, accompanied by one Yörg Purgkhardt, who is described as a man most skilled in the use of the fire-tube, went out chamois-shooting. Coming upon a chamois standing high over their heads on a rock, the Emperor commanded Yörg to shoot the buck with his fire-tube, but the latter declared that the chamois was much too high up, and could not be reached by his bullet. Whereupon Maximilian, taking his cross-bow, said, " Look out, I shall kill that buck with my steel cross-bow," and really brought him down the very first shot, the distance being 100 *Klafter*, or over 200 yards.

But the Emperor's favourite manner of hunting the chamois was with the javelin, which of course was far more difficult than with the cross-bow, for to be successful it was necessary to get to close quarters and tread the dangerous paths and narrow ledges to which the game, when pressed, always takes refuge. This sporting spirit of desiring to come to close quarters with his game, distinguished Maximilian in a high degree. The more dangerous the foe, the greater the zest with which this courageous sportsman entered the fray. Hand-to-hand personal encounters, in which the skill, strength, or endurance of the hunter vanquished the ferociousness or fleetness of foot of the hunted beast, were the joy of his life. Maximilian would journey afar to meet single-handed a great bear or monster boar that had been marked to cover for him. And what enormous sizes those beasts then still attained we know from game registers, that give their weights as up to 900 and 800 lbs. respectively.

These beasts he would tackle on foot single-handed in their lair, armed either with the short hunting spear, with which, gripped firmly in both hands, the charge of the beast was received, or with his hunting sword or hanger. Maximilian's favourite hanger, by the way, is preserved in Vienna.[1] With either in his hand he seems to have feared no beast, and his adventures were of the most thrilling kind. When on horseback in pursuit of a big stag he would, when the cornered beast turned and charged, receive the infuriated beast at the point of the latter arm. But of all these various modes of pursuing game that resulted in dangerous hand-to-hand combats with the fiercest beasts of prey, none, according to his own accounts, brought him so often into deadly peril as the chamois chase with the javelin, or *Schaft*, as was its technical term. Swiftly moving avalanches, showers of stones, set in motion by beaters or by the game itself, shot chamois tumbling down upon the sportsmen from heights above, rocks giving way, the snapping of his alpenstock, the giving way in a most dangerous place of five of the six spikes of his crampon, slipping on narrow ledges and being saved from instant death by a quick leap into the top of a handy tree growing below, or, on another similar occasion, by clinging with one hand to a point of rock, are, one and all, adventures narrated by the Emperor, and quaintly illustrated by the pencil of Burgkmair, Schäuffelin, and Beck.

Maximilian's sporting establishment was very large, con-

---

[1] This sword is one of the finest pieces of armourer's work extant. The blade is 2 inches wide and 34 inches long. For three-fifths of its length the blade has one edge, for the rest of its length it is double-edged. For about two-thirds of its length the blade is "blued," in what was known to the Milan armourers as "alla sanguigna," which gave the steel that red shimmer it obtains when withdrawn from the body of a foe, be it human or animal. The hilt is a plain cross without guard, and is a masterpiece of the metal-chaser's art.

sisting of Masters of the Chase, Master of the Forest, keepers
and kennelmen by the hundred, for he had separate staffs
in most of the Austrian provinces, and in his kennels were
no fewer than 1500 hounds. The latter were, however,
chiefly used when other royal guests were present, to whom
the hardships of stalking were less welcome than they were
to Maximilian himself.[1]

In a few of the illustrations in Maximilian's works,
hounds figure in the chase of the chamois, but it does not
appear clearly for what purpose they were thus used, whether
for tracking the unwounded game, or running it for the
purpose of bringing it to bay, or lastly, whether their assistance was called in for the only purpose that hounds are now
ever used, as track-hounds in leash to follow the wounded
game. On average chamois ground running hounds could
never have been used, for they would speedily have come to
grief, even if they could have followed their quarry for any
distance over the precipitous ground, or along the minute
ledges on which the chamois, but no other animal except the
practically extinct bouquetin, can find a footing. It can
therefore be assumed that hounds, upon which in those days
even greater store was set than to-day, would not be brought
into use except for tracking wounded chamois.

How far this strong-armed old sportsman could throw
his javelin there is unfortunately no evidence, for the faulty
perspective in the pictures is anything but a trustworthy
guide. By the great care taken of these *Schäfte*, it would
seem that the men using them had acquired great skill.
Thus in his " Secret Instructions " the Emperor gives special
orders that, in order to keep the shafts perfectly true and
straight, they should be hung up in special boxes, some of
which by the way, we hear, were kept in the organ-lofts of

---

[1] Maximilian's first wife, Mary of Burgundy, first introduced into Germany
the French manner of stag-hunting.

churches. Very few collections possess specimens of these
chamois javelins; the one I was fortunate enough to secure
many years ago is 7 feet 8 inches long, but is not quite

FIG. 2.—Emperor Maximilian (1459-1519) spearing Chamois,
the Ladies of his Court looking on.

(From *Theuerdank*.)

perfect, the wooden shaft having been cut down by a foot or
two. It has a double-edged, lance-shaped point, 7 inches long
and 2 inches wide at the broadest part. A strong man could
throw it a considerable distance, and no doubt at 25 or 30
yards it was in such hands a deadly arm.

Maximilian appears to have held occasionally great chamois drives, to which the inhabitants of all the nearest villages were commanded to act as beaters. Of one such drive *Weisskunig* gives us details. It was held in the Schmirn mountains, access to which was gained by following up one of the side glens of the Unter Inn valley. There were, we hear, 600 chamois in one drive; on another occasion the bag was no less than 183. Another favourite ground for driving was the Achensee in North Tyrol. Steep mountains rising on all sides from this elevated lake, it was possible, by using a large force of men, to drive the game into the water, where the stags and chamois were killed from boats, the ladies of the court honouring with their presence these spectacular performances.[1] In the picture from *Theuerdank*, of which a copy is here presented, we see the fair audience demurely seated near the foot of cliffs on which the Emperor is spearing chamois. The little wine-keg left to cool in the rushing brook, and the cart with provisions, show that even in those days creature comforts were not forgotten.

Some doubt has been thrown upon the truth of Maximilian's famous adventure on the Martinswand, near Innsbruck, where, in consequence of advancing foolhardily along a narrow ledge, on the face of a stupendous precipice, he at last got to a place where further advance was as impossible as retreat, and death from starvation became imminent. While there is no doubt that religious zealots embellished the final rescue of the Emperor by the intervention of an angel disguised as a superior youth, there is no good ground to call into question the main details of the adventure. The fact that none of the earlier editions of either *Theuerdank* or

[1] This sport reminds one of the description given by Scrope of the manner of killing deer in the old days in Sutherland, viz. by driving them into the sea by means of a large force of beaters, and killing them from boats. Similar practices were employed in the Forest of Glengarry, where herds of deer were driven into Loch Dulachan by a strong cordon of men.

Weisskunig contain any reference to it, is quite possible to explain by the unfinished condition in which many of Maximilian's biographical notes were found after his very sudden death while on a journey from Tyrol to Vienna.

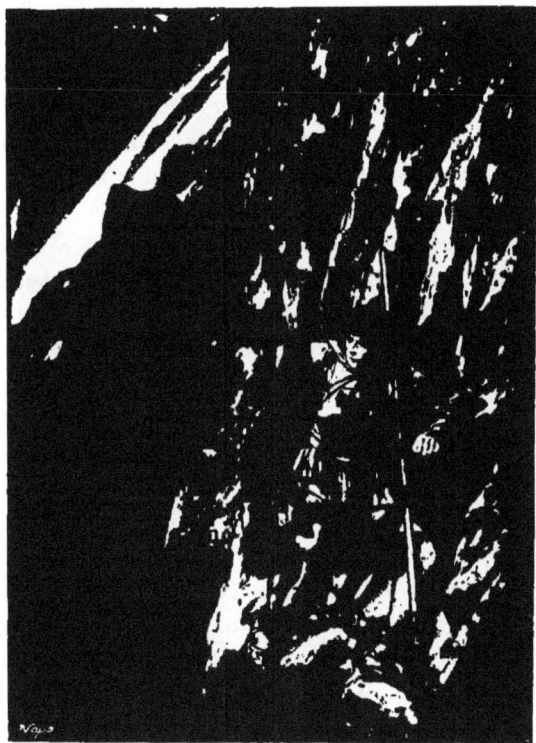

FIG. 3.—Emperor Maximilian's adventure on the Martinswand.

Several authors on chamois, whose opinion carries weight, have stated that 300 years ago chamois were scarcer in the Austrian and Bavarian Alps than they are to-day, mentioning as proof of their contention, that old game registers of sportsmen of high degree, who otherwise showed themselves as keen mountain hunters, are singularly bare of

all evidence concerning a large head of this game. With this
opinion I cannot upon the whole agree, for what is true
in the case of the roe-deer, viz. that 300 years ago
there was but one roe to every six red-deer, while to-day
there are six roes to one red-deer, does not hold good to
anything like the same extent for the chamois. The extermination of the bear, the wolf, the lynx, and the wild cat,
which were deadly foes of roe-deer, and to whose presence
the scarceness of the latter must chiefly be ascribed, was a
matter of less moment to the chamois, owing to the elevated
nature and barren surroundings of the latter's home. It is
quite true that the foes most dangerous to the chamois, *i.e.*
the Lämmergeier (*Gypaetus barbatus*) and the Golden Eagle
(*Aquila chrysaetus*), have shared the fate of the four-footed
beasts of prey named above;[1] but, on the other hand, the
primitiveness of firearms made man a much less dangerous
foe of the chamois than he is to-day. The truth is that to a
great extent the chase of this animal was left to the natives
of the Alpine valleys, and men of standing, who obtained all
the sport they wanted in forests teeming with red-deer and
wild boar, did not bother themselves about a chase which
presented so many difficulties, and round which superstitious
minds had thrown a cloak of myth.

To-day one kills one's chamois at more than ten times the
distances at which javelins proved effectual, and chamois-
shooting, which we have heard was once considered the most
dangerous of all sports, has been rendered to the majority of
sportsmen a very riskless pastime, for " steeple-jacking " after

[1] What great numbers of these birds of prey still existed in the Alps in
the seventeenth century is shown by the registers kept in the monastery
of St. Bartolomeo, a place which visitors to the picturesque Berchtesgaden
lake, near Salzburg, will remember. According to an inscription on a large
wooden tablet, dated 1650, upon which two Lämmergeiers are pictured life-size,
one Hans Duxner killed 127 of these birds, while one Urban Fürstmüller,
hunter and fisher, killed 25 bears and 43 Lämmergeiers, while his two sons
captured 31 of the latter.   .

the nimble mountain game is no longer essential; indeed, as I shall have to show, the qualifications for an up-to-date chamois-shooter participating at drives, need not exceed those of the modest order possessed by sportsmen enjoying a deer drive in the Highlands of Scotland. Different is the case of the lonely stalker who pursues his prey on unpreserved ground, unassisted by keeper or beaters; but of him anon. It is he who has mainly given the chase of the chamois its reputation for danger, for it is probably quite true that the chase of no other animal has cost so many lives.

But a word or two has to be added concerning events in the three centuries that intervened between the death of the great sportsman that saw the Middle Ages merge into Modern Times, and the commencement of the new order of things in the first half of the present century. In the first place, the improvement of firearms must be adverted to. Towards the middle of the sixteenth century the wheel-lock superseded the cumbersome and time-robbing match-lock. Invented in 1515 in Nürnberg, it was a contrivance for eliciting sparks by the friction of a notched wheel against a piece of pyrite. The wheel was wound up by a spanner applied to the axle of the wheel, and it did away with slow matches and other primitive means of ignition. From then on, improvements of the lock, barrel, and of the shafting of hunting rifles, became frequent, so that by the end of the century even the hair-trigger, that abomination for hunting purposes, to this day in general use on the Continent, was invented. But the true spirit of the chase was deteriorating fast. Sportsmen were becoming more luxury-loving, and were surrounding themselves with all kinds of unsportsmanlike paraphernalia. Hardly a century after Maximilian had speared his last chamois, it had already degenerated to such extremes that chamois, after being driven on to ledges on the face of perpendicular cliffs from which they could neither advance nor retreat, were shot at with howitzers from the bottom! Such a feat was performed by Duke Leopold, near Innsbruck, on the occasion of the great festivities which were held in honour of his marriage; the noble knight, Hans von Ferklechen, who narrates the details, going into rhapsodies over the skill exhibited by his liege lord in directing the cannon!

In the two following centuries, the seventeenth and eighteenth, chamois-shooting seems to have become un-fashionable among the ruling classes.[1] All manly pastimes throughout Europe had degenerated in a startling manner. The size of the bag and the minimising of risks to the sports-man became the two premier considerations. Over the whole field of sport, no less than over every branch of the fine arts, there rested a paralysing cloud of torpidity, which seemed to blind the whole civilised world to what was beautiful in nature. The chase was turned into a pageant of stage effects and of ludicrous mummery. Princes vied with each other in the invention of the most bizarre *coup de théâtre*, and sport was travestied in the most grotesque manner. That chamois-shooting under these conditions had but few votaries, goes without saying. It was left to the enjoyment of the hardy and unsophisticated native of the Alps, who had taken no part in the monstrosities committed by their betters in the name of sport.

[1] Among the few isolated records of chamois drives held by great lords in the seventeenth century may be mentioned some held by the Dukes of Bavaria in 1617 in the Berchtesgaden mountains, in 1671 in Hohenschwangau ; one given by the Archbishop of Salzburg in honour of Emperor Leopold I., at which, however, only 16 head came into the drive, of which the latter killed a few, while 4 were caught alive. In 1727 the Elector of Bavaria went hunting chamois in Hohenschwangau, where, as a contemporary says, no princely sportsman has hunted since 1671 "on account of the dangerous mountains." Two great drives were held in July within a day of each other, no fewer than 550 beaters being furnished by three manors and three monastic orders. The results could not compare with those of Emperor Maximilian, for they only got 48 head all told ; but what is remarkable is that 23 were caught alive, of which number 16 reached the game-park at Nymphenburg, near Munich, alive. (F. von Kobell.)

I.

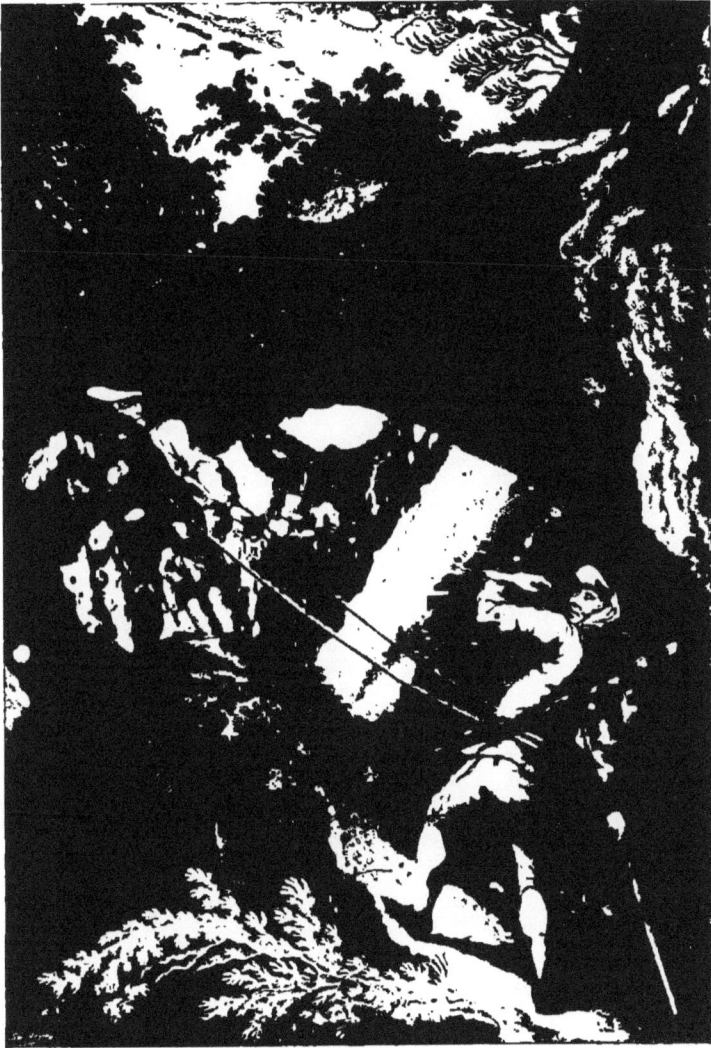

A NOBLEMAN GOING CHAMOIS-SHOOTING 200 YEARS AGO.
(From a copper-plate by J. E. Ridinger.)

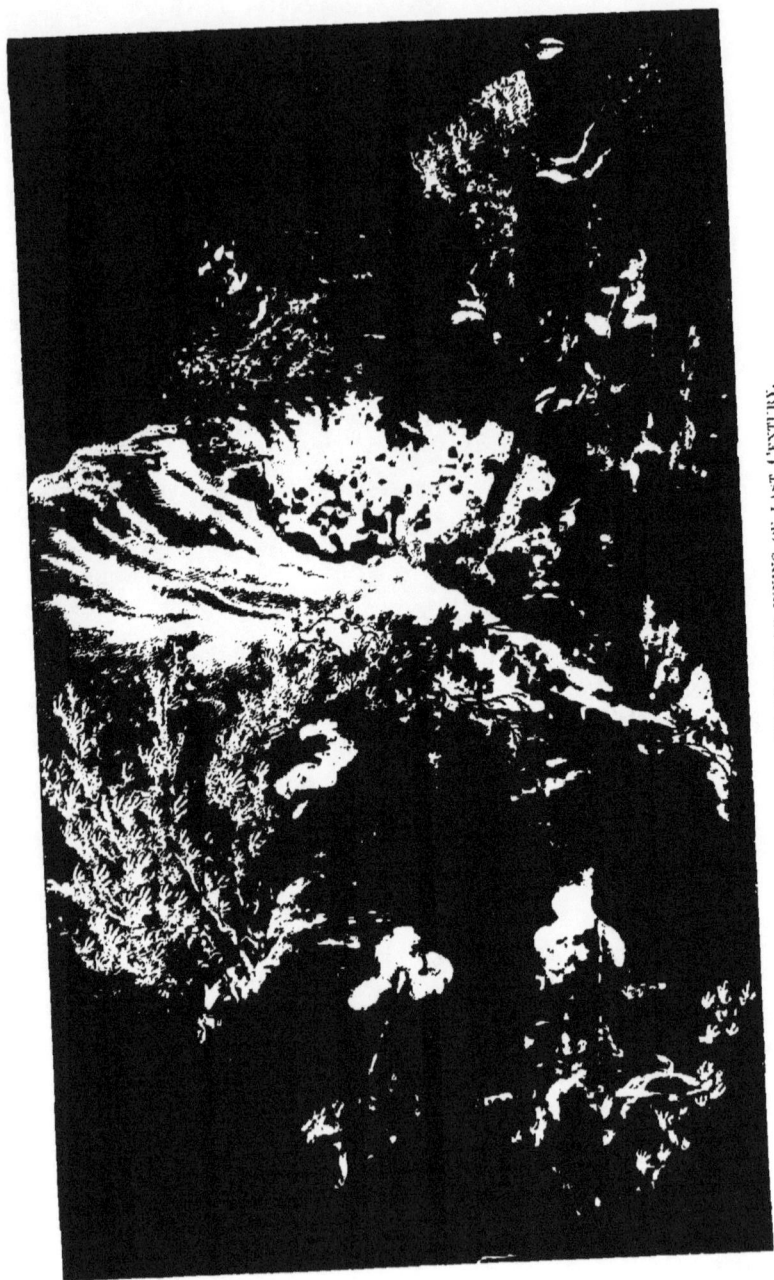

A CHAMOIS-DRIVE IN THE BEGINNING OF LAST CENTURY.

(From a picture by J. E. Ridinger.)

To what depth another branch of mountain sport had sunk, shall be shown in another chapter devoted to red-deer shooting. A glance at one of famous old Joh. Elias Ridinger's copperplates of the early part of the last century, shows what was then the popular conception of chamois-shooting. It represents a noble young sportsman of lusty growth and sturdy limb being dragged up a gentle slope, where the clumsiest cow could easily find a footing. The feat is achieved by means of a rope, at which two natives are tugging like yoked cattle.

Another plate by the same master, shows us how drives were arranged; the cocked hats, uniforms, and white shoulder-belts from which were suspended the bandoleers containing the charges for the rifle, tell their own tale.

It was only in the beginning of the present century that chamois-shooting was again taken up by the upper classes, and, oddly enough, it was again one of the Hapsburgh line who by his example once more popularised Alpine sport. This was Archduke John of Austria, whose earlier career as soldier, made him famous as one of the few generals who relieved by an occasional victory, the dismal tale of defeats inflicted by Napoleon's troops. After the fall of the great usurper and the establishment of general peace, sport in the Alps became the Archduke's chief pastime, and by the time old age put a stop to his favourite occupation, he had become the hero of countless tales of adventure, and was, without exception, the most popular hunter of royal rank that had ever made the Alps the scene of dashing sporting exploits.

He was a sportsman of the good old school, quality and not quantity was his motto, and his maxim, the less display the better the sport, rid his expeditions of all pomp and ceremony. Dressed in the mountaineer's simple but practical garb, and mixing in the most unostentatious and affable manner with the lowest peasant youth or roughest woodman, he shot his chamois in the natives' fashion, that is by stalking, took a hand at their rifle matches, and danced the " Schuhblattler " with the best of them. No half-roofed hayloft or smoky chálet in the timber-line regions of the Styrian or Tyrolese Alps was too draughty or too grimy for this hardy sportsman, and he knew the wide expanse of his snow-mantled playground with a thoroughness few men have had a chance to acquire.[1]

The present Emperor of Austria, unquestionably the foremost royal sportsman of Europe, exhibits a similar genuine love for mountain sport, and despite his almost venerable age, and the exceedingly conscientious manner in which he attends to the toilsome affairs of the Empire, he is to the present day so little of a " shooter," that he still prefers stalking, and only when foreign royalties are present, or for other special reasons, are regular drives held.

Many of the Austrian aristocracy are moved by a similar spirit, even in regard to chamois; the red-deer, as I shall show, when dealing with that game, being almost invariably killed stalking.

In the opinions of some good sportsmen, there is about chamois-stalking one attraction held out by no other species of sport in Europe. It is, that its surroundings are to-day very much the same as they were in the Middle Ages. While some species of game have, in the course of time, become extinct, others have degenerated to a deplorable

---

[1] The romantic morganatic marriage contracted by the Archduke with a daughter of the people, whose father was the keeper of a posting station on one of the Alpine passes, which he frequently passed on his way to Styrian chamois grounds, made a great stir at all the European courts. And though it compelled him to retire from the Vienna Court for many years, pretty Anna Plochel made him an excellent wife, and became the foundress of the still-flourishing race of sportsmen, the Counts of Meran. It was said that the Archduke first saw her, and was struck with the courage she displayed on the occasion of one of his frequent winter journeys across the Alps, when she acted and dressed up as a post-boy and rode the leaders of his carriage, which otherwise could not have proceeded on its journey over the snowed-up Tauern Pass.

degree. The mountains upon which my eye rests as I look up from these pages, and which belong to that great block of rough limestone peaks which were Maximilian's favourite ground, were once stocked with ibex, bear, and lynx, while the deer that frequented the primeval woods that covered their lower slopes, were very giants of their race. Civilisation has swept them away, the game, as well as those vast forests in which it dwelt. But the chamois's home among the rocks, as well as the animal itself, has not undergone any marked changes or deterioration. Indeed, there is evidence that in several regions of the Austrian Alps, there are to-day more chamois than there were 400 years ago. And what is more, the game is hunted to-day in some of these mountains by men who in mien, dress, thought, and bearing might have been humble companions of the hero of the Martinswand, rather than contemporaries of that money-grabbing race of Swiss fellow-mountaineers— save the mark!—who are defiling the face of nature in a manner that disgusts all lovers of what is beautiful.

CHAPTER II

THROUGHOUT the great mountain chain, known to us as the
Alps, that stretches from Eastern France to Transylvania, there
are annually (in average years) shot some 11,000 chamois,
about 15,000 red-deer, and about 100,000 roe-deer.

The Austrian Government has for many years made a
point of collecting in an official form accurate details concerning all the game shot in the Austrian Alps (exclusive of
Hungary), and the subjoined carefully-compiled table showing the total bag for 1892, which was an average year, will
prove of interest.

The numbers given in this list are always less than the
real totals, for the animals killed by poachers, or those shot in
out-of-the-way communes, where no official count is kept,
are not included. The Hungarian Government, unfortunately,
has failed to follow the example of the authorities of Austria
proper, so that there are no official details available concerning the bag made in the sister kingdom, a circumstance
much to be regretted, particularly in regard to red-deer,
of which enormous numbers are killed in the Hungarian
woods.

Red-deer	.	12,385
Fallow-deer	.	2,788
Roe-deer	.	68,110
Chamois		8,144
Wild boar		3,509
Hares .	.	1,309,688
Rabbits	.	95,803
Marmots	. .	647
Bears .	. .	33
Wolves	.	69
Lynx . .	.	31
Foxes . .		26,553
Martins	. .	11,281
Fitchet and polecats		30,668
Badgers	. .	3,870
Fish-otters	.	1,267

Capercaillie cocks { only shot in spring, and only the cocks } 5,143
Blackcocks { } 9,458

Hazel-grouse .	.	10,851
Ptarmigans	. .	2,075
Stone-grouse (*Caccabis saxatilis*)		3,259
Pheasants		141,264
Partridges	.	1,036,836
Quail .		94,995
Woodcocks		26,057
Snipe .		14,756
Wild geese	.	1,245
Wild ducks .	.	52,440
Eagles . .	.	510
Falcons, buzzards, and hawks }		101,960
Owls, horn-owls, etc.		30,855

According to these statistics, the bag of chamois in the Austrian Alps was in 1892 no less than 8144 head, or more than three-fourths of the total in the whole Alps. We find that Tyrol, with 2392, is at the top of the list, then Styria, with 2176, and next Salzburg, with 2039. In the Bavarian Highlands over 1000 chamois are, I believe, annually shot. ·Italy and Switzerland, with a few in the French Alps, bring the annual bag for the Alps to the sufficiently considerable total of over 11,000 head.

These figures do not bear out a fallacious opinion expressed by several writers who, judging from what they have seen or heard in Switzerland, state that the number of chamois has within the last fifty years greatly decreased. With the exception of the last-named country, which is the last locality where game can be expected to thrive, the very opposite has occurred. Thus, to give one instance of which I have personal knowledge, there were in 1860 in the Salzburg mountains about 6000, or at the most 6500, chamois. To-day there are more than 22,000 head.[1] Almost as great an increase has occurred in Tyrol, while even in the Carpathians, where chamois are less preserved, the number, so good authorities assure one, has not decreased of late years.

Speaking roughly, I should say that three-fifths of the total bag of chamois in the Alps are killed by driving, the balance by stalking. There can be no question, of course, which of the two manners of hunting is the more sportsman-like. The one, stalking, might be described, to make use of a play of words, as sport fit for the kings among men, the other, driving, as the sport for the men among kings. A well-known sportsman, belonging to the latter class, once declared that the majority of chamois are killed either by peasants or by princes; and although this must not be taken quite literally, there is a good deal of truth about it. For among the hardy peasant youths who, from their boyhood, pass five or six months every year tending cattle or goats in close proximity to the chamois's home, are found the keenest and certainly the most hardy and persevering stalkers. Among the highest classes, on the other hand, chamois-driving has many enthusiastic adherents. It is a form of sport more in harmony with the great bags landed magnates are accustomed to make when shooting other game, and it does not require the physical training without which the stalker would be foolish to undertake this particular form of

[1] It may perhaps be worth while to give the division of chamois ground in this province as a typical instance. It consists of 1,900,000 acres, of which 480,000 acres belong to the Crown, 1,050,000 acres are commune shoots, and the rest is ground owned by those exercising shooting rights. The chief preserves are those of the Grand Duke of Toscana, who shoots over 150,000 acres, Prince Lichtenstein (120,000 acres), the Duke of Cumberland, Prince Pless, Prince Schwarzenberg, Counts Kinsky, Karoly, etc. In the year 1882 there were shot in Salzburg 1050 head ; in 1883, 1517 ; in 1892, 2039 head.

mountain sport, except perhaps in tip-top preserves, where stalking is also a comparatively easy sport.

Chamois-preserving is for one reason a far less expensive undertaking than is that of keeping up a good deer forest, especially if inhabited valleys are anywhere near the latter. For, while the chamois never descends to inhabited regions, deer do so, and commit more or less damage to the crops of the peasants. These damages must be made good by the owner of the deer, and the peasant, as a rule, does not come off worst. In some great shoots one could name, these damages mount up to more than the rent and wages of the keepers. The owner of a chamois preserve has nothing of the kind to consider; he can foretell his expenses to a five pound note, and he is perfectly independent of the good-will of the peasants, if indeed that class has any rights at all on the ground which harbours his game. Wire fences are fortunately still practically unknown, the few exceptions, where such contrivances have been erected by selfish owners, being too isolated to be taken into account.

There is another good reason why driving has to be resorted to by the owners of larger preserves, viz. that stalking is far too time-robbing. To keep a head of say 1000 chamois down to proper proportions, at least fifty or sixty should be shot in the season. To shoot nine or ten chamois per week stalking, is a very good performance indeed, and there are few preserves where this could be kept up for any length of time, for this game, more than any other, loves perfect quiet, and promptly leaves regions where it is often disturbed, as shall be shown when describing sport on unpreserved ground. Driving therefore has necessarily to be resorted to where the head of game is considerable.

To speak first of stalking, it is necessary to premise a few descriptive remarks concerning the different character of stalking-grounds. To go after chamois in unpreserved ground,

such as are many of the *Gemeinde Jagden* or commune shoots,
owned and shot over by the inhabitants of remote mountain
hamlets, where every youth practically is a born hunter, and
has the right to go out after the game so dear to him, is a
very different thing from stalking chamois in a well-guarded
preserve, where keepers know all the likely haunts of game
and every pass it uses, and where it is disturbed only during
a week or two in the whole year. In the unpreserved ground
the game is not only scarce, but it is exceedingly wary in
consequence of the constant pursuit to which it is exposed
during the five or six months of the open season. Their
vigilance in such places is something surprising. In shooting over such ground, one really enters into competition with
men born to the sport, and who possess an intimate knowledge
of the ground. No keepers watch over such shoots, and there
is no going straight to the spot where game is usually found.
One has to find one's game in precisely the same manner as
were it in some unexplored mountain wilderness in the
Himalayas, or in the Cascade range in North America. Indeed, it is far more difficult than in the latter, where game
is not so vigilant. To stalk a Rocky Mountain Bighorn, or
even the Haplocerus, is easy work in comparison to outwit-
ting a sly old buck in such a peasant shoot. That the
chamois is not by nature so exceedingly wary, but is
made so by constant human molestation, is best proved by
the behaviour of these animals in really good preserves where
not a shot has been fired for a year or two. As I propose to
ask the reader to accompany me on a stalk or two over such
good ground, he will be able to form his own conclusions as
to the correctness of the above remarks.

To the really keen sportsman invading alone such a
peasant's preserve, where he pits himself against the best
native talent, and is handicapped by a less intimate knowledge of the ground, there is added a further zest to his

sport. For to succeed where others have failed is, of course, the keynote of most sports and pastimes. And if these "others" are the flower of mountaineers, the pick of crags-men, with muscle hardened by constant extraordinarily heavy manual labour, with constitutions as of iron, with eyes, lungs, and hearts trained respectively from earliest youth to spy and to climb, then I say, to succeed unaided where they have failed, and to bring down to the valley on your back a veteran buck who has been the object of many a native hunter's well-planned stalk, is a feat of which I think one may be honestly proud.

As a rule, chamois are either stalked or driven. Where there are very few, and the ground is not peculiarly favour-able for driving, this latter manner is not attempted, for not only is it not worth the trouble and expense to drive country where the few animals that are known to exist are, in conse-quence of constant harassing, rendered doubly wily, but the chances of their escaping are much increased by the inexperi-ence of those undertaking the drive. In favourably situated ground there is a third manner of circumventing chamois, by *riegeln* or "moving" the game. For this only two or three beaters—generally the keepers act in that capacity—are required. Everything is done as quietly as possible, and much the same tactics are employed that come into play under similar circumstances, when moving red-deer in the Highlands.

The barren limestone formation of the craggy North Tyrolese mountains is less adapted for this sport than are the Styrian and Salzburg Alps, where, as a rule, game can be approached closer, and success is rendered less doubtful by the more con-fined nature of the individual animal's range, which is brought about by the superior feed it finds on granite and slate for-mation.

This moving of chamois is capital sport, being easier than stalking, and yet entailing enough climbing to satisfy

all but the lustiest. It also disturbs the ground infinitely
less than the noisy drives, and therefore it can be enjoyed
more frequently without damaging the preserve.

To a certain extent the head of chamois is dependent
upon climatic conditions, for of all wild mountain game it
is most subject to that one danger of Alpine regions from
which there is no escape: avalanches. Rapid changes of the
temperature following heavy falls of snow cause in this way
very serious losses. Only too often the remains of whole
bands are found when the June and July sun has at last
reduced the accumulated masses of snow, which held in its
relentless grip the score or more of its victims. To show the
terrible force of a *Lawine*, I may mention an occurrence of
which I receive the news as I write this paragraph. In a
Styrian shoot which I know well, there is high up close to
timber-line, a small loch lying at the foot of a steep slope,
while a bank of considerable height shuts in the water on the
other side. From the former a big avalanche swept down
with such suddenness as to engulf a band of chamois, and
with such appalling force as to force every drop of water out
of the loch over the brow of the bank. The loch being well
stocked with trout, dead fish and dead chamois strewed the
slope below the lake down which the enormous masses of
snow, after filling the depression where the lake once was,
extended its work of destruction, giant pines snapped off like
matches or bodily uprooted, marking the resistless path of the
snow-slide.

CHAPTER III

I ONCE overheard an English tourist in Switzerland describe the chamois as "a sort of wild goat that has a beard and small polished horns, which the natives fasten on the alpenstocks." For incorrectness personified, this account will bear comparison with the famous reply Cuvier once received on asking a nervous student to describe the crab: "A red fish that walks backward."

In olden times, even great authorities spoke of the chamois as a species of goat. Thus we find that the principal author on sport of the sixteenth century, Jacques du Fouilloux,[1] says the Ysarus or Sarris is a goat of like nature and habitus as the domestic goat. But if we read on, we soon

---

[1] Du Fouilloux's description is really not original, but is much older, i.e. by Gaston Phoebus (1331-1391), the famous author of *La Chasse*. The first four editions of Du Fouilloux's *La Venerie* do not contain the very lengthy quotations copied from Gaston Phoebus, and the fifth edition, of which I have a copy (printed in 1573), is the first one including them, a fact not generally known, owing to the extreme rareness of the first four. The entirely over-rated Turberville, than whom no more unprincipled copiest existed, did not scruple to translate practically verbatim Du Fouilloux's work into English (using even his French woodcuts), calling it *The Noble Art of Venerie*, London, 1576, without acknowledging the source. It is therefore quite incorrect to state, as does a recent author on old prints in the *Badminton Magazine*, that Turberville describes English hunting and hunting customs. Text, as well as illustrations, in this pirated book, refer almost exclusively to France.

find that the good Jacques, great *veneur* as he was, and masterly as are his descriptions of the hart and wild boar, knew but very little of our beast. His account of the animal is not only meagre, but entirely wrong. The chief peculiarity to which the greater part of Jacques's description is devoted, is one of those fantastical vagaries of the medieval mind that sound so funny in these days of exact science. He says: " At any time the Ysarus desires to scratch its thighs it sticks its claws in so hard that on account of their being reversed (reuirees) it cannot withdraw them, and thus it falls from the cliffs and breaks its neck." As his account of the manner of hunting the chamois is on a par with what I have just quoted, it is hardly necessary to devote space to it, but rather proceed to give a brief account of the chamois's habitus as we know it to-day.

Though belonging to the antelope family, the chamois forms a specie for itself. Some naturalists pretend that the difference in colour, trifling dissimilarity in the horns, as well as in the size of the whole animal, which distinguishes the chamois, or Atschi, of the Caucasus, as well as the Izard of the Pyrenees and of Albania from those of the Alps, should be marked by the creation of subdivisions. But this view has not been generally adopted, as it is said these variations are more or less attributable to local causes, however undisputable it is; for instance, that the coat of the Izard is far more rufous in colour, and their horns somewhat slimmer and of a slightly different crook, than those of the Alps.

Authors out of number, and comparatively recent ones amongst them, have invested the chamois with certain characteristics it cannot properly claim. The only one to which it is necessary to draw attention in this place, is the generally prevailing belief that chamois only inhabit the highest Alps, living almost permanently on snow and glaciers, far above timber-line. In Switzerland, where the chamois has for centuries been relentlessly persecuted, the region inhabited by it is certainly much higher than in the Eastern Alps. In Styria one can see chamois at home at such comparatively low elevations as 3500 feet, and this during the warmest months of the year. When left undisturbed for a season or two, the chamois loses much of its shyness, and I could take the reader to a dozen places where he can approach in a carriage and pair, small herds of does and kids to within long rifle-shot.

It is, I hope, hardly necessary to take up space with a wearisome description of the chamois's appearance. What in this respect is interesting for the sportsman to know, is that its coat changes colour. Between the appearance of a chamois in July, when the shooting season opens, and that of the same animal in December, when it closes, there is a vast difference. The grayish ochre-brown colour and the short hairs of the summer coat have turned into an almost black, shaggy garb with hairs three times as long, that give the animal, particularly an old buck, a very burly appearance. Along the back-bone of the male the hairs grow in winter to a great length, and, except at the tip where they turn a yellowish white, they are of a glossy black, and stand upright, waving in the wind. These long hairs, most carefully bunched together, form the much-prized *Gems-Bart* or chamois's beard, which the ignorant tourists suppose grows on the lower jaw of the male chamois, as were it a billy-goat's beard. The longer the hairs are, and the whiter the tips, the more valued is the bunch. The extreme length is 9 inches, but hairs of that length are very rare, and I have known as much as £10 paid for such a trophy by those who do not mind adorning their fête-day hats with other men's plumes. The shooting in November or December of one, and in some instances of two *Bart Gams*, viz. chamois bearing these much-sought trophies, is the one perquisite most keepers insist on obtaining. Of course, those having the best beards are carefully picked out by the men who have been watching them the whole year. Imitations are oftener seen than the real article, for good chamois beards

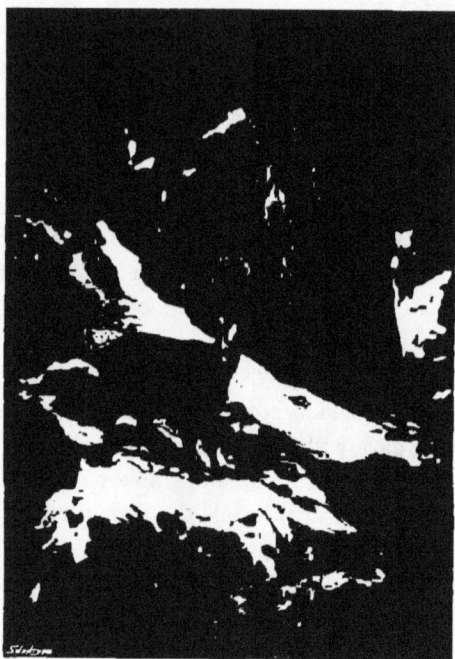

FIG. 4.—A good Buck in his winter coat.
(From a picture by Pausinger.)

are only worn by the genuine *Jäger* on special occasions. Rain or snow very quickly causes the hairs to lose their gloss and the elastic stiffness, without which they do not stand up as they should.

Though the "beard" reaches its highest perfection only during or after the rut, which commences about the middle of November, keepers and beaters will pounce eagerly upon a buck killed in October, for even at that time the "beard," though short and not of the peculiar gloss it obtains later on, has pecuniary value. Very amusing it is to watch, if possible unobserved, the eager and yet careful way in which the prize is secured by the clumsy fingers of a strapping

FIG. 5.—A Chamois Doe with her young in their winter coat.
(Photographed from life by F. Grainer, Reichenhall, Bavaria.)

giant of the mountains, stooping over the carcase and pulling out the long hairs almost one by one! At this time of the year—October—just as the shooting season is at its height, one often is sadly fooled by picking out at drives very dark chamois. In most cases one finds, when too late, that these are not bucks as one expected from their burly look, but

old does, who for some, I suppose good feminine reason, have
seen fit to don their winter garb rather earlier than the rest.

Some peculiar variations of colour, slight in themselves,
but sufficient to impress the seal of rareness, manifest themselves in some districts. Thus in Styria and Salzburg a few
shoots are distinguished by containing animals that even in
summer are much darker than their fellows, and have hardly
any white about the head. These are called coal chamois,
and are greatly prized as *lusus naturae*. In Tyrol, on the
other hand, the silver bucks are a freak of nature, delighting
the heart of ardent sportsmen. They never get such a dark
winter coat as the rest, and there is a peculiar silver shimmer
about the hair. Now and again silver bucks have been shot
in the Hinter - Riss, and curiously enough the only coal
chamois and the only silver buck I have ever bagged, fell
in each case to the second shot fired in the respective
Styrian and Tyrolese preserves. Since the day I fired those
two lucky shots, I have never again set eyes on either kind,
notwithstanding that thousands of chamois have been viewed
by me in the two countries, in the interval.

Albino chamois are even rarer. To kill them is supposed
to be very unlucky, the man who does so surely dying within
twelve months. Strange to say, on the only two occasions
known to me of a white chamois being shot, this superstition
turned out true. One of the two instances was that of a
poacher who was shot a few weeks later by a keeper, the
second one occurring in the Schwarzen See preserve, where
one of the lessees of that shoot, a hale and hearty man, died
very suddenly within the prescribed period. Of other cases
I have read, but do not know further details.

Partially white chamois, which are also rare, are not
believed to be invested with these unlucky powers over the
fate of their slayers, and my fellow-guest who years ago
killed a buck with pure white hind-quarters in the Arch-

duke Louis Victor's shoot near Kufstein is, I am glad to say, alive to-day.

Concerning the horns of the chamois, which are trophies hardly in proportion to the keen interest with which the animal is regarded by sportsmen, a good deal could be said, but the most would only be of interest to the specialist. The most important facts for the sportsman may be summed up as follows. Both sexes bear horns of practically the same length, but the adult buck's are slightly thicker at the base, are usually more parallel to each other than those of the doe, and the pot-hook of the male's horns curves in more sharply than the female's. The longest pair of horns known to collectors measured over the curve are slightly over 12 inches in length. Of the two specimens of that dimension which I have seen, one is a buck that was in the late Duke of Coburg's collection, the other one, which in all probability is that of a doe, being much slimmer, is in Count Arco-Zinneberg's collection at Munich. Of the genuineness of these two heads I have no doubt. Of some others which I have seen, the very contrary is to be said, for by sacrificing two or three pairs of thick-set horns one magnificent pair can be built up, and such frauds take in many an unwary collector. Eleven-inch heads, while extremely rare, are to be got. A buck I killed in 1873 in South Tyrol had horns of that length, with a girth of 4 inches. Ten-inch heads are not too common; roughly speaking, one in fifty bucks one kills under ordinary circumstances, stretch the tape up to that mark. To one rule there is, so far as I know, no exception: that chamois frequenting a limestone formation have bigger horns than those found in slate or granite mountains. This carries out the same principle that manifests itself concerning stag's antlers, as shall be shown in another place. Curiously enough, the contrary is the case with the length of the

3

chamois's winter coat, so far as the prized beard is concerned, the Dolomite chamois having the poorest of any.

In Continental collections, one, now and again, is shown chamois heads adorned not with two, but with four or six horns (see Fig. 6). If the owner is not aware of the fraud that has been practised on him, he will declare it to be a rare and valuable monstrosity. But it is nothing of the kind, only a cleverly-contrived swindle by which many a

FIG. 6.—A manufactured Monstrosity.
(Real chamois horns mounted on a sheep's skull to deceive collectors.)

collector has been caught. The several chamois horns are genuine enough, but the skull is a perfectly *bona fide* frontal bone of a—sheep! Not of the common kind, it is true, but of the Sardinian species (*Ovis aries polyceras*), which have generally four, and often six, horns. By filing down the somewhat thicker core of the hollow sheep's horn, and replacing for the latter, genuine chamois horns, firmly glued on so as not to betray the file's handiwork, the prized *lusus naturae* is ready for the eager collector of such-like curiosities.[1]

[1] The chamois's horns rise at right angles from the skull, while those of

Of a genuine instance of a chamois with more than two horns (with bone cores) not a single case is known to the naturalist.

There is, however, one kind of extraordinary horn-growth to which the chamois in some rare instances has been known to be subject. In outward appearance these horns are not unlike the usual chamois horns, but they have no bone core,

Fig. 7.—Abnormal horn formation.
(A cuticular growth.)

and grow from the cuticle without any connection with bone substance. Only a few instances are known of these cuticular horns. One (Fig. 7) is copied from Keller's monograph on the chamois, where it is stated that the chamois that grew

sheep slant backwards. To prevent discovery by this ready means, the frontal bone of the Sardinian sheep, when intended for these fraudulent purposes, is always cut off close to the base of the horns. The picture here given is taken from F. von Kobell's *Wildanger*.

it, was killed in the Ober Ammergau mountains. A second
instance (Fig. 8) shows a similar formation on the foot of a
buck killed last August (1895) by Lady Loder in Styria. The
buck was in good condition, indeed it was one of the heaviest
shot that season in the preserve in question, weighing clean a
few ounces under 58 lbs.

To the eye of the non-sportsman, chamois horns from
different parts of Europe represent a very uniform appearance. Not so to those who are acquainted with the
peculiarities of his game. To
him the greater or lesser bend
of the pot-hook, the greater or
lesser divergence of the horns,
or the straighter or more curved
outline of the latter, will betray
the home of the animal. Thus
the sharp inward bend of the
pot-hook of the male's horns is
peculiar to the Central and
Eastern Alps. Neither the
Pyrenean, Savoy, nor Carpathian
chamois have it. Count Hoyos,
of whom I shall have to speak
when dealing with the bouquetin, when examining the collection of the late King Victor
Emanuel in his hunting castle Sarre near Aosta, found that
among 700 chamois heads there was not one which had this
sharp "turn-in" which is so prized in "Krickeln" obtained
in the Austrian Alps.

Curiously enough the same superstitious belief which was
in old days attached to the horns of the bouquetin, and
to a lesser degree to the antlers of the stag, meets one when
studying the history of the chamois. Thus even the great

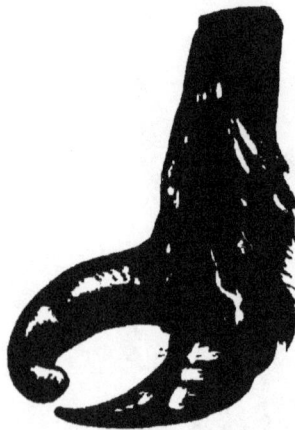

FIG. 8.—Abnormal formation of a
Chamois's foot.
(This Buck was shot by Lady Loder in
Styria in 1895.)

sportsman Emperor Maximilian informs his readers quite gravely, that when the buck chamois feels the end of his days approaching, he will rub his horns off in the middle against rocks, and when he has done so he loses his appetite and dies from starvation!

Chamois are very dainty feeders; the sparsely-growing *Nepidium alpinum*, chiefly to be found on the barren-looking slopes of rocky *débris*, which accumulate at the foot of impending heights, is one of their principal articles of summer and autumn diet, while the equally insignificant-looking *Meum mutellina* is their favourite herb. In the winter, which is a long period of short commons for chamois, their food consists of the withered grass they find under the dense branches of arves and pines, and of fibrous lichen which hangs in long tresses from the branches of these trees under which they also find shelter from snow. Now and again, when exceptionally heavy falls of snow, followed by rain, press these sheltering branches down to the ground, and then become coated with ice, the poor animals are unable to get out and they die from starvation.

The average weight of an adult buck is about 65 lbs., the does being about a fifth lighter. Such extreme weights as 95 and 100 lbs. are known to occur now and again, and the late Duke of Saxe-Coburg killed several of that weight, while Tschudi mentions an apparently quite authentic instance of a certain big chamois known as the Rufeli buck, exceeding that weight by no less than 25 lbs.

A chamois buck of the phenomenal clean weight of 123 .lbs. avoirdupois (56 kilos) was killed, according to the *Waidmann*, in August 1891, by Count Arpad Teleki in Transylvania. The horns measured 11½ inches, and it may therefore be considered the third or fourth largest head known, while in weight it is by far the heaviest buck of this century.

The once famous Bezoar stone, which now and again is

found in the stomach of chamois, and to which formerly
superstition attached valuable curative qualities, is really
nothing else than an accumulation of resinous fibre and
hair. These balls grow, in exceptional cases, to a great size ;
Keller mentions some he has seen with a diameter of
over 7 inches. One which is in my possession is almost
round with a circumference of 8¼ inches. One Adam
Lebwald wrote in 1693 a work in which he treats upon the
high pharmaceutic value of these Bezoar stones, enumerating
some forty ailments for which in his time they were considered a sure remedy !

When the rutting season commences, which it does about
the middle of November, a gland lying at the base and
behind each horn swells up and becomes filled with a pasty
lymph that has a strong musk-like smell. At other seasons
of the year these glands are quite invisible. Curiously
enough the animal, which in the high mountain ranges of
Western America takes the place of the chamois, viz. the
White Mountain Antelope (*Haplocerus montanus*), has
precisely the same glands, which remain inactive at all other
seasons but the rutting time.

Chamois have often been caught alive and kept in semi-
captivity in parks. One of the first attempts known to me,
of acclimatising chamois in a country far away from the
Alps, is mentioned by Landau as having occurred in 1572,
when the Landgrave William of Hesse added some chamois
to the other rare animals, such as Swedish Reindeer and
Elchs, with which he had stocked his large deer park at
Zapfenburg in Hesse (enclosed by a wall 14 feet high).
Another lot of eleven head were received by him in 1591,
and in the letter from the Count Palatine of Bavaria
accompanying this lot, the latter excuses himself for not
sending the promised number of twenty-four, stating that
forty had succumbed while being carried down the high

mountains from suffocation in consequence of the hot
weather (it was in June). In the subsequent centuries, when
princes rivalled each other in stocking their parks and
woods with the rarest game animals—even the ibex being
caught for that purpose — these attempts to introduce
chamois in districts of Central or Northern Europe became
more frequent. Scrope tells us of the Earl of Fife's spirited
experiments to introduce foreign game animals, amongst
them the capercaillie, the wild boar, the reindeer, and the
chamois, into Mar Forest. But it appears from other
sources that the chamois he got, never reached points
farther north than Leith, the king (William IV.) having
expressed a wish to have these chamois in Windsor, so that
the earl made him a present of them. Scrope adds that
they produced young, and that "a wooden tower was built for
them there, and they raced up and down it as if they had been
amongst their native rocks (!) They died from having eaten
some poisonous herb, so that on all accounts it is very much
to be regretted that they were not sent originally to Mar
Forest." In the *Sporting Annals*[1] it is stated that these four
chamois, one buck, one kid, two does, are the first that ever
came alive into this country. Originally they were the
property of Mr. Lowther of Wolvesey, "who during his
sojourn among the Alps was determined to try the experiment of domesticating some of these creatures, hitherto
considered by the natives the most difficult to tame of all
animals in that mountainous region. He may be said to
have succeeded, for they were gradually familiarised to his
château of Blonaz, and to his domestics and people, to whom,
from their novel nature and peculiarities, they afforded much
interest and amusement."[2]

[1] Vol. ix. (1826), p. 236.
[2] Dr. Girtanner has published some interesting notes concerning chamois
in captivity.

CHAPTER IV

THE Alps of North Tyrol are divided topographically, as well as geologically, into two groups ; those south of the Inn river being either of slate or of granite formation, while those north of the river are limestone mountains. This gives the latter also their collective name, "Nord Tyroler Kalkalpen," in distinction to the limestone range of Southern Tyrol, better known as the Dolomites. Confining ourselves to the former, their location may be briefly recalled to the traveller who enters Tyrol from the Swiss side (by the Arlberg railway) as the verdureless mountains, gray in tint, jagged in appearance, which he sees to his left as the train takes him along the somewhat sombre Ober Inn valley to the sunnier and more attractive Unter Inn thal. The mountains that compose the southern flank of this range, form that lofty wall of beetling rock in the shelter of which lies, protected against the northern blast, the capital of the country. Anybody who has visited Innsbruck will remember the picturesque effect of those mountains towering over the quaint streets, as if they were for ever peeping into the dormer windows of the tall old-fashioned houses that give the more ancient part of that town such a medieval look.

The northern flanks of this range, on the other hand, extend into Bavaria, forming the Bavarian Highlands, the scene of Boner's chamois-shooting adventures. The range is divided into several massive blocks of precipitous mountains, that have names of their own. The only one that the reader need remember is the Karawendel range, which is the most important, as well as the most centrally situated. Here eight or nine keen sportsmen, of the rank which tempts one to call the whole range the Dukeries, have made of this sea of inaccessible-looking peaks, a very paradise for the chamois-hunter.

Except in one place, viz. on the Zugspitze at the western end of the range, no true glaciers are to be found in it, and the peaks do not exceed 10,000 feet in altitude. Notwithstanding this comparatively low elevation, many of the peaks in the centre of the chain, invisible from any point to which tourists, with rare exceptions, ever penetrate, are formidable fellows, and afford all the rock-climbing a man can want. For guideless climbing I know no more attractive field than they present, but it is necessary to secure permission to explore their recesses, which resemble in grandeur those of the Dolomites in South Tyrol.

Much of the ground is actually owned by the sportsmen who, by long years of careful preserving and the expenditure of very large sums, have created there a series of sanctuaries for chamois, extending over about 1000 or 1200 square miles, such as there are few in the Alps. Small armies of watchful keepers, well able to cope with their hereditary foes, the dare-devil poachers, are for ever on guard. And though the poaching affrays have of late years lost much of their old ferociousness, many a stalwart fellow has found his last resting-place in the Karawendel Mountains. The ground that is not owned by the proprietors of these preserves, is held on long leases from the Crown, most of the barren ground above timber-line throughout the Austrian Alps being Crown property.[1]

[1] To prevent disappointment on the part of those who would desire to explore this region I must add, that such a plan had better not be carried out,

In the centre of the Dukeries lies the "Hinter-Riss," that unrivalled creation of the late Duke of Saxe-Coburg, now owned by the Duke of Edinburgh, to give the new owner the title most familiar to English ears. As I propose to devote a chapter to a description of this interesting shoot, it will serve present purposes to say, that it was the first preserve in this part of Tyrol, and is to-day still the largest among eight others that have clustered round it in the course of the last half-century. Marching for many miles with the Hinter-Riss, is the shoot of another kinsman of our royal family, Prince Hohenlohe-Langenburg, elder brother of the late Count Gleichen, and nephew of the Queen. On the other side of the Hinter-Riss an Austrian Prince Coburg has a big valley famous for its Alpine stags, while the other sportsmen that retire every autumn to the secluded glens of the Dukeries, are the reigning Duke of Saxe-Altenburg, the Grand-Duke of Luxembourg, the Regent of Bavaria, another Bavarian Duke, brother of the Empress of Austria, several Austrian noblemen, of which Prince Schönburg is the head, the Duke of Alençon, and lastly, at the most easterly extremity of the range, the Landl and Kufstein shoots of Archduke Louis Victor, the Emperor of Austria's brother.

In plain view from any of the peaks of the Karawendel range, but no longer part of it, for the Inn valley is between, one sees at the end of the Zillerthal, where huge glaciers and snowfields betray the presence of peaks over 12,000 feet in altitude, another very famous chamois preserve belonging

for as guides are not to be had, and the keepers are very strictly forbidden to act in that character, the stranger, who of course could not possibly tell what was private and what was Crown land, would expose himself to unpleasant consequences by trespassing on the former. The keepers regard even an apparently perfectly harmless invasion of these game sanctuaries rather more seriously than is pleasant, and considering that one tourist can spoil the efforts of months of the keepers' hardest work, their animosity to the "climbing vagabonds," as they are apt to call the scrambling tourist, is not so very unnatural.

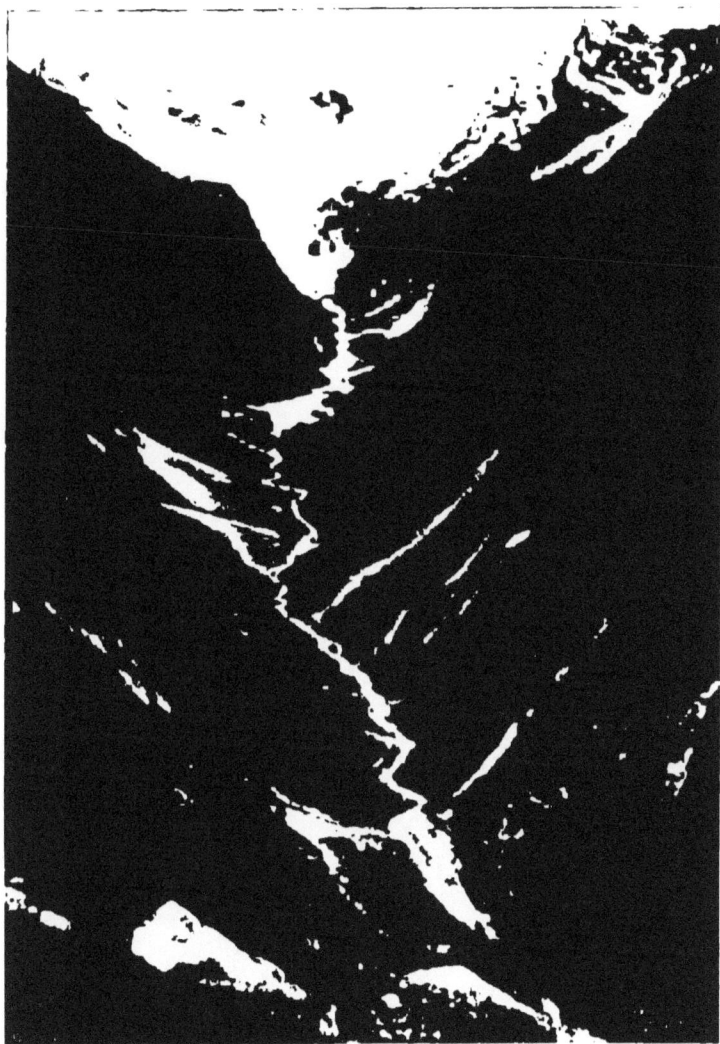

THE FLOITENTHAL FORMING PART OF PRINCE AUERSPERG'S SHOOT
IN THE ZILLERTHAL ALPS IN TYROL.

to the well-known Austrian magnate family, the Princes Auersperg. In their shoot, the largest bag of any in the Alps have been made, viz. the enormous total of 222 chamois have been shot there in six days by five guns. This preserve is of such vast extent that the owner leaves undisturbed for two years running, each of the three great mountain divisions, into which its topography permits the whole to be divided.

Having in the course of the last quarter of a century, off and on, stalked or participated at drives in most of these happy hunting-grounds, I have a fairly large stock of pleasant memories upon which to draw. None are more so than those of the capital sport which the extreme kindness of the hospitable Prince Hohenlohe-Langenburg has enabled me to enjoy for the last twenty years in his sportsman's Eden in the Hinter-Authal. As it would be difficult to find in any part of Europe—and I think I may say I know most regions where chamois are found—ground which comes nearer to what one would call the *beau-ideal* of a chamois shoot, I have selected from my experiences there a chamois drive, which is typical of that form of sport. While the Hinter-Riss, which adjoins it, is as famous for its Alpine stags as for its chamois, the Hinter-Authal contains on account of the absence of forests, roughness of ground and barren wildness, but very few deer, but it excels, in my opinion, all others as chamois ground.

It is reached by a carriage drive of eight hours from the nearest railway station, the last three or four of which are over a narrow Alp-road or cart-track, which ends at the shooting-lodge of the prince. The nearest human habitation —four hours off—is a peasant's hamlet, where the cart-road branches off from the high-road. The only traffic which passes over this rough connecting link with the outer world, is that of the owner of the shoot, who also constructed it, and hence can keep out all unwelcome visitors, such as tourists, whose

invasion of his game sanctuaries would work much damage.
The glen, at the extreme end of which the lodge is situated,
is really a *cul de sac*, and further progress beyond the lodge
is only possible for feet shod in summer with heavy-nailed
mountain boots, and in winter when ice or crusted snow
covers the steep declivities, for feet armed with the crampons
or *Steigeisen*, which are of such essential assistance at that
season.   Boldly rising mountains, towering up in some places
in great vertical precipices 1500 or 2000 feet high, surround
the little glade, consisting of a perfectly level emerald green
Alp-math, some 500 or 600 yards across, and traversed by a
trout brook.   On one side of this perfect little idyl stands
the unpretentious châlet-like building, which annually for
six weeks is the home of the owner and of his family.   So
exposed to the sweep of avalanches is the spot, that the
building had to be erected of stone, and even that did not
prevent the roof being carried off bodily, a few winters ago,
by the mere air-pressure of an avalanche which came down
near the building.

The walk in from the hamlet, following up the rapid
stream, which, by the way, is the Austrian source of the
Bavarian Isar, on the banks of which, many hundred miles
away, stands Munich, has already disclosed the wildest
possible scenery.   But it is only when one has entered
one of the many side ravines which branch off from
the main glen, at the point of juncture of which there is
invariably a vast accumulation of rock *debris* brought down
by the side torrent, that one gets a full view of those vast
verdureless *Kaare*, framed in by semicircular walls of crags
of fantastic shape, which are the chamois's favourite playground.   .

The torrents, which have carved out for themselves these
side ravines, or rather cañon-like gorges in the disintegrating
limestone formation, cannot as a rule be followed.   Those

that invade the recesses of these side valleys have to keep hundreds of feet above the watercourse, on the side which presents the least difficulties. Scrambling, as best one can, over the boulders and smaller moraine *débris* lying at a steep angle, which form the slopes of the glen in those places where absolute precipices do not occur, one's progress is but slow. By keeping on, always heading for the snow-field, which is almost invariably the source of the boiling torrent below, one gradually reaches the top of the moraine at the foot of the cliffs, which latter surround the *Kaar*, like the walls of an arena. If the latter have to be tackled, which is only possible for a practised climber perfectly free from giddiness, real hand and toe work takes the place of mere scrambling. But this the sportsmen participating in drives need not do; their posts are usually near the foot of the cliffs. Only the stalker, if of sufficiently adventurous turn of mind, need try his climbing powers on those towering walls; a fissure or a tiny ledge traversing the face is his path. It is treacherous rock too, and every hand and foot hold has first to be tested ere one can trust one's whole weight to such unreliable support.

In spring, when the frost goes out of the rock, stones often in regular showers are constantly falling, and now and again great blocks, the size of a house, come tumbling down, prised from the mother rock by the expansion of the melting snow, which the fierce winter's gales drove into every cranny and cleft. At that season, as well as a little later, when July thunderstorms are apt to be accompanied by cloud-bursts, these torrents, which at ordinary times can be crossed by a long step, are sights to behold. Rocks hundreds of tons in weight, that have tumbled into the cañon, are borne along as were they of featherweight, to be finally added to the great heap of *débris* at the mouth of the cleft. In no other mountain system that I know, can the appalling force of water be better watched, for on account of the verdureless character of the whole "catch-basin" the water accumulates with astonishing rapidity, the absence of all soil to soak it up assisting, of course, in bringing about these conditions.

In consequence of this, these torrents rise on occasions with an astonishing rapidity, and the volume of water that pours down their courses is vast enough to play at football with masses of rock one can hardly believe it possible could be moved, much less thrown about by that agency. ·

But let us return to that idyllic shooting-box with its green shutters and stag's antlers over the door, standing there on that level bit of bright green sward, the picture of seclusion and peace, as far removed from the turmoil of the great outer world as if seas and continents were between them. No wonder that its sportsman master has for thirty years or more, annually returned hither with the keenest pleasure, and does not allow anything to interfere with those quiet weeks in his picturesque Tyrolese mountain retreat, the year of the Franco-German War being, I believe, the one and only exception to this rule.

The rooms, seven or eight in number, are either plainly wainscoted or whitewashed, while the furniture is all of the very simplest description. Most of it was carried in on men's backs, I believe, in the days preceding the completion of the cart-track, which now allows narrow springless carts to be used for transportation. Only the most necessary servants are brought, *i.e.* a good chef, a couple of men, and a maid for the ladies, everybody enjoying the entire absence of ceremony.

The wise old maxim of "early to bed and early to rise" is rigorously enforced by my host, so that when, after a dip into icy water, and a hearty breakfast by candlelight, we issue forth from the porch, half an hour or so is yet lacking to sunrise. On the hardy Alpine pines that in scattered groups dot the glade—some of the few trees in the valley—and on every blade of grass, hoar frost is glistening ; for here, at the altitude we are, September nights are nipping.

Six or seven of the keepers and some thirty beaters, sturdy sons of the mountains, and greatly devoted to their popular master, await his coming in front of the lodge. All, including the host and his youthful son,[1] no less than the only guest beside myself, a near relation of both my host and our royal family, are dressed in the national garb of weather-worn *Loden* (frieze) jackets, and short black or gray chamois leather breeches, leaving the knee bare. Eight or nine of the beaters have huge bundles of *Lappen* swung on their backs. These are long pieces of stout cord, to which, at intervals of 3 or 4 feet, are sewn oblong pieces, about 1 foot in length and 6 inches in width, of brightly-coloured cotton stuff of a light texture. These cords are drawn, like miniature washerwomen's drying-lines, a little over 2 feet from the ground, on light stakes, along the proposed confines of the drive, so as to prevent chamois breaking out at the side and getting out of the drive. These *Lappen* are very generally used for deer and chamois drives, when the ground is so broken as it is here. For the former they are hung a little higher than for chamois. The very sight of the red, blue, or yellow flags fluttering in the breeze is generally sufficient to keep the latter within the drive. Were it not for them, hundreds of beaters would be required to stand guard along one or both sides of the drive, for when chamois-driving, a vast area of ground is covered, the slopes of two or three adjacent mountains being often taken into one drive.

Half an hour's brisk walk brings us to the entrance of the side glen which is to be the scene of the drive.

[1] Prince Ernst, about to wed H.R.H. the Duke of Edinburgh's daughter.

In solemn glory rise abruptly on both sides grand peaks and lofty walls of rock, perfectly verdureless save occasional dark green patches of stunted *Latchen*. At the end of the glen is a great snowfield, which five minutes ago was of an ashy pallor, but is now overspread by a lovely roseate hue. The tint, gradually extending itself, soon tips with a golden light the eminences of the mountain giants nearer us at the base of which we are standing, still shrouded in the morning twilight. The pale blue of the strip of sky which is visible to us slowly deepens into azure, and then into the profound blue so peculiar to Alpine horizons in the early morning.

The scramble along the steep moraine-covered slope now commences. But there is no hurry; the beaters and the majority of keepers who went ahead have to face some desperate climbing to reach their various posts at the appointed time. While another batch of beaters, the picked climbers of the whole lot, who left headquarters hours before we were turned out of our warm beds, are by this time getting on to the dangerous rocks. The object of their midnight start was to gain the crest from the back of the semicircular mountain ridge that closes the ravine at its extreme end, so as not to disturb the chamois who are on the slope facing us. To do this they had to make a tremendous round, accomplishing the main part of the distance by the light of lanterns, and leaving only the really dangerous climbing till full daylight.

Chamois-driving is an art that can only be acquired by long experience, and in the Dukeries the head-keepers are all men who are past masters at it. Half a century's practice has brought it to a state as akin to perfection as is possible to human beings who still have to learn how to control winds and fogs. The former particularly is a sad marplot, for to get the keen-scenting chamois to face a breeze blowing from the guns in their direction, is an impossible thing. Rather than do that they will break back through the line of advancing beaters, or seek safety by breaking out at the sides, notwithstanding those long lines of waving little flags—anything appears to be preferable in their eyes than facing that tainted breeze. Another consideration that has to be taken into account by those arranging drives, is the amount of climbing, or to give it a more correct name, steep uphill walking, which can be expected from the sportsmen taking part in the drive. In many shoots the arrangements are so perfect, and everything is made so convenient, that the halt and the old can take part. An hour's drive, an hour's ride on sure-footed mules, and a quarter of an hour's walk on a good path, takes the old and feeble to their posts. This means, however, that the chamois have to be driven *downwards*, which, quite apart from the animal's innate objection to go in that direction, presents many more chances for them to sneak out of the drive, and therefore entails far more elaborate precautionary arrangements than if the game can follow its own bent and direct its flight to the higher ground where its instinct leads it to seek safety. To my host, who was a first-class climber in his younger days, and who still manages to stalk his nimble game, no such considerations have to be shown, so that the guns can all be posted on high levels. In consequence of this we keep on ascending till finally we have reached and passed the snowfield at what appeared to be the head of the ravine, from which springs the brook that has worked such destruction below. We now perceive that the ravine does not end here, but that it continues in an easterly direction. A vast accumulation of moraine *débris*, which we have to climb, opens the view to a great semicircular depression, half a mile across, filled with a chaos of boulders, some of which are the size of a house. On the shady side, under the lee of the cliffs, lie patches of last winter's snow. On all sides but the one by

4

which we have gained access, towering crags rise almost perpendicularly. At their base the guns are to be posted. I am to have the highest stand, right on the horizon line, whence every detail of the drive will be visible.

The air is delightfully crisp and keen, and the long slow mountaineer's stride — the very contrary to the skip and jump of the novice as he starts out—has brought us hither in less than three hours from the main glen. After a short rest under the brow of the mound, so as not to show ourselves more than can be helped, it is time for me to start for my post—a good hour's climb. After the usual exchange of greetings passed on such occasions by all German-speaking sportsmen, viz. *Waidman's Heil*—Sportsman's luck to you—which is acknowledged by *Waidman's Dank*—Sportsman's thanks—the company parts, each member repairing to the *Stand* assigned to him.

By the time my post is reached and I have arranged myself comfortably behind a pile of heaped-up stones, and some cold meat with a pint of claret, followed by a nip of something stronger, has been disposed of, there is still half an hour left before the echoes awoke by the signal shot will come rumbling across from yonder ridge where the beaters are to commence their arduous and dangerous work. I am pretty well up, perhaps 1000 or 1500 feet below the top of the highest of those gray giants that surround me on every side. With my glass I can see the three other guns similarly engaged with their lunch or smoking a last cigarette at their less elevated posts ; and now the men drawing the *Lappen* along a giddy ridge of crags flanking the ground also become visible. It is a regular " knife-back " ridge, standing up sharp and jagged like some huge saw with teeth of irregular size. One wonders that the men can go through this tight-rope-like performance and at the same time attend to their duty of fastening the *Lappen* lines on sticks pushed into clefts in the rock. They have done it dozens of times before, and the vast depth of the precipices on both sides seems to have no more effect than were they old laundry-women stretching their lines in the back-yards of their cottages. Plenty of chamois are to be seen, some in positions where they are bound to come into the drive, but the majority are feeding on invisible blades of grass, or lying about on snow patches, quite beyond the extreme point of the semicircle to be described by the route of the beaters. The bulk of the game to be included in the drive is, however, as yet quite invisible to one, for it is on the off-side slopes of the range we have been following up since entering the ravine. That nothing should disturb them till everything is in readiness, was the most essential thing to success. Had the wind, instead of drawing down the ravine since we entered it, chopped round and blown up the gorge, it would have put to flight the chamois in the whole glen, and these again would in turn have alarmed by their precipitate flight those quietly feeding on the off-side, and as the almost certain result, not a shot would have been fired. So dependent is one, when chamois-driving, upon the goodwill of the breezes.

My "stand" overlooked the gap through which presently the bulk of the chamois from the off-side of the range would pass. For obvious reasons I had to be posted at some distance from the gap, for had I been placed in the gap itself the game would have got my wind, and my first shot would assuredly also have been my last one. Only when the game was once over the ridge of the gap and well in the *Kaar*, commanded at different points farther down by our rifles, would it be safe for me to shoot. The drive, being one of the longest, would, I knew, last three and a half or four hours.

Chamois approach one in different manners. At first, when the beaters are as yet far off and no shot has been fired by the guns, they will steal along their wonted paths,

observing the very greatest caution. At this time they are
still in bands of from five to twenty-five in number, headed
by a doe, who acts as an ever-watchful scout. Later on,
when they hear the beaters behind them and shots have
been fired, they generally disperse in smaller bands and
dash along their giddy trails as fast as their legs will carry
them. The older bucks—the great ambition, of course, of
every true sportsman—are rarely with the herd. They steal
away at the first alarm, and, after a prolonged survey of the
ground from some prominent crag, will endeavour to get out
of the scrape in the most stealthy manner. They almost
invariably come singly, keeping a wonderfully sharp look-out.
It is on their account especially that every movement on
the part of the sportsmen lying in ambush must be avoided.
Often have I sat ten minutes or a quarter of an hour as
motionless as a log of wood, hardly daring to move my eye-
lids, and half afraid that the violent beat of my heart
would betray me, while a wary old buck, standing 80 or
100 yards off, only his head and neck showing, would keep
his gaze riveted on my partly visible figure. If perfect
immovability is maintained and the wind is favourable, he
will presently advance still nearer, and then only, while his
attention is attracted in another direction, can the rifle be
slowly raised inch by inch. But let the events of the drive
tell their own tale. At the moment the rumbling sound of
the signal shot struck my ear, I had my glass pressed to
my eye and was counting the chamois in sight. There were
seventy-nine distributed in different directions, most of them
in a state of repose, while one or two little bands betrayed
already by a certain commotion that something had attracted
their attention. The moment the distant signal shot was
fired, the whole scene changed like lightning; the members
of every group were on their feet, and had dashed together
where the scout doe stood anxiously gazing about her. I

know of no prettier sight for the sportsman's eye than the one I allude to. The gay little kids, that a moment before were gambolling about, are now pressing against their mothers' flanks, while the yearlings and two-year-olds, already of a bolder temperament, jump upon the next prominent boulder or crag, to do their share of watching for the common weal. A band nearer to me than the others, is occupying a shady corner close under a wall of rock. They were lying about on a patch of snow, when that rumbling thunder roused them with the effect of an electric shock. They are now bunched round the scout doe, when presently my powerful glass shows me first the head and then the rest of the body of an *Abwehrer*[1] appearing over the jagged crest of the ridge, at the base of which, more than 1000 feet below, the chamois are standing. Faster almost than I can lower my glass and re-find the black dots on the snow, the breeze has carried down the tainted scent from the yet invisible foe. With lightning rapidity the leading doe wheels round, and, followed by the band, dashes off, making for an apparently perfectly smooth wall of rock 800 or 900 feet high. With difficulty I follow their rapid movements with my glass. A small fissure traverses diagonally the perpendicular face of the stupendous precipice. Here evidently lies their favourite path, and they travel up the incline at a rapid rate, their wonderful agility and sure-footedness enabling them to find a footing where apparently a crow could not perch, and where their sole standing room on the perpendicular face consists apparently of protrusions small and far apart. Along the top of the ridge for which the chamois are making, the *Lappen* are drawn; but of course these are not visible to the chamois till they have crested the eminence, where the fluttering rags are right before their noses. Thus it happens

---

[1] *Abwehrer* are men posted in gaps and other favourite passes of chamois, where the *Lappen* alone are not deemed sufficient to keep back the game.

that the leading doe, when suddenly coming face to face with
the startling apparition afforded by the fluttering red and
blue pieces of canvas, is for a second rooted to the ground, as
if sheer fright had turned her into stone. The rest are still
on the face of the wall, where of course there is no room to
turn, and none to allow her to pass. But so great is her
fright that, when she has recovered the use of her legs, she
turns, and, making one huge bound, clears the chamois that
has been pressing on her from behind. An indescribable
scene of terrified confusion ensues; there is absolutely not
an inch to spare to enable the band to turn. And while
the second, now foremost, chamois has with craning neck
approached the point from whence she also can see the
Lappen, and when she does so only to start back with her
front legs wide apart, and terror depicted in every gesture,
the rest stand huddled together on that narrow ledge.

For the moment, till hunger will impel them to pursue
their upward course, they are effectually cornered, and were
a gun posted on the top of the ridge he could, if he chose,
pick off at closest range every head—a proceeding, however,
which, independently of its unsportsmanlike character, and
the fact that the group consists only of does, kids, and some
young bucks, would be absurd, for every one of them would
be dashed to atoms by the fall down the stupendous
precipice.

A right and left from one of the guns below me
warns me to attend to my more immediate neighbourhood.
Opposite my post, within fair rifle range, there is a precipice
about 150 feet in height. Down the face of the rock there
is a chimney-like gully, and I know from former experience
that it is a likely pass for chamois on such occasions. I have
not to wait long. Against the horizon I see clearly outlined
the head of a chamois. I remain quite immovable; so, after
a lengthy examination of the ground, a scout doe, followed

by six other does, each with their kids, rushes down the giddy place. A hasty scrutiny of the long file with my glass assures me there is nothing killable among the lot, so I let them proceed unharmed. A narrow ledge about 80 yards long, 8 or 10 inches wide, affords the only passage to the opposite sides of the chasm where I am sitting. With elegant ease and marvellous sure-footedness they pass over this narrow band, a profound abyss at their side, and with one leap clear a space of some 5 feet where the ledge has been broken off. They pass me not 5 yards off, but as I have remained perfectly motionless, and little of my body can be seen, they do not become aware of my presence till they have passed me, when the wind, of course, quickly betrays me to them. A loud whistle of alarm of the leading doe, a rush down the declivity with an accompanying shower of stones, is the result. They have chosen a fatal course, for my neighbour, the young sportsman, cannot resist the temptation of opening fire on one of the two-year-old bucks, who is rolled over cleverly, as the band flashes past him with lightning rapidity.

A second and third band of does and small fry passes down the gully in the course of the next hour, and some fifteen or twenty shots have been fired by the three other guns, when presently what appeared to me to be a good buck makes his appearance at the top and slowly picks his steps down the slanting chimney.

To tell a buck from a barren doe in early autumn at any but the shortest distance requires long practice, and even then mistakes not infrequently occur, for the latter have also a most misleading propensity to sneak about alone. At the season of the year of which I speak these old dames resemble the bucks in all but the position of the horns, which very slight difference can, of course, only be detected when the animal is fairly close. Only the day before I had killed a barren doe, mistaking her for a buck, and though they are perfectly legitimate game, yet it is always the ambition of those "who think they know all about it" to kill only bucks.

My glass assures me, however, that not only is the animal a buck, but unquestionably one among the very largest—the so-called "capital Böcke." I let him proceed half-way down the gully, bringing meanwhile my rifle very slowly up to the shoulder. Here he halts, apparently to again survey, for the last time, the ground. This is the desirable moment; and, though the buck will get a nasty tumble, for he has scanty footing, I prefer a fairly long and steady shot to a much closer running one. My Express gives forth its loud report, and the solid bullet (a preferable missile to the usual expanding bullet for such small game as chamois), propelled by what Continental sportsmen consider a terribly large charge, *i.e.* 5½ drachms, pierces the wary old fellow from end to end, sending him to the bottom of the precipice, where he lands with a dull thud. Twice more do I shoot at chamois coming also singly, but from different directions.

By this time the drive is drawing to a close, and wherever one looks one sees, generally in the most impossible places, beaters descending from the heights above. As one watches now one, then the other edging barefooted, or with crampons buckled to his boots, along fearfully narrow bands of rock, giddy abysses yawning at their side, one must acknowledge that these men are not moved so much by sordid lucre (about half-a-crown per diem) as by an inherent love for sport, to follow such an exceedingly dangerous vocation, when they could earn as much, if not more, by their ordinary calling.

The results of the drive, after the numerous reports of the keepers had been heard, were the following: About ninety chamois were in the drive to start with. About forty broke back through the line of beaters, or escaped at the sides, while the rest came to the four guns, who, with twenty - one shots, killed eleven head, viz. seven bucks, all, with the exception of my first one, of moderate size, three barren does, and, unfortunately, also one mother doe, who, having lost her kid in the frantic rush, appeared quite alone, and hence, being mistaken for a barren doe, paid with her life her unmatronly conduct.

From the foregoing, the reader must not fancy that on every occasion do a warm and balmy autumn sun and a bright cloudless sky, join to make the long four or five hours one has to remain at one's post, a pleasurable time. Unsettled weather, as I have already hinted, is the bugbear of chamois drives, while bad weather, which in September at these altitudes means a snowstorm, though quite as fatal to good bags as shifting winds, is decidedly more unpleasant for the guns. On many occasions I have sat four long hours while a snowstorm, of a violence such as one never experiences outside of the Alps, covered me complete with drifting snow. On such occasions misses are the rule, for, hard as it is to hit so small a beast as the chamois rushing past you at double-quick speed, it becomes next to impossible to accomplish this feat while your whole body is a-tremble with cold, and your frost-cramped fingers fumble clumsily with the triggers.

Strange as it may seem, it has happened that chamois driven to the last extreme of fright, make a bold dash at the *Lappen*, either clearing with an easy bound the obstacle that has caused them so much alarm or bodily charging it. In the latter case, however, the thin but strong rope, and the pliant nature of the stakes to which it is fastened, are generally too much for them. Entangling themselves with their horns, they are hurled, after turning a complete somersault in the air, with great violence on their backs to the ground; or if, as now and again happens, they get the rope round the throat, they throttle themselves in their vain endeavours to get away. The very year I am speaking of, a chamois perished in a neighbouring shoot in this fashion.

A somewhat ludicrous adventure illustrating the blind fright of chamois, when charging the *Lappen* lines, occurred to me some seven or eight years ago in the very same preserve. And though I have already mentioned it in a place where it is more likely to meet the eye of the sportsman,[1] it may be worth repeating in these pages.

On the occasion in question we were only three guns, and as the line of fire was a long one, where six or more guns were really needed, flag-lines had to be used between the three guns so as to converge the game as much as possible to the "stands" that were occupied.- I was posted on a rock at the bottom of a steep slope of loose stones stretching many hundreds of feet upwards, my range of vision and of fire being unusually confined in every other direction. Two shots fired in rapid succession by my host, who was the nearest gun above me, put me on the *qui vive*, and not needlessly, for there, flying down the slope at a terrific pace, bounded a chamois straight for my post. On getting closer I observed, to my utmost surprise, that to one of its horns was attached what appeared to be a scarlet handkerchief, which fluttered like a pennant in the air as the animal pursued its headlong flight. The fluttering rag made it impossible to determine the sex of the animal by its horns, but its large size and strongly formed neck, as well as the two shots which I thought had been fired at it, confirmed me in my belief that it was a buck. On it came with the speed of a ricochetting cannon-ball straight down towards me, and would have passed me within a couple of yards had my rifle not ended almost *au bout portant*, the

[1] Badminton Library, *Big Game Shooting.* 2 vols.

days of what, on going up, turned out to be an old and unusually large barren doe ! It afterwards transpired that several beaters had seen her in her wild flight dash against the *Lappen*, which were new and strong, and after turning a double somersault and being flung on her back, dash away with one of the red rags, pierced by one of the horns, fluttering from her head. What made the matter worse, and earned me some chaff, was the fact that it was my hundredth chamois, and only that morning I had expressed my determination that the animal making up my century should be a big buck !

CHAPTER V

"LET the drive commence!" were the last words, as I was
told by one who was at the bedside, uttered by the unconscious
and dying sportsman that sultry August night of 1893, which
witnessed the passing away of one of the foremost and
keenest sportsmen produced by the present century, H.R.H.
Duke Ernest II. of Saxe-Coburg-Gotha, elder brother of the
Prince Consort of England. As fitting as these final words
was the act that closed this long and distinguished sporting
career, for less than an hour before that fatal attack of
apoplexy, his master hand had brought down two royals!
That the dead prince was a just and very popular ruler of his
two Duchies, a well-informed and generous Mæcenas, and
an enthusiastic patron of everything connected with Natural
History, is generally acknowledged; moreover, it does not
concern us in this place as much as do his qualities and acts
as a sportsman. In this character he was certainly the most
interesting and genial personage it has been my privilege ever
to meet. His ideas about sport, it always appeared to me,
were shaped more in accordance with English ideas than with
those of the Fatherland, where the practical in connection with
sport is apt to be lost sight of by men somewhat apt to regard
sport through the spectacles of a professor or through those

H.R.H. THE LATE DUKE OF SAXE-COBURG-GOTHA.
(From a sketch from life.)

of a master of ceremony. The duke was a great admirer of England and of England's sportsmen; the only exception, and about which he liked to quiz one, being the poorness of Scotch deer antlers, a subject with which he had ample opportunities to become familiar during his frequent stays at Balmoral, in the earlier days of his brother's royal union.

Springing from a dynastic race, which for eight centuries had furnished some of the most liberal-minded sovereigns and many a doughty warrior, the Saxon electors and dukes were, however, principally distinguished for their devotion to the chase. His own partiality for it lay, therefore, in his blood.

Nature had endowed him with the frame of a Hercules; and one has to go back to past centuries to find among royalty those broad shoulders, huge limbs, and knightly bearing which made him such a conspicuous figure at all distinguished gatherings of a nation where martial demeanour and well set-up men are rather the rule than the exception.

The duke was owner of some of the best shooting in Europe. Most of the wooded portion of his Duchy of Gotha was one great deer preserve; numerous shooting-lodges, distributed in various spots, affording the necessary accommodation to himself and his guests. The principal one was the beautiful castle of Reinhardsbrunn, a few miles from Gotha, amidst sylvan surroundings of exceptional beauty. They resembled those of another of his seats, Rosenau near Coburg, of which the Queen, when describing her visit to this her favourite holiday ramble, writes : " What is so beautiful, is that between the noble and solemn forest of silver and spruce firs you come to the greenest and most beautiful little valleys, overshadowed by these deep green firs, with here and there some beeches and oaks among them. These reminded us of Windsor, only the latter seems stiff and tame after this."

Built by the duke's father, Reinhardsbrunn occupies the site of an ancient Benedictine abbey, founded 800 years ago, in days when the Saxon dynasty furnished more than one Emperor to Germany. For many centuries the great forests which clothe the hills of this part of Thuringia were famous hunting-grounds. Vast numbers of deer, wild boar, and even bear stocked them, for the crops of the peasantry were entirely at their mercy, the killing of an antlered marauder being visited in olden days by the loss of limb and even of life. At one time of its history Reinhardsbrunn severely felt the consequences of this oppression, for in the sanguinary peasants' war of 1525 the buildings were razed to the ground by the rebellious peasants. The great lime trees are there still, under which the masterful abbots were wont to entertain the sovereign on his frequent hunting excursions. In the corridors and halls of the picturesque castle which now rears its walls under those groves of 700 years old limes, there is a most interesting collection of trophies of the chase, the like of which can only be seen in two or three places in Europe, though in one respect it is without a rival. For no sportsman, at least of modern days, can boast of an equal number of stags, chamois, and wild boar brought down by his own rifle. The duke's bag is nothing like that of his famous ancestor of the seventeenth century, the Elector John George I. of Saxony, who is said to have shot, in forty-five years, 47,239 red-deer. But the duke's 3500 red-deer and 2000 chamois stand, so far as the writer has ascertained, for this century at least, at the top of the score.

As the duke was in the habit of annually visiting all his sporting estates, and was, moreover, a frequent guest at the shooting parties of royal kinsmen, every day of the season was carefully planned out months before. The year began for him, as he would say, with a three weeks' visit to Tyrol, where the season for chamois opens on 15th July. On returning to his Thuringian forests he usually devoted the four weeks following the 15th August to his deer, their antlers being then "clean," and the animals themselves in perfect condition. As stalking at that season of the year is, of course, impossible in dense forest, driving had to be resorted to, and for this purpose the ground was divided into districts separated by avenue-like cuttings through the forest, in which the guns were posted. Each of these blocks of forest was driven separately, the following being a favourite manner of his. The first time, the beaters walked as noiselessly as possible away from the guns till they reached the other end of the beat, when, at a given signal, they turned and retraced their steps with loud halloas and the beating of bushes with sticks and cudgels. The first part of the manœuvre was often more successful than the latter, for old stags, who attain great cunning, have a way of breaking back through the line of beaters. As the rides were narrow, and stags invariably "rush" these open spaces, the shooting was not the easiest. The duke generally occupied a *Hochstand, i.e.* a platform raised some 8 or 10 feet over the ground, from which elevation he, of course, commanded a wider field. The Thuringian stags, though in size nothing like to the Hungarian red-deer, are considerably larger animals than the Scotch deer, and carry finer heads. In the fifty-six years in which the duke shot these forests, he killed seven stags of from twenty to twenty-four points, and over 200 of from fourteen to eighteen points. He was one of the finest game shots with the rifle I have ever met with, and he used to make some marvellous shots with his favourite ·450 Henry Express. Thus I saw him once get a right and left across a valley at two deer in full flight. Some discussion arising as to the distance, he ordered it to be measured, and it was found to be 440 metres, or about 480 yards.

On one occasion, when he was the guest of the old

Emperor of Germany in the well-stocked forests of Letzlingen, the host was prevented by indisposition from going out, and the duke, as the oldest royal personage present, was given the post usually occupied by the Emperor. The drive lasted three hours, and, when it was over, thirty-two stags were found lying in front of the duke's "stand." What was remarkable about it was that every stag, however speedy the rush of the animal may have been, had been laid low by the " master shot " through the shoulder, just over the heart. It was a performance which the rest of the guests thought so marvellous that they suspected some trick about it; and Prince Frederick Charles, " the red Prince," then the best shot at the Prussian Court, and another guest, made the most searching inquiries when their kinsman's back was turned in the hope of discovering the secret of his success. But, needless to say, it was simply the remarkable skill of the sportsman (at the time almost sixty-five years of age) which made this feat possible.

On another occasion, a few years before, when driving the Inselberg in the Thuringian forest, the duke with two double shots killed four stags (three of them of fourteen points) while in full flight, the first being over 200 yards off.

The duke's bag during the four weeks' sport in the Thuringian forests were usually from 80 to 100 stags. From there, with the Duchess and a small suite, he again repaired to Hinter-Riss, which, as he frequently said, was also his favourite. This shoot was a creation of his own, for when he and the father of the present Prince Leiningen started it, more than fifty years ago, the great tract of mountain country, they leased from the Crown, contained but few chamois and fewer deer, and the subsequent devastations by the peasants in the Revolution of 1848, when so many well-stocked preserves were utterly ruined, undid the result of many a year's preserving. But for the last thirty years it has certainly proved to be one of the best chamois and deer grounds in the Alps. Not so extensive as some of the Emperor of Austria's preserves in Styria and Upper Austria, and not containing the enormous head of chamois to be found on Prince Auersperg's probably unrivalled chamois preserves in the neighbouring Zillerthal, the Hinter-Riss can yet more than hold its own in other respects. Upon none have such large sums of money been spent in making carriage-roads along the narrow mountain-skirted valleys, and in cutting bridle-paths up the precipitous slopes, where it often seems impossible that approach could be thus facilitated. The main lodge, a small but picturesquely situated Schloss, guards the entrance to the wilder part of the shooting, and numerous châlet-like lodges built high up near the timber-line, enabled the duke to pass many days consecutively in the very heart of his preserve, where chamois and deer could often be seen quietly grazing in close proximity. A large staff of keepers, all fearless cragsmen, guarded the game during the rest of the year; while for the chamois drives as many as 100 of the boldest climbers in the country received employment for several weeks as beaters. In his younger years the duke was a first-rate climber himself, and stalked his chamois in the orthodox manner. Many a story is told of the popular prince's prowess in this respect. I remember on one occasion when walking with him over an open *Alpenlichte* —grassy clearing—he pointed out to me a spot where, notwithstanding the exceptionally open nature of the ground, he had contrived, during the rutting season, to stalk up to within 100 yards of a herd of red-deer, consisting of thirteen stags, none of which carried less than ten points, surrounded by over forty hinds, and to kill a royal out of the herd with the single shot he fired. " It was one of the sublimest pictures I remember," he continued, " for yonder," pointing to some rocks only a couple of hundred yards above the spot where

5

the deer had stood, "I saw over fifty chamois, which had noticed me long before the deer did, and were peering down as if curious to watch me circumvent their antlered fellows."

Of late years, when his increasing corpulency made it impossible for him to indulge in that most arduous of sports, the chamois were driven and great bags were made, close upon 200 being killed in some years; 149 head to his own rifle being, if I remember rightly, his best score. Considerably larger bags might have been made had mere slaughter been the duke's object, and had the rule been less strictly respected that, if possible, only bucks should be shot. Mistakes in distinguishing the minute, and at a distance almost invisible marks of distinction between the adult buck and doe were, with him, far rarer than with most sportsmen. The chamois drives commenced usually just after the stags' rutting season was over. During the latter he was always quite alone, for, to the Continental sportsman, the short fortnight of the red-deer's mating season is the *ne plus ultra* of the whole year's sport. So passionately fond was this veteran sportsman of deer-stalking, that even during the very last season which he lived to see, he succeeded in killing several stags. He managed this by having himself drawn up in a sort of chair on wheels, before dawn of day, to the vicinity of the spot where the stag was calling, and doing the last bit of stalking on foot as best he could. The chamois drives lasted almost invariably until the end of October, and those who know how inclement that season often is in the high Alps, will appreciate the hardiness and pluck shown by the aged duke on such occasions, when he would often have to stand three or four hours in a raging snowstorm, on the top of some knife-backed ridge, exposed to the full fury of the marrow-freezing tempest.

Leaving Tyrol in the first week of November, the boar forest in Elsass, which he had leased, and his great Upper

Getting a Shot at a Stag in the Rutting Time.

Austrian estates on the Danube were visited. The last year
I was privileged to be his guest his bag was: August 16 to
September 15, in Thuringia, 82 stags, 18 hinds; September
21 to October 31, in Hinter-Riss, Tyrol, 48 stags and 149
chamois; November 3 to 7, Wallersee in Upper Austria, 115
boars, and between 4 guns, 22 roebucks, 132 hares, 1113
pheasants, 2 woodcock, and 6 partridges.

There was so much to interest the sportsman in the
Hinter-Riss, that a short description of its chief features as I
saw them on the various occasions when I was a guest of the
late owner, may not be out of place in this little volume
devoted to Alpine sport. Under the late duke, the Hinter-
Riss certainly was the beau-ideal of a mountain shoot, made
so by an intimate knowledge of every detail and of all the
requirements, no less than by the expenditure of sums large
even for the ducal purse, considering the number of shooting
estates in the prince's possession, and which were all kept up
with a lavish hand. The most convenient approach to the
central lodge, the charmingly situated château, to which I
have already referred, and of which the sketch I am enabled
to give conveys a fairly good idea, was from the Bavarian
side, for the several streams that rise in the various parts of
the estate all flow into the Isar in Bavaria. The deep glens
worn by these watercourses through an otherwise exceedingly
precipitous "sea of mountains" afford in such a country the
only practicable approach. Hence the narrow carriage-road,
built, as were one and all the roads and paths in this mountain
wilderness, by the late duke, follows up the rushing stream
towards its source. Here the sportsman devoted to the rod
could find excellent sport, when once the water runs clear.
This latter occurs later than might be wished, for in the
mountains drained by this stream, snow lies late—in fact, in
some places it is to be found all the year round. The
principal room in the castle was the dining-hall, a lofty

chamber of great size, the walls of which when I was last there were adorned by some 1500 trophies, principally those of the chamois, though some fine antlers of mountain stags shot in the Hinter-Riss (some of twenty and one of twenty-two points) were not wanting. A large open fire-place, an institution unfortunately too rarely seen on the Continent, and the finish of the oak wainscoting gave the stately room the home-like appearance of an English hall.

The only building on the whole property which did not belong to the duke was an ancient little chapel and hermitage, which latter had for centuries been the one and only human dwelling permanently inhabited in the unbroken solitude of a vast stretch of mountains. When the duke came to build his shooting-box, he selected, as the site most suitable for it, an eminence a couple of hundred yards from the lowly little hermitage inhabited by a solitary monk. Here the descendant of the great Elector of Saxony, the redoubtable fighter for the Reformation, and the cowled Benedictine friar, settled down in peaceful neighbourliness, not as much as a fence separating the castle grounds from the bit of grass where the cassocked hermit turned out his one cow when he had finished ringing matins, and from which he drove her back to her diminutive shed, when vespers had been tolled by his busy hands. Here, in the supreme solitude of the great forest, rows upon rows of craggy gray peaks looking down as silent auditors upon this little settlement, the great Protestant prince and the lowly friar lived for nearly half a century side by side in peace and goodwill. Once or twice during the two or three months which the duke spent annually in the Hinter-Riss, the friar would dine at the castle, where the kindly prince would have him at his right and show him all honours; and the same number of times the duke's huge form would darken the small doorway of the hermitage, where his genial voice would sound like a lion's roar in the tiny cell where the monk

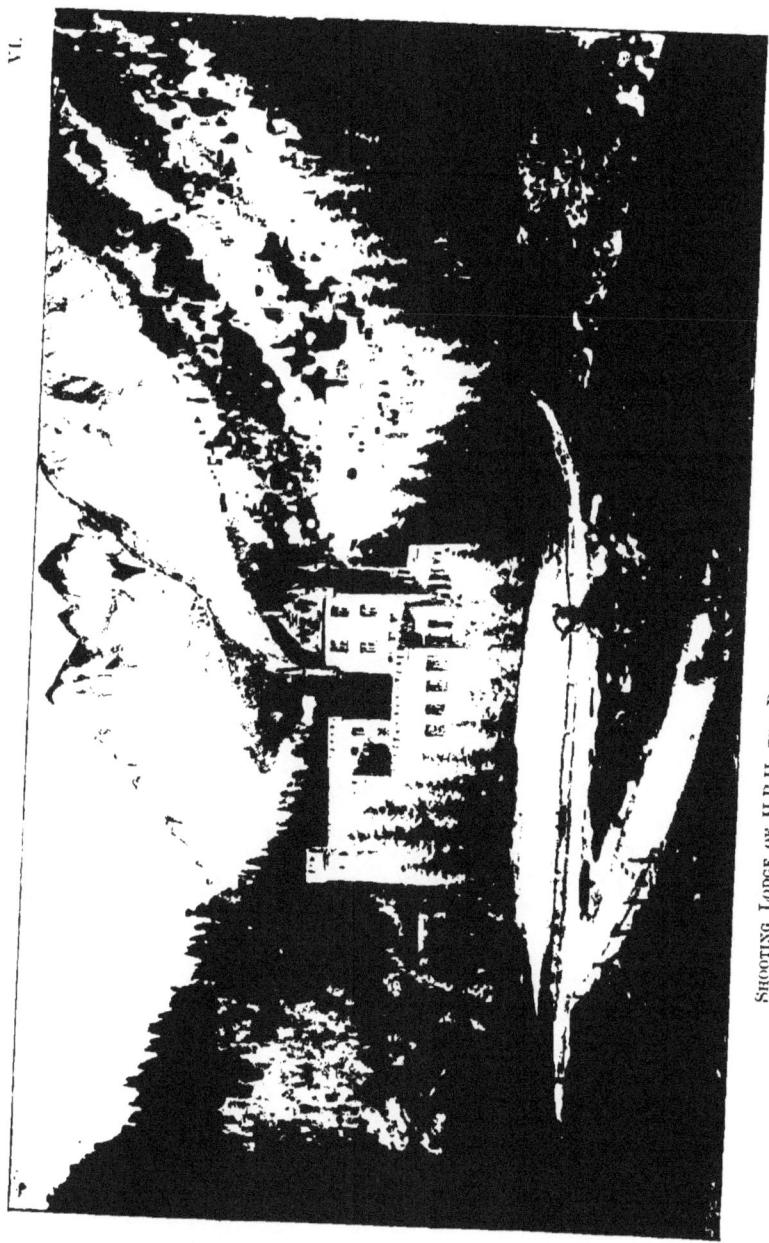

VI.

SHOOTING LODGE OF H.R.H. THE DUKE OF COBURG IN THE HINTER-RISS, TYROL.

received his visitor. A loaf of the coarsest brown bread, some fresh home-made butter, and a sip of some raw native cordial, no less than a freely offered grimy snuff-box, constituted the return hospitality. Twice or thrice I happened to be present when the friar dined at the castle, and on one of these occasions he was permitted to bring with him an unsophisticated friar who happened to be paying him a visit at the hermitage. To the latter, everything he saw, heard, ate, and drank was as novel as had he just dropped from the moon. Not the least ludicrous incident on that occasion was the cowled guest's perplexed face after gulping down the lukewarm contents of the finger-bowl, the use of which he did not know. While the very frequent indulgence, during dinner, of snuff dipped from the interior of a vast snuff-box which, when not in actual use, was deposited in the hood behind the wearer's neck, was not less amusing. But I must not take up too much space with these reminiscences, though they are among the pleasantest, for my pen would easily outrun the constable of my readers' patience.

Scattered about on the mountain slopes, on clearings that were either natural or made by the woodman's axe, were a number of *Alp-hütten* or *châlets*, each tenanted during the three summer months by a male or female herder, and a dozen or two of cattle or sheep. These belonged to peasants living in other parts of Tyrol, who had acquired the grazing rights on these secluded Alp-maths in old times when a great part of this portion of North Tyrol belonged to the rich Benedictine monastery of Ficht in the Unter Inn valley. When Emperor Josef, more than 100 years ago, abolished all monastic orders in Austria, the land reverted to the Crown, and many of the peasants who had held long leases of these Alp-rights from the Abbot of Ficht, now bought the land outright from the Crown. Originally intended only for cattle-grazing, in the course of time sheep

took the place of the latter in many of the highest grazings.
To sheep, chamois have a particular aversion, which causes
them to leave the neighbourhood. The duke soon recognised
that if the shoot was to be made a really good one, such as
all the other features gave promise it could be made, these
sheep-rights had to be abolished. As this could be done only
by purchasing the land, large areas were bought by him in
the course of time, at what were then considered extravagant
prices, but which in the end proved to be most judiciously
invested money. When these Alp-maths passed into his
hands the grazing of cattle and sheep was stopped, and the
spot reverted to its wild state, to the great benefit of the
game in the surrounding mountains. Chamois were no
longer disturbed, and the red-deer found the best of grass on
patches of soil that had been manured for upwards of a
century. The utterly barren rock above timber-line, which
in extent forms the largest part of this shoot, and which is
Crown land, the duke leased from Government not only for
his lifetime, but for a series of years beyond his demise. In
consequence of this wise foresight on the late duke's part,
his successor, the Duke of Edinburgh, will enjoy the preserve in its entirety for many a year yet, till the Crown
leases fall in.

　　Though my first visit to this lovely mountain retreat
occurred almost a quarter of a century ago, the late duke was
then already past his prime. His increasing corpulency, to
which, curiously enough, another great mountain sportsman,
the late King Victor Emanuel of Italy, was also a martyr,
compelled him to take his chamois-shooting rather more easily
than was his wont in the days of his lusty youth, when he
could hold his own with the best amateur mountaineers of
his day. Thus it came about that every year more and more
attention was paid to the construction of bridle-paths, by
which he was enabled to reach high levels on the back of

his sturdy shooting-ponies. Stalking chamois had to be altogether forsaken, and driving the game was, for many years before his death, the only possible method to give that deadly double barrel of his a chance to prove the unerringness of the hands that held it.

In his home forests in his own Thuringian principality, the chase was conducted in the usual German style. The keepers and foresters, of which there were a great number, were all dressed in the dark-green tightly-fitting frock-coat which gives the sporting brotherhood in North Germany that stiff and unpicturesque look so strange to English eyes, to which such an assembly gives the impression of militarism masquerading in the guise of sport. Very different in this respect were matters conducted in the Hinter-Riss. There the master, keepers, and beaters, as well as many of the guests, appeared in the easy, workmanlike shooting costume of the Tyrolese and Styrian mountaineer, which is universally worn on such occasions by all Austrian sportsmen, from the Emperor down to the youngster eager for the blood of his first chamois. The more weather-stained and worn-looking the black chamois-leather knee-breeches, the more scarred and sun-browned the bare knees, which are visible between the latter and the gray stockings, the more ancient and shabby the hat, the more faded the green binding on the coarse gray frieze jacket, the more convincing the proof that the wearer has served a long and faithful apprenticeship to mountain venery. In this respect the North German differs somewhat from the Austrian sportsman. The former has fewer of those genuine sporting qualities the Englishman instinctively associates with the pursuit of game. These qualities, more or less prominent in the Austrian and Hungarian, are also those that lead the latter to seek, like the Englishman, sport in India, Africa, and America, in each of which fields they have distinguished

themselves. The Prussian, on the other hand, enjoys sport
from an academic rather than from a practical standpoint,
and he can rarely unbend sufficiently to exchange his stiff
military pose for one more natural to the pursuit of sport, or
take off that tight frock-coat of his, and in its stead don
the loose workmanlike *Loden* jacket of the Austrian *Jäger*.
The late Duke of Coburg wore his Austrian shooting-dress
also in his Thuringian woods, and well did it suit those broad
shoulders and Herculean limbs. But he was one in ten
thousand, and his open, clear mind instinctively acquired
and adapted to its own use the best of every country.

In the old days, when the late prince was active and
lithe, his keepers were famous throughout Tyrol as the best
climbers and most dare-devil fellows. Several of them had
been poachers in their youth, and the far-seeing duke secured
their lifelong devotion by saving them from prison when
captured red-handed in his mountains. An old saying has
it, that those who have attested their innate love for sport,
by risking liberty and life as *Wilderers* (poachers), make in
the end the best keepers. Only one or two of the old guard
are alive to-day, living by their master's generosity as
pensioners in remote villages. Several of them were, however, still doing active duty when I first came to the Hinter-
Riss, amongst them famous Rieser, the *Wildmeister* or
Master of the Game of the Hinter-Riss. What that man
did not know about chamois was indeed not worth knowing;
and I have certainly never met any man who could approach
him in the successful planning of chamois drives. His
intuitive expertness in this respect bordered on the wonderful,
for he seemed even to be able to outwit that arch-enemy, a
suddenly changing wind, which, as a rule, means ruin to the
most skilfully laid plans for the day's drive, where such
keen-witted game as the chamois is concerned. The most
sudden change of weather, with consequent change in the

NEUNER: A FAVOURITE KEEPER OF H.R.H. THE LATE DUKE OF
SAXE-COBURG-GOTHA.

wind, would yet find old Rieser master of the circumstances.
Without altering the prearranged position of a single gun,
success would be brought about by a changed disposition of
the beaters and of the lines of flags. To think all this out
on the spur of the moment, miles away from the spot, required
the most minute local knowledge, not only of the ground, but
of the play of various currents of air, that puzzle the most
astute in such a maze of mountains.

  With such masters of the craft at his elbows, chamois-
shooting in the Hinter-Riss was like witnessing a *Kriegs-spiel*
managed by a Moltke; and none understood the difficulties
and appreciated the skill that had overcome them, better
than Rieser's master. Sprung from humble peasant stock,
Rieser remained to his last day the typical free-spoken,
simple-minded mountain man. It was said that in his
earlier years of service under the duke, when even the
commonest forms of intercourse with royalty were rules he
little understood, he would, when excited by some question
concerning which he and his master were not at one, drop
into the colloquial form common among peasants, and address
his royal highness by the familiar "thou" (*du*), to the
latter's great amusement. When reprimanded by his superiors
for these lapses, he would excuse himself by asserting that,
as the duke always told him to tell the truth and shame the
devil, he thought the personal pronoun which he used when
praying to his God, was good enough when he spoke the
truth to his master, who was after all only a man. " You
fellows," he would fearlessly say to his shocked North German
monitors, " you think because you bow and scrape and say
' Herr Herzog,' you needn't tell him but the truth that flatters
him." Of the tales told of Rieser's adventures and early life
many a chapter could be written, but as several of the persons
that would figure in these tales are still alive, the time for
this has not yet come.

For the last twenty years of his life the duke and duchess, when staying in the Hinter-Riss, did not reside in the castle itself, in which the guests lived, but in a picturesque little cottage close under its walls. The dinner-hour, which varied according to the exigencies of the day's sport, united host and hostess and their guests in the great dining-hall. These repasts, to which every one sat down with sharpened appetites, for the days were mostly long ones, were delightfully cheery meals, for the duke was one of the liveliest and most amusing conversationalists imaginable, while a perfect freedom from the stiff court etiquette, so invariably enforced at the gatherings of German royalties, was not the least of the causes that made these occasions so memorably pleasant. The duke was passionately fond of whist, and the invariable rubber was not even omitted on those evenings which were passed in one or the other of the small lodges high up above timber-line, where, to avoid a long ride in the dark down to the castle and an uncomfortably early start on the following morning, the night was passed in the primitive little huts. As there were always at least three guests present, and most of the higher lodges contained, besides a sitting-room, kitchen, and the duke's bedroom, only one other room, which was used by the guests as a common bedroom, the quarters were very close; but ah! what delightful evenings were passed there in spite of it, or rather on account of it. On more than one occasion, winter surprised one during that last week of October, and after the usual premonitory signs in the shape of a flurry of snow, driving before a bitter gale, which made those four or five hours at one's posts desperately cold waits, we would find on rising next morning after a night of the most terrific storm, one side of the house half-buried under heavy drifts of snow 8 or 10 feet deep. The coming of winter at those bleak altitudes beyond the growth of timber is no joke, and a speedy retreat to the castle, 3000 or 4000 feet lower down,

A *Stand* at a Chamois-drive in the Hinter-Riss.

was the only course open. To continue the drives was impossible, for the peril to which such a snowfall would expose the beaters, when climbing in dangerous places, was altogether too serious to be risked. But for that consideration, I am convinced the duke would have often continued his hunt in the severest weather, for in spite of his age he was exceedingly hardy, and thoroughly inured to the hardships inseparable from sport in the high Alps in late autumn.

The most distant of these outlying lodges, though it was not in an elevated position, occupied an historical spot, namely, the *Pertisau*, on the shores of the Achen See, which was one of the favourite retreats of old Maximilian. Here, we know from documents in the Innsbruck archives, the old sportsman had erected a great timber lodge and caused numerous boats to be built for use on the mountain-bowered lake. To please the ladies of his court, the chamois and stags were on occasions driven by a great force of beaters down the precipitous mountain-sides into the lake, where they were shot or speared by the Emperor. The duke's lodge, standing a few hundred yards from the lake-shore, and slightly more roomy than some of the lodges higher up on the mountains, was annually visited for two or three days, as some good chamois and deer ground could be reached from there. So favourable is the lie of the country, that the spots where the guns were posted could almost be reached by a four-in-hand. Let me describe one of these shoots in a valley called the Gramai, which I happen to remember more particularly, for I killed a fine royal, the best that had been obtained for several days, on that occasion. We had come over from the castle on the previous day, a high pass over which the duke had constructed a bridle-path, facilitating communication with the castle for all but carriages. A couple of country vehicles hired in the nearest village, a good day's drive off, were waiting at the door of the lodge when, after an early breakfast at candle-light, we were ready to start for the glen we were to hunt that day.

But for that often - mentioned vital consideration at chamois drives, viz. the wind, there would have been no necessity to make such an early start, for a two hours' drive took us to within a rifle-shot or two of the posts we were to occupy, and as the drive would not take longer than three hours, the day's sport was over soon after noon. But in this outlying part of the preserves where the duke owned no land, the stalking-paths were few and far between. It was therefore necessary to drive the game *down* the mountains to points low down which the duke could reach. This is always a difficult job, and only possible in the morning hours before the rays of the sun strike the slope frequented by the game which is to be driven. The drive into the glen was all the way up a gentle rise, and the farther we penetrated into the heart of the mountains, the higher and more precipitous did the peaks on both sides become. The *Granai* itself is a level stretch of green Alp-math, clear of timber, except a few isolated groups of fine old sycamore trees that have managed to escape the vicissitudes of winter and the avalanches of spring. From this level space, a few hundred acres in extent, the mountains on the west rise almost perpendicularly to one of the highest peaks in that part of the range; while, on the other side, tier upon tier, the lower ones covered with stunted pine, the upper ones of bare rock now covered with the remains of the last snowfall, rise in amphitheatre shape towards heaven. A few log-huts, the summer residence of cattle-herders, occupying the centre of the math, had long ago been deserted by their occupants, and other human habitations there were, of course, none within many a mile. The duke's post was a little way up the lowest tier, where it commanded a favourite *Wechsel* or pass of old bucks. The other guests were posted along the border of the math, at the

foot of several long strips of slope where avalanches had
cleared off the timber, and which enabled them to shoot
upwards at game crossing these clearings as well as out
towards the math, across which it was anticipated some of
the game would attempt to direct their flight in order to
reach the mountains on the other side. My own post was
farther out towards the centre of the math, at the base of a
huge old sycamore. From there I had not only a splendid
view of the whole drive, to me a most desirable addition to
the pleasure of actual shooting, but also an unusually
extensive *Aus-Schuss* or range of fire, covering practically the
whole clear space of the math. It was one of the mixed
drives, *i.e.* red-deer as well as chamois would be in it. And
though it was the 24th October, and therefore nine days after
the close of the season for harts, the special permission
obtained from the proper authorities to prolong the open
season to the end of the month, enabled one to shoot the
stags too. Half an hour after our arrival the commencement
of the drive was announced to the guns by the far-away
signal shot, and soon afterwards one could perceive with the
telescope the long line of beaters breast the jagged sky-line
which they had gained after a long detour from the opposite
side of the range. On the one flank the line of coloured flags,
drawn during the previous afternoon along a shoulder of the
mountain, was visible through the glass. For some time no
game whatever came into sight, then little troops of black
dots, hurrying across snowfields or down invisible ledges
traversing the face of precipices, came into view. They all
seemed to be pressing towards a well-known gap in a sharp
ridge, whither escape from the encircling line of beaters
seemed assured. But one knew well enough that a vigilant
keeper had for hours been occupying this post of trust in the
gap, for on him depended to a great extent the bag of the
day so far as chamois were concerned. Nearer and nearer to

this gap drew the foremost band. Now they are not more than half a mile from it, and would soon come in line with the current of air drawing down from the man stationed in the gap. With the glass glued to my eye, I watched for what I foresaw would happen. "Ah! there they have got it!" rose involuntarily to one's lips, as suddenly that tainted whiff reached the foremost doe. Wheeling round as if on a pivot, the startled animal suddenly faces those behind her, and it did not tax one's imagination to fancy the whistle of alarm that sends the warning of danger along the whole line. Like chaff picked up by a strong gust of wind, the alarmed animals fly in different directions. Some make for the ridge where descending beaters soon turned them downwards, others take a bee-line towards the math, where they expect to be able to cross to the opposite range of mountains. Soon the easily recognisable report of the duke's Express rang out, but as he was invisible to me, it was impossible to tell the effect of his fire. Also the other guests' turn comes in due time, but chamois on a dead run across an open space are not everybody's meat, and the most got off scot-free, an escape shared also by a three or four year-old buck who goes scooting across the level at his best gait, some 200 yards off. I had evidently, so I thought, not held far enough in front of the moving target, for the hardly perceptible duck he made, plainly showed that my bullet went skimming over his back, cutting off, perhaps, a few hairs without further injury to him. My next neighbour, who had missed two bucks at what appeared to me to be less than half the distance at which I had fired, now greeted my performance with a polite but derisive bow and doffing of his hat, to which I, of course, signalled back the superior number of his misses. But the chance to repair my bungling soon came. Two fine stags I saw were making for the duke's post, the lesser one, a good ten-pointer as it afterwards turned out to be, a couple

of hundred yards ahead of the other. When my host's
Express rang out, the second hart, taking fright at the
leader's tumble, turned round, and made for the math, following a slanting direction downwards. Will he escape the fire
of those two Prussian Excellencies between whose posts he
had perforce to run the gauntlet? Bang! goes the first one's
rifle, and bang! follows suit, a second later, the second
sportsman's rifle. The only result of the shots, so far as I
could see, was that the stag's flight is slightly turned away
from me, and that instead of passing me within 50 yards or
so, he swerved off, and I had to take my shot at a distance of
quite 200 yards. A huge block of rock, hundreds of tons in
weight, was lying on the math in the direction for which the
deer was heading. At the moment the stag, now broadside
on to me, passed it, which he did within a foot or two, I
pulled the trigger. Warned by my late experience with the
chamois, I took time rather too much by the forelock, and
my bullet reached its mark a trifle too quickly. Instead of
inflicting a mortal wound, it only grazed its chest. A subsequent examination of the smooth face of the boulder demon-
strated that the bullet, after inflicting the slight flesh
wound, struck the rock, and "splashed." Some of the
particles of lead glanced back, and hit the deer on the
opposite side from whence the shot had come. The animal,
no doubt, confused by all the shooting, and feeling the sting
of the lead, turned off at right angle, and came straight
for me. My second shot was an easy one enough, for I
had the noble beast at 50 yards when my ball doubled him
up. After a few kicks he joined the majority, whither his
mate, felled by my host's bullet, had preceded him. Mine
was, however, the better stag of the two: a "royal," superior
in weight as well as in points to any of the other deer grassed
in Gramai.

   With chamois we had only indifferent luck that day,

nothing like the anticipated number being brought to book. Though more than a hundred were in the drive, only a few were bagged. The old difficulty of getting the chamois downhill, was one which even astute old Rieser could not surmount on that occasion.

In all matters appertaining to venery and the natural history of game, the duke took a keen interest. He was undoubtedly on these subjects a foremost authority, and spent money in a lavish manner where he thought improvement was possible. With a herd of wapiti, imported from America, he freshened up the blood of his Thuringian deer, and the large public ornithological museum in Gotha, begun by himself and the Prince Consort when they were mere boys, owes its present completeness almost entirely to the duke's later efforts in different parts of the world. The Dark Continent was visited by him in the Sixties, with several distinguished men of science in his suite, amongst others Brehm. Antler lore was a favourite study of his, and a more enthusiastic collector and admirer of the stag's proud trophy it would be difficult to imagine. At the sight of a fine head he would evince the excitement and joy of a boy gloating over a much-desired toy. An instance of this came under my personal notice, when on returning from a shooting trip to the Rockies, where luck had favoured my rifle, and I had bagged some very fine wapiti and bighorn heads, the duke, on his next visit to Tyrol, honoured my trophies with an inspection. The wapiti heads took his fancy more particularly, and when I offered him the pick, his pleasure was great. He was half an hour making his selection, walking round the heads and dilating upon the merits of each, and subsequently jumped up several times from the whist table to inspect and reinspect the antlers.

With the Tyrolese in the Hinter-Riss the duke was immensely popular, notwithstanding the bigoted prejudice often entertained by these staunch Roman Catholics against Protestant strangers. His urbanity and his keen devotion to the sport so dearly beloved by themselves, won their hearts in the same way that their sturdy independence and naïve simplicity of mind gained his own good-will. Numerous stories of the duke's *bonhomie*, as well as of the natives' guileless frankness, which latter contrasted so strikingly with the servility to which royalty is accustomed, might be told in illustration of the cordial relations which existed between the duke and the lowly Tyrolese peasants. One little incident will suffice. Ragg, one of his favourite keepers, while trying to secure a chamois wounded by the duke, followed the not very seriously injured beast on to some dangerous shelving rocks, where he finally overtook it. He had left his rifle behind, and proposed to finish off the animal with his knife. In the struggle with the chamois, the latter managed to stick one of his horns through the tendon of Ragg's right heel, where it remained hooked in. Being a strong buck, the man, thus handicapped, was incapable of saving himself from being dragged by the fiercely struggling buck down the shelving rock, which ended a yard or two off in a profound precipice. Death stared him in the face, but at the last moment, when the chamois had already slipped over the brink, he managed to clutch a *Latchen* branch, and so arrest his fall. Suspended in the air with the kicking buck hanging from his heel, Ragg passed some terrible minutes, till the duke, who had watched the whole affair, could reach him with a helping hand, and, in spite of the risk he was running, extricate him from his perilous position. Notwithstanding his lacerated foot, Ragg walked down to the Alpine hut in which the shooting party were to pass the night, and insisted in joining the group that assembled after dark, as customary, round the blazing fire in front of the hut. When dinner was over, the duke, surrounded by his guests, was wont to join his stalwart keepers

6

and beaters, to discuss the events of the day, as well as the arrangements for the morrow. Calling limping Ragg out of the group of keepers, and forgetting for the moment the tenacity with which these simple-minded people believe the doctrine of their Church, that none but those of their own belief can go to heaven, he addressed him in his cheery way : " Well, Ragg, my man, that was a close shave you had to-day ; I did not think your life was worth much when I saw you hanging to that bit of a branch ; and now that I think of it," he added jokingly, "you had better, in future, avoid making me risk my own neck in that way. We were both of us nearly going to heaven together, eh ?" Ragg's reply was as unexpected as it was amusing, the effect being heightened by the perfect seriousness of the man. " Well, Highness, 'tis not for me to say nay, and though no two men stood nearer death than you and I did to-day, it isn't my belief, if I have your permission to say it, that we would have gone to the same place if that branch *had* broken," and quite unconsciously, as if to give further emphasis to his words, he crossed himself. Over the duke's expressive features stole a hardly repressible smile, and he endeavoured to pass it off by remarking : " Well, Ragg, we can't all hope to go to the same place, can we ? "

When the news of the duke's death reached the secluded Hinter-Riss, the deepest consternation took possession of the people, amongst whom the prince and the duchess had passed, as they often used to say, the happiest days of their long, eventful lives. In him they lost a kind, dear master and a good friend, who was for ever willing to help where help was needed. If it took half a century to win the affection and confidence of these self-retained hardy mountain people, his memory will a century hence be as green as are the firs and pines that cling so tenaciously to their native rock ; and the deeds and words of the popular " Herr Herzog " will there be spoken of when in the outer world his name will be remembered only by the historian.

A pathetic little incident, showing the place the duke had won for himself in the heart of even the lowliest peasant, may fitly conclude these desultory reminiscences. Happening to be near the Hinter-Riss when the news of his death penetrated into this mountain retreat, my intention of attending the funeral ceremonies in distant Coburg became known among the people. I was about to step into the Rom-Berlin express at the nearest railway station, which is a good day's walk from the Hinter-Riss, when a bare-legged little peasant girl, pale with fatigue, rushed up to me and pressed a little bunch of Alpine gentians and rhododendrons into my hand, saying: " They are the only ones I could find still in bloom, and I spent all day yesterday on the rocks to get them. Please put them on the ' Herr Herzog's ' coffin— he was so fond of them ; and once he was so good to my mother—mother, who died last month. I've been walking pretty well all night to get here in time." Among the multitude of gorgeous floral offerings from the crowned heads of Europe, which covered the coffin and the floor of the mortuary chapel—where for the last time I saw the calm features of the great sportsman—that little bunch of half-withered Alpine flowers was certainly the most humble. But I know which would have pleased the dead prince most.

The dead sportsman's hunting-knife, which I saw so often in his strong hand, is now lying before me, a cherished memento, kindly sent me by the stricken dowager-duchess a few weeks after the funeral. It will ever remind me, not so much of a sportsman prince, as of a prince among sportsmen.

CHAPTER VI

THE pursuit of chamois in unpreserved ground, which in the Austrian Alps is, as a rule, either Crown property or belongs to peasants who have not leased their shooting rights to wealthier sportsmen, but exercise their rights themselves, gives one all the hard work even the lustiest Alpine enthusiast can desire. Of the hundreds of lonely stalks after chamois in such sparsely stocked ground, enjoyed by me in past years, I propose to describe a couple, so as to make the reader acquainted also with that form of sport.

The scene of both lay in the X——Valley, a favourite haunt of mine. It is one of the least known *Hochthäler* of Tyrol, and branching off from the Unter Inn Valley in a northerly direction affords an easy pass from the latter to Bavaria—a pass which formerly was much frequented by smugglers. Its population, numbering some 500, live in picturesque broad-eaved houses, made of sun-browned timber, which are scattered about in the lower part of the long, but not very wide mountain valley. The upper and much wilder parts of the 25 miles long glen, as well as half a dozen side valleys, are one huge uninhabited natural game district, in which occasional Alp huts, tenanted during the summer months, afford convenient places of shelter, so that sleeping out is not necessary. With the exception of one fine limestone peak of about 9000 feet elevation, the ground is really more suited for red-deer than for chamois, for it chiefly consists of great tracts of fine woods of spruce covering the slopes of the minor peaks, interspersed here and there by clearings or by expanses of undulating Alp-land where hardy cattle find summer grazing. Above timber-line the slopes are either bare or are covered with a dense, shrub-like growth of *Latchen* or dwarf-pine, that form an intermediary belt between the bare rocks and the timbered slopes below.

The X—— Valley shoot marches for many miles with the Bavarian royal preserves, the Austria-Bavarian boundary line running along a sharp ridge, of which the northern slopes are Bavarian, the southern Tyrolese. Also to the east and to the west has this fortunate peasant shoot the best of neighbours who assiduously preserve game, which, in some instances, no doubt, strays over the boundary, and is shot by the peasants instead of by princes of the blood royal. Thirty or forty years ago poaching affrays were frequent, and many ended fatally, but they have now ceased almost altogether.

Mountain game in those regions of the Alps inhabited by German-speaking races is divided into two classes. The first is the *Hochjagd*, which embraces red-deer and roe-deer; the second is the *Nieder* or *Reis Jagd*, to which the rest of fur and feathers belong. The chamois, strange to say, is often included in the latter. In Tyrol, where in many respects the game laws differ from those in the other provinces of the Empire, the *Hochjagd* is generally in the hands of the Government, while the *Reis Jagd* in the same place is owned by the peasants. This is a most undesirable state of things, for it holds out temptation for poaching, and control by the Government keepers is, of course, rendered much more difficult.

The X—— Valley is not one of these, for both sporting

rights belong to the inhabitants of the glen.   The *Reis Jagd*,[1] which here includes chamois, was granted to them 200 years ago by the emperor, as a reward for the conspicuous bravery they displayed in the capture of the neighbouring fortress of Rattenbérg during the wars of the Spanish succession.   Every owner of house property in the valley has the right to shoot chamois, capercaillie, and blackcock, and he may depute his right to his son or other near male relation, but he cannot sell it.   The game he shoots is his, and he has only to pay a small fee into a fund for every head he shoots.   The *Hochjagd*, on the other hand, is owned by twenty-six peasants who, in the first half of the present century, first leased, and finally bought the *Hoch Jagd* from the Crown.   At the time there was very little big game left in their mountains, and the fact that the forests are now full of deer, speaks well for the measures these twenty-six hunters took.   It is one of the few, if not the only exception I know to the rule that peasants are indifferent game preservers.

The following will explain how these simple peasants manage their shoot.   Before the beginning of the season the twenty-six settle definitely in solemn conclave what is to be shot, for, in consequence of the variable character of the winter, and the fact that they do not feed or provide shelter for their deer, the losses after a heavy winter with a late spring are now and again very heavy.   In the season following such disaster much less is shot than in ordinary years.   Throughout the season two, and if necessary three, of the twenty-six take it in turns of a week each to act as keepers, so that the preserve is constantly patrolled by the

---

[1] In Maximilian's time the division was different.   The most important class was the *Hohe Bann Jagd* or High Proclaimed.   It consisted of red-deer, chamois, ibex, wild boar (of which great quantities still existed in the Alps), bear, capercaillie, and blackcock, as well as eagles, hawks, and every kind of falcon.   All other game was spoken of as *Reis Jagd*.   Frederick, Duke of Tyrol, Maximilian's predecessor, passed strict game laws, the killing of a stag being punished with loss of all property, and death for a second offence.

owners, who, of course, are the best able to protect their property. During the season any one member of the twenty-six may shoot as much as he likes until the total fixed before-hand is reached. A large town being within 50 or 60 miles

Fig. 9.—Tyrolese Peasant watching for Chamois.

from the shoot, a good market can always be found for the game killed, which is sent to one of the game-dealers there with whom the twenty-six entered a contract at the be-ginning of the season. In the hot months of the year this

is fraught with a good deal of hard work for the fortunate
shot, who, after killing his stag, has to carry it at night for
8 or 10 miles to the nearest point to which a cart or a mule
can be got. But they are a sturdy lot, and there is many a
man among the twenty-six who will shoulder his stag and
carry him down unassisted, if it is not one of the largest
animals, when two men will share the burden. Even the
girls in that valley are as strong as an ordinary man, and to
carry three chamois, weighing a hundredweight and a half,
from the village to the nearest railway station, is not considered anything extraordinary.

Half of the proceeds received for red-deer or roebuck
belongs to the man who killed the game, the other half goes
to a fund which is equally divided at the end of the season
between the twenty-six. In consequence, those who have not
had the time, or who were otherwise prevented from shooting,
receive a substantial dividend of from £5 to £8 each, which,
to these frugal, hard-worked people, is quite a large sum.[1]
Twenty-five or thirty years ago shares changed hands at
£30 each; to-day they fetch almost £200 each. Some
of the men devote themselves more than others to the
chase, and if attended with fair luck, they can make a
fair living at it. The annual bag, of course, varies; I have
known over 300 head of big game killed in the X——
Valley shoot in one season, but that was before a most
disastrous winter (1874-75), which destroyed a great quantity
of the X—— Valley game. At present the annual bag varies,
I believe, between 150 and 200 head of red-deer, roebucks,
and chamois. The latter have decreased there in the last

---

[1] The elevated position of the valley makes the people almost entirely
dependent upon their cattle, and almost every essential is made at home.
Cash is therefore anything but plentiful in that self-contained little com-
munity, and the hard silver florins received for their game are most welcome
means for providing little luxuries, such as tobacco, and the wherewithal to
make merry at rifle-matches and other festivities. A happier and more
cheerful people it would be difficult to find.

TYROLESE PEASANT GETTING A SHOT.

ten or fifteen years, chiefly in consequence of the general introduction of breechloading rifles, with which at first one man occasionally killed four or five from one spot—a feat which was practically impossible with the old single-barrel muzzle-loaders. Besides this, they now can shoot much farther. In the central parts of the X—— shoot there are now but few chamois left, but in late autumn the southern aspect of the boundary ridge works advantageously for our peasant friends. Many a king's buck who, notwithstanding the keeper's constant watch, crosses in the latter part of November that invisible line separating the two countries, falls victim to their sure rifles. Unfortunately for the peasants, the shooting season in Tyrol for chamois closes on the 1st December, a fortnight earlier than in Styria and elsewhere. But for this they would kill many more, for it is only when really heavy snow begins to tell that chamois will leave the range to which they are accustomed in order to seek one with a southerly exposure.

The annual accounting and division of dividends by the member to whom the important duties of secretary and treasurer have been entrusted (for many years the school-master of the village, an ardent old sportsman, has been holding this dual office) occurs always on the last Sunday of Carnival, which is the least busy season for the peasants. It is *the* event of the year in the valley, a great dinner of the most substantial type begins the feast, and a rifle-match at a running deer, with a ball to follow, keeps things very lively for three days till midnight of Tuesday, Ash Wednesday being usually ushered in by an all-round *Katzenjammer*. In former years, when not away in Transatlantic shooting grounds, a couple of days' railway journey did not deter me from being present at these quaint and characteristic merry-makings. Dancing two nights running, with rifle-match, shooting in the daytime, followed by a long tramp back through 2 or 3 feet of snow, was a performance from which I did not shrink.

The reader, from what I have said concerning the financial details, must not carry away the impression that pecuniary benefits are the chief motive of this arrangement. All the peasants are deeply attached to their old rights, and when some years ago the Government wanted, right or wrong, to re-purchase the shooting rights of the X—— Valley peasants (one of the Austrian archdukes, I believe, being in want of a good shoot with easy ground), the owners unanimously refused to listen to its offers, which, of course, were far in excess of the price at which the shares change hands among themselves. It would be an unfortunate day for the valley that witnessed the sale of their rights, for many of the young generation, all keen sportsmen, would assuredly turn poachers, and probably many a life would be sacrificed in affrays with the keepers.

This shoot is, as I have said, an exceptional instance of a well-managed peasant's shoot. As a rule, if a commune does not let its ground to a wealthy sportsman, who turns it into a regular preserve with keepers, a lodge, etc., the ground is generally wretchedly stocked, not the slightest attempt being made to keep shooting within reasonable bounds. Everybody goes after what little game there is, and a few of the most skilled manage to occasionally bag a chamois or two.

As the law does not permit persons owning less than 200 *Joch* (284 acres)—and it must be in one tract—to shoot over their land, the commune has the leasing of all shooting rights over properties smaller than the above area. These rights must by law be put up to public auction, and the shortest term for which they can be acquired is five years. The lessee must be a person of reputable character, or the magistrate will refuse to issue to him the license, which everybody must obtain before they can exercise shooting rights. In Tyrol, a province which has always been distinguished by the freedom of all regulations hampering the peasant population in becoming proficient rifle shots, the law that every person carrying firearms must be provided with a gun license does not come into operation, but in all other Austrian provinces the *Waffenpass* should be in one's pocket-book when out with rifle or gun. The cost is very small, less than two shillings, and any reputable resident can get one for himself or for a friend.[1]

But now to those stalks which I promised to the reader at the very beginning of this chapter. The first expedition had for its object a nearer acquaintance with a couple of old bucks that I knew haunted a certain very wild gorge known as the *Weisse Gries*.

One of these I had seen some weeks previously, and my glasses enabled me to perceive that it was of rare size. Ascertaining from the man who had last visited this locality that this veteran was still among the living, I resolved to do my best to bag the prize.

Chamois do not by any means, as I have already said, live exclusively on ground above timber-line. During the summer and early autumn the old males keep aloof from the females and young fry, which latter, as a rule, prefer the elevated ridges and barren rocks where vegetation no longer thrives. In these breezy regions they are difficult to approach, as their surroundings do not offer cover to the hunter to hide his approach. And while the female chamois' innate watchfulness leads her to select just such open and exposed playgrounds, where she can spy danger from afar, the old bucks prefer to roam solitary through the upper fringe of arboreal vegetation. Here, in the cool shade of cliffs, in the near vicinity, if

---

[1] Sportsmen proposing to enter Austria with rifles can avoid all trouble at the custom-house at the frontier if they provide themselves with such a *Waffenpass* beforehand. Any person domiciled in Austria can apply for the document for an acquaintance.

possible, of snow-patches, which, in the lee of rocks, remain
protected from the devouring rays of the summer sun, these
sly old stagers lead a peaceful if lonely existence, showing
themselves as little as possible during daylight, and instinctively avoiding open spaces, where watchful eyes could
detect them. No gambolling about ledges or frisking on
knife-back ridges for these lazy old recluses, who naturally,
in consequence, put on weight in much the same way as
portly old gentlemen whose daily exercise consists solely in
walking from their chambers to their club.

The only chance of seeing these old stagers with a chance
of a shot, is to be on the ground at the first peep of daylight,
when they are still out feeding, frequenting for this purpose
spots where the sparsely growing but exceedingly succulent
herbs, which are their favourite diet, are found growing on
ledges and steep slopes, while the ranker grasses, flourishing
in the woods proper, are rarely touched by these epicures of
the Alps. As they stop feeding, and almost immediately
retreat to dense cover, where they remain till dusk, as soon
as the sun shows up, the above chance is the only one—
with the exception, perhaps, of a few moments in the middle
of the day, when they rise from their couch to stretch their
limbs—upon which the stalker can count. But to be on the
ground at peep of day means either sleeping out under a
handy tree, or a tedious and often risky scramble over
dangerous ground, or along the brink of deep precipices in
the dark, aided, at best, by the fitful light of a small lantern,
and that only if the stalker knows, so to speak, every inch
of the ground before him, or broken bones, if not a broken
neck, will add another victim to the list of those who have
paid dearly for their venturesomeness in the chase of the
chamois.

The *Weisse Gries* is a deep gorge a couple of miles long,
consisting of precipitous slopes of considerable height, at the

bottom of which flows a mountain torrent, to which the rays of the sun but rarely penetrate, so deep is the channel which the stream has worn for itself in the course of ages. It is accessible only in a few spots; but from one or two ledges about halfway down one side, to which, by a careful use of the branches of dwarf-pines, a practised climber can let himself down, an extensive view of the opposite side of the gorge can be gained. This latter precipice is seamed by numerous little ledges too narrow for human foot, but safe enough for the sure-footed chamois. Here and there are dense patches of stunted dwarf-pine, ensconced under overhanging bits of rock, and thus practically unapproachable save by means of a long rope and men to let one down from above. In these patches the bucks lie up during the day, and there they are as safe from human molestation as were they dozens of miles from the nearest *Jäger*.

My *Rücksack* — a canvas bag with two strong straps through which the arms are looped, thus distributing the weight the bag may contain on the small of the back as well as on the shoulders—filled with "grub" for twenty-four hours, a cape and a rug of *Loden* (the native frieze, which turns rain), and my favourite single-barrelled ·450 rifle, made up my kit. Light enough not to impede climbing, a five hours' tramp from the main Inn valley brought me early in the afternoon to the Alp hut nearest to my goal. Here, in a borrowed frying-pan, I cooked for myself a substantial *Schmarn*, a native dish consisting of butter, flour, salt, and water, the first-named preponderating, and after a chat with the cheery peasant lass, the guardian of her father's cattle in this elevated solitude where for weeks she would not see a stranger's face, I proceeded on my tramp. A couple of hours' walk, first through fine forests, then across some rocky slopes, brought me to the brink of the gorge of the *Weisse Gries*. Some 500 feet below me lay the stream, and, at the first glance, descent to it seemed a matter of impossibility, for apparently there was not an inch of foothold visible between the point one stood on and the bed of the stream below. But by going a few score of yards to one side and craning over the brink, one perceived that a sort of gully or chimney, almost vertical in direction, but supplied at brief intervals with stunted dwarf-pines growing in the cracks of the rocks, and pushing their branches out horizontally into space, offered the means of descending. A hundred feet down ledges of varying breadth, but always of an uncomfortable slope outwards, enabled one to gain a " nose " of rock, which was one of the places already alluded to as affording a view of the declivity on the opposite side of the gorge. As it was impossible to descend in broad daylight to this spot without exposing oneself to the view of any chamois lying up on the opposite side, I decided to defer my descent till dawn next morning, when I hoped to effect an approach without being seen. The remaining daylight—the sun had gone down by the time I reached the brink of the gorge—I used to spy the ground from above and to hunt up the most inviting tree under which the night might be passed with least discomfort.

It was a lovely evening, perfect in every respect, and as star after star became visible in the pale blue heavens, the absolute stillness that reigned made the scene all the more impressive. It was only when the chilly mist rose from the profound depth, now yawning dark and gloomy at my side, that I was reminded of the necessity of getting back to my camp-tree before it was quite dark. A little spring close at hand, and a small spirit-kettle, enabled me to cook a cup of cocoa, which helped to wash down my supper of cold meat. A layer of pine boughs, piled in the scientific manner one had learnt in the Rocky Mountains,—a capital school for learning all kinds of camping-out dodges,—made a comfortable bed,

on which, covered with my *Loden* cape, I soon was fast asleep.
I woke up somewhat late, for it was already almost " shooting
light," and had it not been that rising mist promised to
hide my descent to the " nose," there would have been no
time left for the light breakfast with which it is always
pleasant to fortify oneself before starting out. It was chilly
and decidedly damp work getting down to the "nose," for
the bushes, to which one had to cling for dear life, were
dripping with dew, and the dense mist that kept rising from
the depth of the gorge chilled one to the bone. Long before
I reached the point of view there was hardly a dry stitch on
my body, for there was no escaping the heavy shower of wet
that came down from every branch as one caught hold of
bush after bush. Where the chimney ended the ledges
commenced, and to get from one ledge to the next one below
one had to depend again on dwarf-pines to assist the descent,
and as these were often wide apart, it was slow, zigzag work,
requiring surefootedness and knowledge of the ground.

Louder and louder one heard the rushing torrent in the
gorge below, which, however, remained hidden from view
by the mist which hung heavily between the chilly walls
forming the cañon. As several years had elapsed since I
had been to this spot, it was not so easy to find the one
and only route to the point of view I was striving to
gain; but, finally, I saw the shape of the " nose " or pro-
montory faintly outlined through the dank mist. Just
behind it, under an overhanging rock, there was a miniature
cave-like recess, to which, by going on hands and knees, and
creeping along a narrow ledge, one could gain access. Here
I determined to await the lifting of the mist, which I knew
would occur as soon as the rays of the sun struck the upper
strata of air, for down to the "nose" itself only the slanting
rays of the afternoon sun could penetrate. As the layers of
fleecy mist overhead gradually became more luminous, and

dawn slowly gave way to full daylight, one could watch those sublime effects produced by the lifting of the filmy haze, and its gradual melting away under the influence of warm sunshine upon the upper aërial regions.

Rift after rift in the haze disclosed details on the opposite precipice. Not more than 150 yards across from side to side, the distance seemed much less. Thus when a stunted bush, growing from a crack in the rock opposite me, became visible, it seemed almost close enough for me to hit the little bird sitting on one of the upper branches with a stone. But the little bird was not so small after all, for when with a harsh croak it flew off, one saw it was a large Alpine jay.

Looking again, one's eyes, no longer misled by optical delusion, the bush was discovered to be a pine that had thrust its gnarled trunk far out over the precipice. But all this was byplay, hardly noticed at the time, for one was anxiously peering into the slowly dissolving haze out of which the farther-off details took shape only too slowly, for the object one was looking for was neither tree nor rock, but game. Cold work was this waiting for the mist to clear away, sitting on a bit of rock with not an inch of room to spare, not even enough on which to perform a cabby's shuffle. But everything has an end, and even down that clammy gorge mist and cold finally felt the effect of a glorious sun and bright sky, to which the more favoured regions above were being treated. But my gaze ranged in vain along the nearer ledges and protrusions of the opposite cliff: "not at home to visitors" appeared to be the orders of the old buck with whom I was so anxious to renew acquaintance. But if anybody has to be patient it is certainly the chamois stalker, for might not the very animal one is looking for be quietly grazing behind yonder bed of dwarf-pine, which is just high enough to screen it from one's view? Or might not that protruding knob of rock, with a patch of grass the size of a

CHAMOIS AHEAD! THE AUTHOR STALKING.

dining-table set on edge, be hiding that wary buck? A hasty step from one's ambush, a whiff of tainted air, or a pebble loosened by the foot, would assuredly be answered in that case by the ominous whistle, wherewith the alarm is carried to its companions, be they ever so distant.

The telescope sank wearily from my eyes, and I was about to give up further spying into what appeared a perfectly gameless region, when suddenly I perceived a dark spot in the middle of what, I felt sure, had but a minute before been a spotless little snow-patch, occupying a ledge close to the commencement of the gorge. A brief examination with the glass showed the spot to be a chamois, concerning the identity of which I had but little doubt: it was the patriarch of the gorge! How to get at him was, of course, the next question, but it was easier asked than answered, for the intervening ground was a precipice bare of all cover, even had it been possible to find a ledge along which one could creep till shooting range was reached. No such approach being available, I had to take refuge in the only remaining stratagem, and try to get down to the bottom of the gorge, out of sight of the chamois, proceed along the watercourse to a point beneath him, and then trust to luck to find means of getting sufficiently high up on the opposite walls. I am very sure that had I known what was in store for me, I would have given up the plan, but never having been right to the bottom of the gorge, I was unaware of the real nature of this route. Dwarf-pines, festooning with their pendent boughs my side of the precipice, assisted me materially in effecting the descent into the chilly depth. When I reached the water's edge—if, indeed, there was such a thing as an edge to a body of water flowing most of the time between perfectly smooth walls of rock rising up sheer, and showing plainly by parallel lines of slimy moss the high-water mark of the previous spring—I saw at once

7

that the only means of proceeding was to take to the water and wade. The latter was disagreeably cold, uncomfortably deep, reaching in the pools nearly up to my waist; but the picture of the buck at the end of the 400 or 500 yards of wading was too attractive not to outweigh the discomforts. And watery it was in all conscience, for the descent of the stream was rapid, causing numerous miniature waterfalls. It is true they were only a few feet in height, but considering that the smooth, water-worn walls on either side failed to offer any foothold, one had to climb as best one could up the waterfalls, clinging to protruding stones or cracks in the rock, and getting, of course, drenched in the process. It must have taken me more than an hour to get over the intervening 400 yards, and to succeed in reaching a point where I judged I was beneath the buck. From there it became necessary to ascend again. A side stream coming in at this point at right angles made possible what otherwise would have been so only to winged creatures. A quarter of an hour later I was well up on the walls of this little side cañon, and about to turn the corner, which, according to my calculation, would bring him into full view. I was not far out in my forecast, but, alas! he had in the interval moved to another patch of snow a trifle beyond. The buttress of rock was a good place to shoot from, and the buck was standing perfectly motionless, regarding something that had attracted his attention in the direction away from the one where now real danger was threatening him. He was nearly broadside on to me, and the distance was under 200 yards; so, putting my hat on the rock to rest the rifle on, and waiting a minute or two to let lungs and heart resume their normal action, there would have been but little excuse for missing him. The spasmodic leap, as my bullet struck him a trifle high and 6 inches too far back, told its tale; but he was not yet my meat, for he made off, coming towards me. He evidently was endeavouring to return to his usual home in the more inaccessible part of the gorge. Two or three minutes later, however, when he was already almost opposite me, he came tumbling down the cliff and lodged on a ledge not far from the bottom. Death had overtaken him suddenly, and his legs collapsing under him, he had toppled over, and was now lying in about as unapproachable a spot as there was in the gorge. Entirely un-get-at-able from beneath, for the ledge practically overhung the watercourse 50 feet below, the sole means of reaching the body was by means of a rope from above.

It was only late that evening, when, assisted by three men and a stout rope, half the time scrambling along ledges where, unassisted by the latter, I would never have dared to tread, I at last succeeded in reaching the spot, and, slinging a line round the body of the buck, saw him hoisted up, whither I soon followed him. Fortunately, his horns had remained intact, though there were few bones in his body of which the same could be said. There, on the wall at my side, the former hang, the black, polished-looking, sharply tapering *Krickeln*, fastened on a shield of oak, upon which, in a Gothic scroll, stands inscribed the date and locality of that interesting stalk.

The second stalk in the X—— Valley had for its object a somewhat mysterious old vagabond buck, who for some years past had been known to haunt, off and on, a low mountain called the *Rosskopf*, and then suddenly disappear no one knew whither. In this way he had fooled many a stalker who had paid a Saturday to Monday visit to the ground in the hope of finding him at home. I had been out shooting one hot July in a different part of the X—— shoot, and after three unsuccessful days was returning to the village thoroughly disgusted with the hot dry weather, which made stalking next to impossible. I had reached the first stragg-

ling group of peasants' houses, lying near the foot of the
Rosskopf, but just then it would have been the height of folly
to expect to find chamois on its slopes. One of the houses
being an inn, I was soon sitting in front of my second
bumper of beer, for on that scorching July afternoon there
was nothing "small" about my thirst, as a Yankee would
say. I had not been there long when in walked one of
the Government under-foresters, and, in the free and easy
manner of the country, joined me at the table I was occupying. I knew the fellow but slightly, as he was a new
man. Moreover, as these officials, whose duty it is to
guard the Government forests from wood-thieves, make,
as a rule, no pretension to be sportsmen, I came rarely in
contact with them. In answer to his friendly query what
I had shot, I told him what bad luck I had been having,
for in those days game was plentiful, and I rarely returned
with an empty *Rücksack*. "You needn't have gone so far
to get nothing," the man replied, "it's not half an hour ago
that I saw on the *Graue Wand*, on the *Rosskopf* yonder, the
biggest old buck I have seen many a day." I laughed. "What,
you mean to say you saw a chamois out feeding at half-past
three o'clock on a scorching July afternoon on the sunny
side of a hill less than a couple of thousand feet over these
houses?" The man's predecessor was known as a fairly tall
old prevaricator, and this story sounded rather like an attempt
to keep up the reputation. But the forester stuck to his
story, and, moreover, mentioned the particular point on a
mountain opposite the *Graue Wand* from where he had seen
the buck with his glasses while scanning the mountain-side
for a stray heifer a neighbour had lost. "Come up and I'll
show him to you," he added, and up the steep pitch to the
said outlook we promptly went. With my glasses I soon
spied him, and sure enough it looked a good-sized animal.
By the time I got back to the inn where I had left my

rifle, and had eaten a hasty bite, it was six. Having been on my legs since three o'clock that morning, I was paying that old buck something of a compliment in starting out afresh, but I did. An hour and a half later I was lying panting on the brink of the *Graue Wand*, carefully peering over to discover his whereabouts. "There he is, by Jove, not 200 yards below me, quietly feeding on some green patches that shelved out from the declivity. But how slim he looks ! Can it be the old veteran I had heard of but never seen before ?" Almost before I had time to get my glass fixed upon the dun-coloured animal, which might have been a goat, so near was its range to permanent human habitations, when another brown animal, a shade darker in colour, but infinitely smaller, raised itself upon its tottering little legs and approached the side of the larger beast. The slimness of the latter was no longer a riddle; it was a doe chamois with her kid ! "Fooled, by Jove, and probably with *mal perpense* by that forester who, as likely as not, well knew that it was a doe." But there was no use crying over wasted breath. Feeling tired after my fast climb, I made myself a comfortable seat on some boughs of *Latchen* and lighted my pipe, proposing to take half an hour's quiet rest. The point I was on was high enough to afford a good outlook over the great stretches of forest and rocky peaks constituting the bulk of the shoot I was in, while in the background the main chain of the glacier-mantled Central Alps towered up in snowy billows. The Ave Maria evening chimes of the village church, softened by the great distance, came floating up from the glen at my feet. It was the only sound that broke the solemn eventide stillness that lay over the whole landscape. But no, now and again the little bleat of the chamois kid became audible as it pressed up to the side of its mother, and impatiently butted her patient flank in its hungry impatience. Not getting my wind, mother and

offspring were quietly continuing their evening ramble.
Leaning back comfortably on the springy boughs that formed
my seat, now watching that interesting still-life scene below
me, then gazing at the view, or watching the ever-changing
shapes of the fleecy white clouds in the rosy-tinted sky,
time passed in pleasant reverie. A quarter of an hour more
and it would be dusk, and high time to retrace my steps, if I
wanted to reach the nearest Alp hut, where I proposed to
pass the night before it was absolutely dark. The occupier
of the hut, Lois, as fine a specimen of a Hercules of the Alps
as an admirer of physical perfection ever set eyes on, was
an attached ally of mine, with whom I had enjoyed many
a good stalk in the X—— woods. Many a night I had passed
in the hayloft of his particularly diminutive châlet, which was
so low that no grown man could stand upright in it, and,
being windowless, so dark that even when the door was wide
open at mid-day one could not read the sooty peasant's
almanac, which was the only literary pabulum it contained.
Indeed, when one saw the young Hercules standing outside
the door, one wondered how he possibly found room to
attend to his cheese-making and other duties inside a
dwelling which it almost seemed he could have picked up
and carried off on his immense shoulders, as I saw him once
hoist a two-year old steer. With a last glance at the doe,
I was just in the act of raising myself from my lounge of
boughs, when I caught sight of a third fawn-coloured speck at
the farther extremity of the semicircular buttress of rock.
Whipping out my glass from its leather sheath, it was focused
on the chamois with the rapidity given by long habit. "By
Jove, it was the big buck! But what a distance off; 350
yards if it was an inch! Not a moment was to be lost,
for the light was failing fast, and in another five minutes it
would be too dark to venture the shot. But for this I could
have got much closer, but there wasn't time to make the neces-

sary circuit. It was in the old days of muzzle-loaders that the event I am speaking of occurred, and the old rifle, reliable as none other I ever had at distances up to 150 yards, would throw that 24-bore spherical ball yards short at what was then still an unheard-of distance. But the temptation to try my luck at fluking was hardly to be resisted, for youth's fault to venture what more mature judgment would pronounce foolish was a failing to which I have to plead guilty. Squaring myself on my seat, a strong bough giving me a good back, and resting the rifle barrel on my knee, I took steady aim at a stone which I judged was about two and a half or three feet above the shoulders of the quietly-grazing animal. Just then the latter shifted its position a bit from a full broadside to a quartering one, without altering, however, its relative position to the stone above it. The next second the shot rang out. When the smoke cleared off the chamois was quietly walking away! A miss? Yes, it was one, and served me well right for thus muffing a capital chance of getting him next morning at break of day. With that handy hut, wherein to pass the night, not a quarter of an hour off, and everything else favourable, it was indeed a piece of stupendous folly to venture what I knew, or should have known, was hopeless. But there, what is that buck up to? A few staggering leaps, as if trying to throw off some great superincumbent weight, a slip backwards, a sudden collapse of the vital forces, a last attempt to regain his precarious footing on the shelving rock that juts out from the great buttress, and death has claimed that old veteran after all! Toppling over the brink and turning feet upwards in the air, the body lands with a heavy thud among some bushes at the bottom of the cliff—dead before he reached the ground. I had not killed then so many chamois as I have when writing these lines a quarter of a century later, and sitting at my writing-table, at my side a window

from which I can see in the far distance the very rocks that
were the scene of that big old fluke, it is no very hard task
to recall the supreme joy of that moment.

But I was not to have that old veteran on my back quite
as quickly as I expected. Leaving my coat and rifle close to
the spot from where I had shot, I hastened down to my quarry.
But the shortest was, as is so often the case, not the quickest
road, and my attempt to proceed down the face of the cliff, by
taking advantage of ledges and of occasional *Latchen* bushes,
by which I thought I could let myself down, was not a
success. I had to return to my starting-point after the loss
of a quarter of an hour, and, after all, make the circuit I had
wanted to avoid. When I got to the spot where the buck
should have lain, I found ample traces of his fall, but the
slope was so steep that the body had begun to roll down,
and in spite of a frantic search it was impossible to find it in
the rapidly-increasing darkness. With bleeding shins, for I
had been rushing about, vigorously kicking the bushes in the
hope of thus discovering the body, my shirt almost torn off
my back, and blood trickling down my face from a cut which
a sharp bough had inflicted, I saw it was useless to prolong
the search for the present. Neither was it very wise to
retrace my steps in the dark over the ridge to Lois' hut,
picking up on my way rifle, coat, and *Rücksack*. So I thought
it best to try and gain a hut, half an hour off, but lower
down the mountain, which I knew was also tenanted by
a young fellow I knew. Great was his surprise at the
battered appearance of his belated visitor; but matters were
soon explained, and after a four or five hours' sleep in the loft
of his châlet, filled with fragrant new-mown hay, we started
out at daybreak to look for the buck. We presently found
him tightly wedged into the branches of a tree six or
seven feet from the ground. The body had rolled down the
steep slope in which here and there little precipices intervened,

and finally landed in the branches which were close to one of these sheer declivities. In the dark I might have looked for a year without finding him. It was the old buck right enough, and though his horns were only middling ones, I was not a little gratified at my success. Had I fired at 35 instead of 350 yards, I could not have made a better shot, grand old fluke as it was.

CHAPTER VII

LAST August I was whiling away a hot afternoon under the grateful shade of a gnarled old pine on the banks of a certain picturesque loch hidden away at the farthest end of a remote glen in picturesque Styria.[1] The tarn, a couple of miles in circumference, was surrounded by steeply rising mountains, the tops of which towered about 3000 feet over the mirror-like surface. On the slopes of these peaks I had been enjoying for the last three or four days some capital chamois-stalking; indeed, the result of that forenoon's stalk in scorchingly hot weather, in the shape of a fine five-year-old buck, was hanging by the crook of his horns to one of the protruding cross-beams supporting the roof of the weather-browned log-built lodge, a couple of hundred yards behind me. Stretched out on the soft moss within a foot or two of the water, I was enjoying in delicious *dolce far niente* not only the view framed in by blue clouds from my pipe, but, above all, a certain interesting article which I had just discovered, as an unexpected *bon bouche*, within the familiar brown covers of *Blackwood's*, which latter I had withdrawn from the heap which the postbag had disgorged on the grass at my side.

[1] Styria contains some of the choicest preserves. According to the official returns, there were shot in Styria in 1894 : 2109 chamois, 4219 red-deer, and 10,398 roe-deer. The real totals would have been somewhat larger.

A few hours previously the aforesaid buck was still calmly surveying his rocky realm from yonder *arête*, hardly more than 1000 feet over the placid surface of the tarn. The latter, I may as well at once reveal, was but 3500 feet over the sea-level. And even down to the latter very low altitude did chamois in this instance descend, for on the previous evening, while enjoying a dip in the lake, two old does, each with her buck-jumping young kid at her side, had actually watched my proceedings quite unabashed from a point not 100 feet over the water, and within a distance which, had their sex been but a different one, a ·303 or a Mannlicher would have shown to be a fairly easy range. If I further add that the buck I had bagged that morning was the fourth I had shot in that preserve, the four falling to a total expenditure of four cartridges, it will be seen that I was in the heart of some really excellent chamois ground, where game was as plentiful as it was undisturbed. Not only was it the beginning of the season, but, with the exception of a few days' driving in the previous September, not another shot had been fired for two years within the confines of that strictly preserved and carefully guarded preserve.

But what has this to do, the reader will ask, with the interesting article in *Blackwood's Magazine?* Those who have read last August number will not need to be told that I am referring to a capital paper entitled " Chamois-Hunting in the High Alps," in which Mr. Stutfield gives a very readable account of some sport he enjoyed, and not by any means for the first time, on the Italian slopes of the Pennine Alps. Fortunately I knew enough of the region in question—high and difficult stalking ground, if there is any—to be able to draw a mental picture of the scenes described by the writer, and to compare them with the *mise-en-scène* of my own much easier sport on the grassy slopes of the Styrian slate mountains. I say " fortunately," for otherwise I probably would

have patted myself complacently on the back when proudly
comparing my four bucks bagged with four cartridges, and no
misses, with the result of Mr. Stutfield's sport, where, according
to his own words, " failures rank with successes in the proportion of about four to one." This somewhat bad average, let
me confess at once, is the peg upon which I shall venture to
hang a few remarks anent the missing and hitting of the
nimble little mountain antelope.

While it is not perfectly clear whether the writer of the
article means this proportion of four to one to express the
proportion of misses to hits, it is certain that he lays greater
stress upon the difficulties of hitting chamois while stalking
than tallies with my own experience in this respect. I would
almost go to the other extreme and declare that, given a well-
stocked chamois preserve in Tyrol, Salzburg, or Styria, a spell
of fine weather to usher in the season and to ensure a welcome
immunity from shifting winds and unsettled weather, a rifle
that one can depend on, and the reputation of which is too
dear to one to lightly father a miss upon it, and I think
that there are few wild animals easier to kill than your wily
old buck chamois, if—and it is a big if—the hand that holds
the rifle be only steady. I refer here to the effect which the
climbing of steep slopes has upon the steadiness of one's aim,
and upon this factor, I am inclined to think, the writer I have
alluded to has laid too little stress.

People often assume that the climbing powers of a chamois
stalker must necessarily be of the very first order. Under
ordinary circumstances—such, for instance, in which an
English sportsman would be likely to be placed when shooting
chamois as the guest of some hospitable Austrian friend—
nothing of the kind is required of him. On the larger shoots,
where there are often guests present who have never seen a
chamois, the keepers have by long practice become past
masters in the art of getting their " Herr " his shot. Men

who are long past their prime, and by no means of a firm
" understanding," or men who for all the chamois in the world
would not face a *mauvais pas* entailing ordinary freedom from
giddiness, will be dragged, pushed, and tugged into a position
from whence at last the shot, according to the keeper's
opinion, can be safely risked. But what chance of hitting his
game has that thoroughly blown wretch, whose hands shake
as if stricken with palsy, and whose lungs and heart go
pumping and thumping at a rate which would make his
doctor blanch ? Bang! goes the rifle, and away goes the buck.
In nine cases out of ten the misses scored by the tyro are
caused by this undue haste, and not so much by buck fever—
if perhaps the very first shot at the first specimen of the
race one has ever pulled trigger at is excluded. For, even
in the case of really good and experienced shots, it is remarkable how rarely the first attempt of all at a chamois's life is
crowned with success. Apart from this little passing weakness
of the sportsman misses usually result, as I say, from shooting
too quickly. And this, again, is the consequence of over-
excitement, not so much on the part of the sportsman as on
that of the keeper, who, born and bred in the mountains, is
apt to forget that the panting victim behind him does not
possess either his training in the art of scaling mountains, or
his physical strength, and who, on bringing his " Herr ". within
range of the game, expects him at an instant's notice to steady
his wobbling hand, to calm his heaving breast, to stay the
200-to-the minute throb of his heart, and bring his front
sight to bear upon the sufficiently small mark with vice-like
steadiness. The would-be chamois stalker will, however, soon
learn that he must steel his nerves to the more or less intense
excitement which the native in front of him or at his side, as
a rule, manifests. The latter's anxious clutch at his shoulder
and eager whisper, as the game is at last spied, must leave him
as calm as the proverbial cucumber, and he must learn to

disregard the injunction, "Shoot! shoot!" which the over-
anxious native hisses into his ear until such good time as he
has regained his wind, and a four or five minutes' rest has at
last allowed his respiration and his heart to resume more
normal beats.   To many sportsmen, under such circumstances,
the very presence of a keeper at the supreme moment of
firing is a disturbing element.   However useful a second pair
of eyes often is to mark the effect of the shot (in nine cases
out of ten when stalking chamois you have the wind in your
face, and hence the smoke, if one uses ordinary powder, is
liable to blur one's field of vision), no advantage thus gained
can outweigh the disadvantage of nervousness at the moment
of firing.   This the novice suffering from this species of
nerves can easily avoid by instructing the keeper to remain
some distance behind when once game has been sighted.   To
sportsmen of this type, when chamois are driven, the presence
of a keeper at their post, which is often imposed by hosts
over-anxious to reduce to a minimum the number of does in
the day's bag, has the same objection.   An acquaintance of
mine, as good a rifle shot as one wanted to meet, had a
deeply-rooted objection to this, and so, in order not to offend
his host by telling the keeper to leave him altogether, he
seated him some twenty yards behind him, and by a string
tied to his foot, the other end being held by the man, the
latter used to signal to him the sex of the approaching
chamois.

   Stalking chamois in well-stocked private preserves, and
stalking the same game in unguarded shootings belonging to
communes where there are no keepers, and where every able-
bodied inhabitant has the right to turn stalker, are, as I have
repeatedly remarked, two very different things.   For learning the art there is nothing like such difficult ground.   In
such localities game is not only scarce, but is exceedingly
wary and difficult to approach.   I have been five or six days

on such free ground without getting a shot, but when a chance at last did offer itself, I took great pains to make as careful shooting as was possible. There is no school like it to make one a careful marksman. The privations and toil of several consecutive blank days, while possibly forgotten during the last supreme moments of the stalk, have nevertheless left their impress upon one's mind, and one instinctively fires with more deliberation than one would under circumstances offering frequent chances to make good a miss. The most valuable lesson it will teach the novice is to rely upon one's first shot, and not upon the rapidity with which one can "pump" bullets at the vanishing game. In this respect the old muzzle-loading rifle was the very best tool with which a youth could pass his apprenticeship to the craft, and I am very sure that my averages made with breech-loading rifles in the last fifteen or twenty years would have been very much worse had I not killed my first half hundred deer and chamois with this now antediluvian arm. Whatever the demerits of the muzzle-loader, and they were considerable, the drawback of frequent misfires being the most vexatious, their accuracy up to 150 yards has always seemed to me to be superior to that of the Express. One advantage they certainly did possess, viz. the greater quantity of blood which usually was the result of wounds by the large spherical ball—results rarely attained by breech-loading rifles of small bore and high velocity. To the lonely chamois stalker, far from assistance in the shape of a good tracking hound, a large blood spoor is, of course, a matter of great moment. As a matter of fact, I do not remember losing more than one wounded chamois in my muzzle-loader days. I can by no means say the same thing regarding my subsequent experience.

At drives, in those days, one rarely got more than one shot at a beast, and this one remembered. How different are the feelings with which the average stalker of to-day

goes forth after chamois! The fact, always present in his
mind, that his pockets or the magazine of his repeater are
full of cartridges, gives him a false confidence, derived
from the fact that he can fire half a dozen shots before
the beast is out of range. Thus he looses off his first shot,
trusting more to luck and to the number of cartridges he
has in reserve than to the details of marksmanship. As
he pulls the trigger his thoughts are centred, not so much on
the result of the shot, but more on the necessity of reloading
as quickly as the mechanism of his arm will allow him to
do. And he is not wrong—the fluke did not come off, and
it is a case of fast loading. But now his quarry is thoroughly
alarmed, and there ensues a very different condition of
things so far as aiming is concerned. No more chances to
shoot off the knee, or to rest the rifle on a handy rock, with
the *Rücksack* under the barrel to take off the jump. He has
now to aim at an animal pursuing a most erratic flight, now
scampering along narrow ledges, then tearing down steep
moraines with the speed of a rocket, or taking flying leaps
of prodigious extent across *Couloirs,* a shower of stones, torn
from their places by the speeding hoofs, rattling down upon
the sportsman if he happens to be below. Now the buck, as
he tops a tiny ridge, has come to a halt as sudden as it is
brief, and he gives the stalker a chance as he stands end-on,
spying down the ravine, which he is about to cross. But to
hit a chamois in that position—in fact, in any—at 250 or
300 yards, requires some exceedingly fine sighting and steady
shooting, to neither of which arts the tyro stalker has given
sufficient attention. As a matter of fact, he has probably
never taken the trouble to try his rifle at those distances.
His last chance is thus also lost, he has emptied his magazine,
' and his fusillade, re-echoed from side to side by the precipitous slopes, has disturbed for days to come the game in half a
dozen as yet unvisited corries and glens. Such men have no

business in chamois preserves—certainly not where stalking is the main feature. In drives such pyrotechnically inclined shooters do less harm, for noise is, of course, an inseparable feature of chamois-driving, and as good ground is disturbed in this manner never more than once every year or two, a score or two of shots more or less on the great day do not count. Some very bad shooting is often to be noticed at chamois drives, the majority of guns one usually meets having but little experience. Last year, in a Salzburg shoot, one man fired upwards of 200 shots in a few days' driving, but bagged only thirteen or fourteen beasts, and those by no means all bucks. A kill to every two shots is a good average in drives; when stalking the average should be even higher, at least, in the case of those who have had experience, and who claim to be rifle shots. A capital way of schooling oneself to keep up averages is to limit one's supply of cartridges. Thus, to start out for a day's stalking with only four or five makes one careful how they are expended. Now and again, on those dark days when everything will go wrong, when bad luck hovers persistently about one, and in spite of one's best efforts, one either misses or only wounds; when the beast, which one could have sworn was a good four-year-old buck, turns out to be, after all, but a barren old doe, one curses, it is true, the want of a few more cartridges, but on such occasions it is just as well that a self-inflicted curb should make itself felt. It is, after all, the only way of keeping up the average, and good days cannot make up the leeway if it is too considerable.

But I have wandered far away from the slaying of those four bucks, incidents which I proposed to describe to show how easy chamois-stalking in good ground really is. And even now I must crave for further patience, so that I can premise a few remarks concerning the character of the preserve to which I am inviting the reader to follow me, and

8

which will give him some idea of the usual surroundings in
such shoots. In area the S—— preserve is not among the
large shoots, for its extent is rather under than over 20,000
acres. But it is astonishing how many gorge-like glens,
how much slope standing up at angles of from 50° to 65°,
how many rocky precipices of an even steeper pitch or of
absolute verticalness, can be crowded into a poor little
20,000 acre shoot in the heart of the Alps. In what is
practically the centre of the ground lies the loch spoken of
at the commencement of the chapter. The lodge, occupying
one of the few level spots, stands close to it, and is therefore
conveniently situated in the centre of the shoot. "Lodge" is
hardly the right name, for it consists of four quaint little
detached log houses, the fronts of which form a square about
15 yards across. One of these buildings, the oldest of the
four, now turned into the kitchen house, can almost claim
to be of historical interest, for it was built in 1808 by Archduke John of Austria, who dwelt in it, and shot from it on
many an occasion, the shoot being well known for its scenic
attractions as well as for its sporting qualities. The four
rooms it contains are now devoted to the domestic uses
indicated by its name. Next to it on one side is the stable-
house, if indeed the shed-like structure, the home of two
mules, deserves that descriptive term. The other buildings
are the sleeping-house, consisting of five rooms, of which one
has been made the gun room; the other, and the smallest
of the four dwellings, is known as the Prince's house, having
been built by the former lessee of the shoot, the head of the
Austrian Coburg family. It consists of one good-sized
sitting-room, with a tiny anteroom. All the windows are
small, the doors are low and narrow, for in bad weather
there is a good deal of air about. The four keepers are
domiciled in two pretty little lodges, one close to the lake,
within call from the lodges; the other, two hours off, at the

point where the cart road leading into the glen first enters the boundaries of the shoot.

The nearest post office, shops, and railway station are 20 miles off, the connecting link with this outside world consisting of a very rough cart road, passable only to the narrow, springless waggons in which the enormous cheeses are brought down from the Alp huts.

The shoot is surrounded on all but one short side, less than a couple of miles in length, by the best of neighbours, viz. the ardent sportsman who, during his former tenancy of the ground I am describing, had added to the existing lodges the little building to which I have already briefly alluded. On this one vulnerable point, the S—— preserve marches with a commune shoot, in which the peasant owners, in spite of offers which much exceeded the value of the ground, persist in exercising their rights. If they did no more nobody could complain, but, unfortunately, the neighbourhood of well-stocked preserves had made them daring poachers, and a constant watch along the dangerous boundary was therefore essential, while occasional affrays between them and the keepers proved to what extremes the passion for sport could lead. As is so generally the case in the Alps, the ridge of a knife-back range formed the boundary. One of the favourite tricks of these undesirable neighbours was to climb the ridge from their own side, poke their heads over, and shoot down at any chamois that happened to be within rifle range. If the quarry fell they would let it lie and return at night when, notwithstanding the character of the rocks, dangerous even for passage in daytime, they would fetch their prey when darkness screened their approach.

And now to the events of those four stalks, or rather five, for one stalk, which was undertaken in unsettled weather, ended with failure, as most one's endeavours are apt to do if the wind, now blowing from one side and five minutes later from the opposite direction, does its best to convince one of its omnipotence.

The first buck, which rewarded a ludicrously easy stalk, fell victim to a feeling of security engendered by long immunity from man's molestation. Such instances one now and again comes across in preserves that have remained undisturbed for a long time.

We left the lodges on the morning following my arrival at S——, on what was my first visit to the place, at a fairly early hour. The tops of the peaks that surrounded the lake were tipped with the first rosy tints of morning, when Kals the head-keeper and I ferried ourselves across the tarn in a cranky old boat, on our way to where we were to begin stalking. This spot, where a side ravine branched off from the main glen, was not many hundred feet higher than the loch. And being quite a short glen, half an hour's walk would have taken us to the end, where rose great walls of rock which enclosed the semicircular *Kaar*, on the upper part of which one saw a small snowfield. This latter was the source of the little brook which coursed down the glen. The rock escarpment, which towered up at the end of the glen, and which I expected would have to be climbed in order to get near game, since the small extent and low elevation of the glen seemed to hold out but poor chances for sport, were after all not to be tackled, for game was much closer than I anticipated. I must mention that these very rocks I saw ahead were the one vulnerable point of the preserve to which I have already referred. In consequence of this circumstance, one or the other of the keepers was almost daily in the habit of passing up this glen on his way to convenient points of outlook, from whence to watch the boundary. Kals, on our way up, had told me that a fine buck had since the preceding summer made this glen his home, and that hardly a day passed that he was not seen by the man who took that particular beat. "At this time of the morning," said Kals, " he is generally feeding on one or the other of the steep slopes of the glen, and very often, if the wind is all right, he will let us pass within 200 or 300 yards, without moving away more than a few yards, and perhaps whistling once or twice." This I could hardly believe, for nowhere had I ever seen chamois evince so slight a fear of man. But events showed me that one is never too old to learn. We had not proceeded far up the glen, following a sort of rough path worn by the feet of the keepers, who were practically the only human beings who ever set foot there, when we spied the buck quietly feeding at a point some 400 yards farther up the ravine. He was about half-way up the slope, or, in other words, about 200 yards from the bottom, where ran the brook and the keeper's path. Retiring under cover of a handy *Latchen* bush, of which a few dotted the otherwise quite barren sides of the glen, a council of war was forthwith held. The following plan was decided upon. According to Kals there were only two alternatives possible, and either was bound to give me the chance of a shot. One was that the buck, when he perceived the apparition to which he had become accustomed, would follow his usual custom and remain where he was, or he would show us his heels and make for the farther extremity of the glen. " This latter he is sure to do if you come with me," said Kals, "for he is accustomed to see only one man, and so suspicious do these wary old fellows get, that the slightest change in what they are accustomed to see would bring about the very thing we want to avoid. So you must let me go ahead; if he stays where he is, you can follow me shortly afterwards, and you will get a capital shot. You must walk on quite quietly till yonder big boulder, which lies close to the path, and which will hide you for an instant from the buck, and then you must fire as quickly as you can, for if he sees you peeping round the corner he will be off like a shot. If, on the other hand, he takes it into his head to move away as I approach him, I know that as soon as he is out of sight I can run ahead and cut off his only escape up those walls of rock, and thus force him to turn back, when he is bound to pass you somewhere or other." Thus argued long-headed Kals. The walls that flanked the gorge, and from the base of which ran down the slopes of loose rock upon which the buck was standing, were, as I could see, so precipitous that it hardly needed Kals's assurance, that if the buck did turn back he would in all probability follow the base of the cliffs, within range of which I could manage to get by running up the slope a bit while the buck was out of sight. "Mind you walk on quite slowly, with your rifle slung over your left shoulder as I carry mine, and don't stop or look about till you get to the boulder," were Kals's last injunctions as he started out to put his ruse into execution. I felt convinced that the second alternative would be the one that would occur, for the test to which he proposed to put that buck was one of those experiments that usually don't come off when they are most ardently desired. But I was wrong; the buck saw Kals as soon as the latter turned the corner round which we had been peeping. A whistle, a few leaps to one side, where a rock with a small *Latchen* bush at the top offered a good point of view, was all the buck did. Slowly, with the steady swing of the mountaineer, Kals pursued his way along the rough path, getting with every step nearer to the beast that, from his point of vantage, was watching, as I could see with my glass, every movement of the approaching man. Now Kals had reached the boulder, which was about the size of a railway truck, and that made him, for a step or two, invisible to the buck. While thus screened the keeper took off his hat, and bowed low in the direction of the unconscious beast, hardly 200 yards distant. Thirty or forty steps more and a bend in the path took him beyond the chamois's range of vision. With beating heart I set forth some ten minutes later to follow Kals's tactics, the buck having in the meanwhile resumed his old place on the moraine slope, feeding on the fine blades of his favourite, sparsely growing herbs. When he first caught sight of his second visitor he seemed rather more uneasy than in Kals's case; his whistles were oftener repeated, and for the first moment he seemed inclined to make off in real earnest. But second thought—a fatal one for him— prevailed, and he jumped on to the same rock from which he had reviewed the march-past of Kals. Mine was a more painful one, for to keep a calm, nonchalant air, and to walk at a slow, steady gait in plain view up to a good buck, as I was doing, was a nerve - trying experience. The noise of the bubbling brook at my side seemed to grow louder and louder, and yet it appeared insufficient to drown the thumping of my heart. Nearer and nearer got the haven I was steering for, and immovable, as if carved out of stone, became the buck. Now he was 300, now 250, and now, as I threw myself on my knee behind the boulder, I had him, sure enough, as fair a mark as a sportsman could desire. But when I cast my eye over the rifle-sights I found it was not quite such a big bull's eye as I thought it would be. For, of course, the buck was not broadside on to me, but only end- ways, and the small bush covered all but the neck and head, which at 200 yards are too small a mark for the best marks- man in the world to safely risk a shot.

There was not an instant to lose, for the buck, rendered uneasy by my non-appearance on the other side of the boulder, was, as I could see by the turning of his head, casting glances to the right and left as if preparing for instant flight. But for that my Express did not give him time, and my aim at the boughs, which I knew hid his chest, was true enough to fell him as had he been struck by lightning. My bullet, as I was shooting upwards, entered between the front legs and came out above the tail. It was a fine six-year-old buck.

Next morning's stalk was almost as easy, except that the light was rather dim, the hour being an early one, so that the morning mist was still hanging heavily over the clearing where we spied my second buck. It was also a fairly long shot, and it was only when I got up to the dead beast that I discovered I had been lucky enough to bag one of the rare "coal" chamois, a *lusus naturae*, of which I have already spoken. And not only that, but the horns were abnormal, one horn being a mere stump. Kals's joy at my luck was a thing to see.

The events of the third stalk illustrated the necessity of always carrying one's own rifle, a practice from which I very rarely swerve, and only in the most exceptional cases. I had on this occasion another keeper with me, who said he knew the whereabouts of an old veteran. But we came upon him long before we got to the crags the patriarch usually frequented, and that in a most unexpected and sudden manner. I was leading, and just in the act of topping a little ridge 10 or 15 feet high, when I saw not 10 feet from me the horns of a buck, whose head and body at that instant were still hidden from my view by the intervening crest of the ridge. Fortunately I had just before slipped a cartridge into the barrel, for had I not done so, or had I not had the rifle up to my shoulder without an instant's loss of time, the buck would have got off. He must have seen the top of my hat the same moment that I caught sight of his horns, for, when I gained the crest, which I did by a couple of quick strides, he had already turned, and I shot him while he was in the air, crossing with one huge leap the small ravine-like watercourse on the brink of which he had been standing.

So great was the impetus of his bound that, though he was practically dead before he touched ground—my bullet cut his heart almost in two—he rolled over the bank, and was out of my sight before the powder smoke cleared off, so that for a moment I thought my snap-shot had missed him.

The fourth buck fell to my rifle the next day but one, the resultless stalk occupying the intervening day. The first three bucks were all shot by me at the low elevation of about 4000 feet, the lowest at which I have ever killed chamois in the Alps. For the fourth buck I soared a bit higher, for the weather was glorious, and I wanted to combine with my sport a bit of climbing, in order to make myself familiar with the lay of the country, which the scaling of one of the higher peaks, some 9000 feet in altitude, would enable me to do.

This peak threw out towards the lake a great shoulder, and this latter was the sanctuary where neither keeper nor stalker ever disturbed game. In consequence of it there were lots of chamois on it, and, as the slopes were in plain view of the lodges, there was always some band or other to be seen from the windows, often so close that one could make them out quite plainly with the naked eye. The keeper and I, therefore, tackled the peak from the rear, so as not to disturb the sanctuary, and, in three hours of steady climbing, had got within 900 or 1000 feet from the top. At the last water we came to we halted, and brought the glass into use. The slope which faced us was exposed to the full glare of the August sun, so there was little hope of seeing anything. According to the keeper, there was but one place where a buck, who had been often noticed in that vicinity, might be now holding his siesta. It was a deep ravine, with sides that

fell off in most places in sheer precipices. The side of the
gorge we could see was in the shade; upon it our two glasses
were soon fixed. "There he is!" and "I have got him!"
were exclamations that came from our lips at the same
instant, though, truth to say, considering the vast superiority
of my capital deer-stalking telescope over the diminutive and
cheap glass that the keeper had, and which, I am convinced,
cost fewer florins than mine did pounds sterling, I should
have discovered the quarry sooner than he did. But of
course he had the pull of me in knowing exactly where to
look, while I had to scan the whole side. The buck was
lying on a minute projection of rock, about on the same level
with us, with a high wall at his back, a point from which he
commanded a good view of the whole slope below him. He
had evidently seen us, for, as he was not farther than a mile
or a mile and a half at most from us in an air-line, one could
plainly see that his head was turned in our direction. "Can
we get at him where he is, Steinkogler?" was naturally my
first question. "Certainly not from here or from below, but
if you don't mind those steep grass slopes and the rocks on
the ridge, you might get him from above," was the keeper's
answer. While we were yet discussing the pros and cons of
the approaches, the buck raised himself very leisurely from
his couch, and, after standing for a minute or two gazing in
our direction, turned, and bounding on to a narrow band
that traversed the wall of rock, from the top of which he had
been watching us, followed its downward course, and in a
few seconds disappeared into the gloomy depth of the gorge,
where he was lost to our view. "That's the most awkward
thing he could have done," said the keeper, "for now we
don't know whether he'll go up or go down the gorge." The
best thing to do, under the circumstances, was to separate,
and by letting the keeper take a much lower level (by descending 700 or 800 feet), enter the gorge at a point where

this was possible. The buck would then get his wind, and, in making for the top of the gorge, pass within rifle shot of a certain point to which in the meanwhile I could have ample time to make my way. Capital plan! If only he would keep in the cool gorge till the keeper had time to enter it from below. But this was exactly, as the sequel will show, what the old hermit took into his head not to do. The ground that intervened between the buck and us, and which I would have to cross in a slanting and upward direction, consisted of an exceedingly steep grass slope without a bush or shelter of any kind on it. It was not an even surface, but, like a square mile of ocean rollers set at an angle, consisted of a series of wave-like rises and depressions, some of the deeper ones being dry watercourses, while others were simply shallow gullies. It was advisable to get over this desperately bare slope as speedily as possible, for if the buck should happen to leave the gorge before I reached the cliffs for which I was making I might as well have left my rifle at home. These steep grass slopes are often awkward places to traverse without crampons on one's feet, and these iron "friends in need" I had not with me, so I had to do the best I could to combine speed with safety. When I got to the rocks above the gorge I had to be careful not to set the smallest pebble rolling, for, till I reached the gap from which the keeper assured me I could look down into the gorge, it was essential that the buck's attention should not be attracted to my approach. At last I reached the spot, and with bared head carefully peered into the chasm below. Not a sign of life of any sort was to be seen in that wild chaos of rock strewing the bottom of the fissure. Pulling out my watch, I found there were five minutes wanting to the time agreed upon for the keeper to enter the gorge, when the buck would get his wind and probably come my way. While intently watching the chasm for the expected inmate, I was paying

no attention to the ground I had recently crossed, and to
which I was turning my back. Suddenly a chamois's whistle
coming from the latter direction made me turn round. What
was my surprise to see the buck standing on the grass slope
I had recently crossed. He had perceived, or had got the
wind of the keeper far below him, and though he could not
possibly apprehend any danger from that quarter, he was
giving vent to his annoyance at this unwonted invasion of
his realm. The direction he was taking showed that the old
fellow's curiosity had been awakened by seeing us sitting at
the spring, and he was now cautiously stealing up towards
that place to investigate at closer quarters the apparition,
unaware, of course, that while he was out of sight in the
ravine, we had left that place and were approaching his old
quarters in much the same stealthy manner in which he was
nearing ours. The small dips and rises in the grass slope
accounted for our passing each other unseen, probably within 100 yards. He was now some 250 yards off, rather farther
than I liked to risk shooting, particularly at a steep downward angle, so long as there was a chance of getting closer
to him. This, owing to the dips in the ground, was possible,
and by a series of short runs across each "wave," while the
buck was moving on at a more leisurely pace, his attention
riveted on the keeper, I managed to reduce the distance by
nearly 100 yards, and after a brief halt to recover my breath,
I sent that over-curious old stager rolling down the slope.
He was a five-year-old, with a moderate head.

As I had to leave next day I had no chance to spoil my
clean record in the —— shoot. What the next season has in
store there, in the way of averages, remains to be seen. In
easy and well-stocked ground such as I have described, there
is less to be proud of in bagging four bucks with four cartridges than in the limestone mountains of Tyrol. For the
game is wilder, the ground more difficult and more noisy on

account of the brittle rock formation. Fortunately, the older one gets the easier it seems to shoot steadily, and not allow oneself to be flustered, a trial of nerves to which youthful ardour is more apt to fall victim.

Critics have a habit of finding fault with the compiler of sporting literature for only describing their successes. " He is usually," they say, "a person of unfaltering purpose and unerring aim. All his stalks are conducted without flaw or mistake, his cartridges are loaded with the straightest powder only, and every bullet finds its proper billet." Similar criticism, I remember, was passed by a really good sportsman, when reviewing, in an influential journal, the chapters on " Big Game " which appeared in a standard publication to which I had also contributed. It is true that the first impulse of the average sportsman-writer, human as he must plead to be, is to deal only with the good days, with his successes, to the exclusion of all his failures; but, on ·the other hand, it cannot be denied that the novice can learn, under certain circumstances, quite as much from occurrences which demonstrate how not to do things, as he can from the narration of invariable successes. Let the following, therefore, tell its own tale, and teach its own lessons, for it narrates the worst run of bad luck I have ever experienced.

From the hospitable owner of a capital chamois preserve, well known to me for the last twenty years, I had received an invitation to stalk six bucks. To have taken with me more than twelve cartridges for this purpose would have been an insult to my favourite single barrel, for I knew game was very plentiful, and I was familiar with every inch of the ground. The latter was far harder stalking ground than the slate mountains of Styria. The mountains were of the disintegrating limestone formation, and of the roughest and most craggy forms, and, though not as high as the Pennine Alps described by Mr. Stutfield, they could hold their own for ruggedness with any chain in Europe. Selecting the end of October for the time of my visit, when the weather looked settled, a two days' carriage drive brought me to the lodge at the farther extremity of a *cul de sac* that penetrated far into the range.

The mountains which formed this gorge rose on both sides very precipitously, forming in places huge precipices of great height, where golden eagles were wont· to build their eyries. Smaller glens opened off on either side, and these again ended in great arena-like *Kaare*—*i.e.* semicircular moraines, bare of the faintest vestige of vegetation. These *Kaare*, splendid places for chamois-driving, but the worst possible ground for stalking, had some weeks before been driven, and as the weather, moreover, was fine, and the rutting season not far off, all the chamois, even the solitary *Latchenböcke*, had retired to the tops of the mountains. Wherever one directed one's glasses in the direction of the sky-line, one could see bands standing about on the ridges sharply outlined, good glasses disclosing, in the case of old bucks, the play of the breeze among the long hairs of the *Gemsbart*.

It was altogether ideal weather and ideal stalking ground, and as I sat in front of the lodge on the evening of my arrival, and watched the shadows of night gradually sinking down on the familiar scenes of many a grand stalk or memorably successful drive, the outlook could not have been happier. A change of wind during the night made things, however, look different, and when an hour or so before dawn the head-keeper David and I set forth from the lodge for the Spitzhüttenkopf, a chilly breeze and clouded sky warned one that a break in the weather was imminent. A level walk of about two or three miles was followed by a sharp burst up the already-mentioned declivity of some 2500 or 3000 feet. This latter we accomplished in little over an hour, so that

when the threateningly hazy sun topped the far-off snowy
main chain of the Central Alps, where old friends reared
their white heads, we had already got far beyond actual
timber-line, and were dodging about in the highest belt of
Latchen in the endeavour to reach the clear rocks' beyond.
It takes fairly good lungs to climb at the rate of 2000 feet per
hour. Fifteen or twenty years ago it was child's play, for in
this respect I was well able to hold my own with any native
I have come across, but the frugal fare and constant practice
of the native hunter, whose whole life is spent in the mountains, manages to keep lungs and heart longer in good training than is the case with one who devotes but a few months
to the pastime of ascending and descending steep slopes at a
fast pace. To the former this is a daily duty, which he
never dreams of shirking, and hence he is always in the
fittest condition.

By the time we got to the last straggling clumps of
dwarf-pines and came to a halt, the perspiration was streaming off friend David's forehead as profusely as from mine;
unfortunately, however, it was I and not he whose steadiness
of hand was almost immediately to be put to the test. I
was in the act of levelling my telescope at a band of chamois
grazing on a ridge some 800 yards off, using my *Bergstock*
to steady my hand, when an uncomfortably vice-like grip
fastened itself on my thigh, and the words "Don't move"
were whispered into my ear. Slowly turning my head
while gradually lowering the telescope, I saw not 70 yards
off as fine a buck chamois as can gladden the heart of the
stalker. He had that instant stepped from behind a buttress
of rock and stood there almost broadside on, gazing quietly
in our direction, though still unconscious of the danger that
threatened him from that quarter, or rather, I should say,
that would have threatened him had I followed my first
impulse and reserved my fire till I had recovered my breath

a bit. Friend David was, however, much too excited to realise that even he would not have found it an easy job to keep his front sight steadily on the beast. " Shoot ! shoot ! " he hissed into my ear, " It's the big Spitzhüttenkopf buck, and you'll never get a better chance." And shoot I did in spite of heaving chest and shaking hand. The moment I pulled I knew I had overshot the brute, and the few long hairs we found lying on the thin sprinkling of snow showed that I had grazed his backbone. Another shot with the same result while the buck was flying down the slope, and a third miss at 250 yards, and good-bye to my chance of getting that 10-inch head. Three cartridges gone and nothing on the ground, was something that had not happened to me while stalking for many years, but worse was to come. David, of course, expatiated at great length upon the size of that veteran buck, and of the various times he had successfully run the gauntlet in drives, and had got off unharmed when made the object of special stalks. This, naturally, did not increase my good humour, but I knew it would be useless to attempt to convince him that I laid my miss at his door. Under ordinary circumstances calm to imperturbability, the sight of game made David a changed being. His master told me that on one occasion, when out stalking with him, in the intense excitement of the last approach, David so far forgot himself as to turn round and scold him for clinking with his ironshod boots against a stone. " Take off your boots, *verfluchter Kerl* (confounded fellow) ! " he gruffly exclaimed, and then, recollecting himself, almost fell upon his knees in the abjectness of his apologies to the Prince.

There was no use following the buck, even had the weather looked less threatening, for now that he had got below us he had also got our wind, and probably would not stop till he had put many miles of rough country between himself and his pursuers.

The look of the weather had in the meanwhile got most unpromising. Sleety snow, driven before a furious gale, had commenced to fall, and made the rocks dangerously slippery, while the cold on that exposed and elevated flank forcibly reminded one that a fall of some 40° or 50° had occurred during the last twenty-four hours—a change in the temperature for which we were by no means prepared. We kept on, however, and in an hour had crossed a ridge, and · had reached another slope, upon which we soon spied a band of chamois. Great masses of mist came sweeping down, hiding the animals, and enveloping us in fog of icy chilliness. On one side we had a vast precipice, and the rocks we were on shelved down to the brink of the jump-off rather more steeply than was pleasant, considering their condition and the high wind, so that we had to move along very slowly. Now and again, as the furious gale for a moment got the better of the supply of seething mist, we obtained momentary glimpses of the rocks ahead, so that, with a little care, it was possible to keep a fairly straight course. As we got closer to them these chances got scarcer, and we finally halted to await the next rending of the mist. We knew we were close upon our game, but how close we discovered only when too late, for suddenly we seemed to be in the middle of the band. While we had been waiting they had moved off their old ground, and had approached us with the wind. In the dense mist they looked huge, each looming up like some gigantic African antelope, of treble their size. Owing to the fact that the fog, which is usually densest close to the ground, hid the latter, the animals looked very much farther off than they were. There must have been quite thirty beasts, but of course they only came into our field of vision by twos and threes. The whistles of alarm and rattle of stones in all directions, made the unknown number appear much greater. What to shoot at was a most puzzling question; to tell the

9

difference of sex by the horns was practically impossible in
the haze ; and they all looked so large that one lost all sense
of comparison. They were dodging about in the most aggra-
vating manner, probably quite as much puzzled as we were.
With the cocked rifle in my hand, I was turning hither and
thither, irresolute at which to fire, and what to do. David
was quite as nonplussed as I was, and had laid his hand
instinctively on my arm as if to stay my fire till we could
single out the biggest of the lot. But this he could no more
do than I could. Presently what appeared to be a big buck
suddenly bounded into our view, and stood like a vignette
with his four feet brought close together on some projection
high up on the slope, but which the fog hid from us. The
distance appeared to be some 60 yards. "That's a good
buck," exclaimed David; "make sure of him anyhow." I
hastily brushed the snow from my foresight and barrel and
let drive at the beast. I hardly knew that the rifle had
gone off, so inaudible was the pop in the turmoil of the
elements, and the form I had aimed at disappeared that same
instant. I loaded as quickly as my fingers, which were
almost uselessly stiff from cold, could accomplish the feat,
and we continued to stand shoulder to shoulder gazing into
the mist in the hope that a second chance might present
itself. This occurred almost instantly, a flying form of even
more gigantic dimensions presenting itself at what appeared
to be the same distance off, but below me. "Shoot! shoot!"
exclaimed David, "it's a buck, too." And shoot I did. Reloading with all possible speed, I took a third snap shot at
what I thought was also a big buck 70 or 80 yards
off. A few minutes later a stronger gust than any of the
past drove the seething masses of mist with magical rapidity
to one side, and the field of action lay revealed before us.
Of chamois not a sign was to be seen, and though the next
ridge behind which they had probably vanished was scarce

100 yards off, the interval of time after my last shot was so short that it seemed almost incredible, and the whole scene with its sudden transformation gave one rather the impression of some fantastic Fata Morgana having been enacted to tantalise us poor wretches with visions of "Brocken" spectres. But what is that little object lying there above us fifteen, or at most twenty, yards off, on the top of a rock not much larger than a good, honest ant-hill? With dismayed looks we stared at each other as we recognised that it was a diminutive young chamois, and worse, a closer inspection confirmed the worst fears; it was a two-year-old doe, with puny little horns, such as in more than thirty years' stalking I had never bagged! I must plead the recentness of that cruel event, as an excuse for not entering here into my feelings! The silence which fell upon us, the rapidity with which that slight little form vanished into the capacious folds of David's *Rücksack*, as well as the angry hitch with which the bag was slung on the latter's shoulders, spoke eloquently concerning our feelings.

Six cartridges of the twelve gone, and only one miserable little doe! was the practical summing up of events, for the absence of even the faintest sign of blood on the snow showed that I had missed the two others. What was perhaps funniest of all was that we saw by the tracks that the band had passed us within the same ludicrously short distance as lay my solitary victim. Scores and scores of times dense mist has "blanketed" my progress in Alpine timber-line regions, but it has never fooled me quite so badly, and I am sure David would say the same were it not an ill-natured act to refer to the events of that day—a day, too, which, as the following will show, very nearly terminated fatally for him. As the weather improved a bit, we decided to go on stalking. So far the fog had played us tricks; might it not, we asked ourselves, if we persevered, once do the same to the chamois?

Not far from the scene of the late events there was a favourite corrie where, even in the hottest summer, patches of never-disappearing snow made the cool recesses of the gorge-like glen a sure find for the stalker. The only fear on that day was that my shots had disturbed its denizens. But high wind had favoured us, and when, after a nasty creep up some very steep slabs of rock, we cautiously, after removing our hats, peeped over the edge, the sight of a little band standing about in the narrow ravine rejoiced my heart. The animals were almost directly below us, the side of the glen at the top of which we were, falling off in a sheer precipice, though not more than some 200 feet high. There was just enough mist about to blur our view of the animals and make the picking out of the one best worth shooting, a matter of difficulty. After a whispered confab the choice fell upon the one standing closest to the base of the cliff we were on. "If that isn't a buck, I'm no *Jäger*," asseverated David, and as it was also my opinion, I settled the matter by letting drive at the beast. My firing position was about the most uncomfortable imaginable, for, in order to get the rifle to bear upon the beast vertically under me, I had to push myself far over the brink, David holding on to my legs. The chamois fell to the crack, the rest of the frightened band fleeing down the gorge. We had to make a considerable detour to get down to the dead chamois, and did so by entering the glen from below, following back the downward tracks of the chamois. What was our surprise to find blood on these tracks, and we were cudgelling our brains to find an explanation, when, on getting up to the place where the buck should have been lying, we found him gone, and instead of his corpse only a considerable quantity of blood. The explanation was then easy enough; I had shot him high, or possibly had only "creased" him, and after recovering from the shock, he had got up and betaken himself after the others. The quantity of

blood made the former seem likelier, so we decided to institute
a search. Returning on our tracks, which for several hundred
yards followed those of the wounded animal, we presently
caught sight of him. There could be little doubt that he was
hard hit, and could get along slowly only. It was, however,
too far to shoot, and when David discovered the direction in
which the buck was making off, some strong language betokened his vexation. "We must stop him as soon as possible,
or he'll get into the *Wand*, where he will be lost to us," he
remarked, and rushed off up a narrow chamois track which
led up one side of the glen. While following him he explained
to me his plan of action. To understand what happened, a
word of explanation must be premised. The place we were
on was like the steep slope of a mansard roof on a vast scale.
Below us, representing the wall of the house, was a vast
precipice, which fell off perpendicularly to the main valley,
2000 feet below. Across the upper part of this stupendous
wall of rock there ran, slanting slightly downwards, an in-
finitesimally narrow ledge, consisting in places only of small
projections separated by gulfs, across which a chamois when
hard pressed could leap, but which were quite impassable for
human foot. This ledge was well known to the keepers, for
numerous chamois, wounded in the drives, had been known
to seek it as a last resort. They were invariably lost, for
they almost always got to places where they could not turn
round, and when too weak to keep on their legs, they would
topple over and be dashed to atoms at the bottom of the
vast cliff. The height was so great, that the velocity of the
fall would even cause the sheath of the horn to become
detached from the core, a feat of strength which a strong
man can accomplish only by the exertion of his full force in
the case of a recently killed animal. David hoped by following a cut-off to get within range of the buck ere he could
reach the ledge. Close to this point there was a pulpit-like

projection, from which a great part of the face could be seen,
but it was out of rifle range of the face itself. David, who
knew the ground better than I did, asked me to proceed to
this " nose," and from there do the necessary signalling should
the buck succeed in reaching the ledge, which was evidently
the goal the animal was making for. While he, on the other
hand, proposed to give the buck his *coup de grace* if possible
in such a place where, if the worst came to the worst, by
dint of a climb with bared feet the animal could be recovered.
For this purpose I gave him my rifle, for he had left his own
at home. On separating I made my way as quickly as possible
by a somewhat giddy ledge to the extreme point of the "nose."
Our bad luck was, however, still following on our heels, for I
was soon almost level with the buck, who was harder hit than
we had supposed, and was making his way very slowly towards
the face of the wall. I could have finished him off ten times
over had I only had the rifle. As it was, my following him
only acted detrimentally, for instead of lying down, never to
rise again, as he assuredly would have done had nobody been
behind him, he kept going, and every minute brought him
nearer the dangerous ledge.

To cut short a long story, David's stratagem did not come
off, and the buck, before David could reach the desired point,
had got out on the face of the precipice, where he was standing
on a tiny projection invisible to the eye, as if glued to the
rock. All chances of getting him were now gone, and the
only thing that could be done was to end the poor beast's •
sufferings by a shot. To do this, David, after taking off his
boots, walked, or rather "sidled," out for a few yards on
the ledge in order to get a better view of the animal. The
band upon which he stood was not wider than 10 or 12
inches, and where he happened to stand there grew a small
Latchen bush (*P. pumilio*), the main stem not being larger
in circumference than a sixpence. He was carrying my rifle

slung by the leather strap over his left shoulder, his right
shoulder scraping along the wall. The tiniest slip on
his part would have sent him at least 1000 feet, and
possibly double that depth, to the very bottom of the
vast cliff. While thus standing, peering forward to catch
sight of the chamois, he suddenly felt that something about
the rifle had given way, and that it was in the act of falling.
To throw his left hand backwards and downwards in order
to save it, was an instinctive act, but it was one which very
nearly cost him his life, for by so doing he lost his balance,
and, as the smooth rock presented no hold, he toppled over.
Had it not been for that slender *Latchen* stem, nothing in the
world could have saved him. As it was, he made one con-
vulsive grasp at it, caught it, and so tough and tenacious are
the branches of the "Stalker's Friend," as more than one
man has had good reason to call this hardiest of Alpine
bushes, that for some seconds the heavy man was hanging
to it, clutching with one hand that life-saving bough, his
body dangling clear of the rock over the terrific abyss.
Singularly to say, he never let go of the rifle which he
held, probably quite unconsciously, in the other hand, until
by drawing himself up he deposited it on the ledge above
his head, doing the same with his own body, when he had
thus freed his hand. For half an hour he sat on the ledge
totally unnerved ; every drop of blood seemed to have left
his blanched face. What had happened was this. The
English gunmakers who had built the rifle had omitted
to rivet the long thin screw which fastens the stirrup-
shaped buckle (through which the leather strap passes) to
the "nose," which is soldered on to the barrel half-way
between hammer and muzzle ; the screw had worked loose
and had come out, with results so nearly fatal. On another
occasion, many years before, the breakage of this pin caused
an Express, which a friend was carrying, to fall down, with

the result that the rifle went off, smashing the man's knee, a wound to which the strong young fellow succumbed within twelve hours. As the use of the strap (in Continental fashion) is little known to the average English sportsman, who, until he has tried it, can form no idea of its great usefulness on all occasions where both hands have to be used for climbing, David's adventure may serve as a warning to have this pin well riveted down.

Silently we returned to the lodge, for both of us had lost all desire to tempt Providence any further that day. The wounded buck, I must still mention, had scrambled out of our field of vision, and though no doubt by next morning the hoarse croak of the Alpine raven (*C. corax*) would betray the spot at the bottom of the great cliff where his mangled remains lay, I naturally did not include him in my bag. To obtain the remaining five chamois I had now six cartridges left, for I had discovered that I had a thirteenth cartridge in the hollowed-out receptacle, just large enough to contain it, which I always cause to be put underneath the heel plate of my rifles, a tightly-fitting trap lid holding the cartridge in place. So that, as a matter of fact, I had started out with the proverbially unlucky number, which, in the eyes of the superstitious, may account for all the bad luck on that expedition.

The next two days' bad weather, with mist and shifting winds, made stalking very hopeless work. In the evening of the third day, David, another keeper, and I were returning, after a blank day, towards the main glen where the lodge is situated, when we passed a spot where a well-known big buck was usually "at home" during the summer and early autumn months, when these old stagers seek the coolest spots in the depths of glens where the rays of the sun rarely penetrate. It was almost dusk, and a filmy mist was hanging about, clouding smaller objects at a greater distance than 100 yards or so. We were trudging along the path, the noise of a rushing brook drowning the sound of our steps, when suddenly I saw, half hidden in a thick bed of *Latchen* bushes less than 100 yards off, the form of a big chamois. I dropped to my knee the same instant, and the two men behind me, who by this time had also seen the game, did the same. There was no occasion to pull out telescopes, for there the beast stood as plainly visible to three pairs of hunters' eyes as the failing light and filmy mist would permit. "It's the big buck," exclaimed David, in an anxious voice; "take care you don't take your bead too coarse." The smoke of my black powder hung heavily over the damp ground, and it was a second or two before we got a clear sight of the spot where the buck had stood, was standing, and, for the matter of that, is probably still standing. The half-light and the mist had played me the first and only trick of the kind to which I have ever fallen victim. Those six eager eyes had all mistaken a tree stump covered in a most life-like manner with long, dark lichen, for the old buck who had so often been seen in that spot. A more perfect optical delusion the deft hand of Nature had never shaped—that all three of us are prepared to make oath to. We were, nevertheless, thoroughly ashamed of ourselves, and the tale would not be told were it not a pity to deprive that chain of bad luck of one of its amusing links. That evening, David, after counting up the shots already fired by me, remarked, "Well, if this kind of thing is to go on, I only hope you have enough cartridges with you." My reply, that I had exactly five left with which to kill five good bucks, led him to beseech me to send one of the keepers at once to the nearest telegraph station with a wire for more cartridges. "In three days you can have them here, and, after the bad luck we have been having, there is no telling what 'pech'—misfortune—may have still in store for us." But I declined — at any rate,

for the time—to give that man a long night's walk, for it
seemed preposterous not to be able to kill six chamois with
thirteen cartridges. Next day, after a blank morning's stalk
with David, I went out in the afternoon by myself, and,
coming upon a good buck, my ninth cartridge made my
Rücksack his temporary home. The following morning we
had another stiff climb, failed to get near a big buck, and
had to be satisfied with a three-year old beast, which fell to
my tenth cartridge. The events of the next day were again
of a somewhat extraordinary kind, for to start out chamois-
stalking and come upon a big bear is a most unusual occurrence in the part of the Alps to which I refer. But again
bad luck was to the fore.

The way it happened was this: On our way up to fresh
ground on the following morning, a tempting shot at a
moderately large buck presented itself, and, as I could not
afford to throw away fairly easy chances, my eleventh cartridge ended his career. Expecting to get another chance
on the other side of the ridge, we pursued our way, when
suddenly to my inexpressible surprise I saw before me in
the fresh snow—it had been snowing a little an hour or so
before—bear tracks, as big as any I have seen made by a
black bear out West. The death of the last bear in this
part of North Tyrol was an event which even the memory
of the oldest man could not recall, but there had certainly
been stray paragraphs in the local papers during the preceding
half-year concerning the misdeeds of a big bear in the mountains of the Stubai Valley, where he had killed many scores
of sheep. But between that valley and the region I was in,
lay the main Inn Valley, where towns and railways would
seemingly have prevented Bruin from skipping across. But
this he must really have done, for there were the tracks,
and some droppings we presently came upon were unmistakably quite fresh. We covered a good bit of ground that

day following those tracks, but Bruin was a tiptop traveller, as they always are at that season of the year. Enormous distances are covered by them, as is well known, in those parts where they are still to be found, for every year a few are killed in South Tyrol and on the borders of Switzerland. One is told that no human being has ever overtaken a bear when disturbed at the setting in of winter while he is looking about for winter quarters. The following day, for curiosity's sake, I followed the tracks back from the point where we had first struck them, and found the cave in which he had evidently passed one or more nights. Had that unlucky easy shot at the chamois not presented itself that morning, we would, in the course of our stalk, have assuredly come upon his old tracks, which were easily discernible under the thin layer of the fresh snow, and in all probability would have been able to surprise Bruin at home. Singular to say, the bear is still about, as I am writing this twelve months afterwards, he having been seen a short time ago in the Vomperloch, a very wild region adjoining the shoot where occurred the events I have described.[1]

My twelfth cartridge did its duty satisfactorily the following day, so that for the last of the six chamois I had that unlucky thirteenth cartridge left. And unlucky it proved to be, for with it I shot something I had never shot before.

David and I had started out very early that morning, intending to reach at sunrise the home country of a certain big buck he knew of. We had not got anywhere near it, when it was beginning to get light enough to shoot, though the usual autumnal mist was still hanging about, the result of a frosty night. We were crossing a little glade in the upper fringe of gnarled old arves and larch trees, talking in

[1] The bear at last met its fate the following November at the hands of the head-keeper of the Glairsthal shoot, which marches with the one I was shooting in. It proved to be a fine old male, almost 6 feet long, and reported as weighing 470 lbs.

fairly low tones and smoking our pipes, when suddenly we
were right upon a big chamois, not 60 yards away. The
animal was feeding, and had its head down, so that we could
not see the horns. What I should have done was to wait
till it raised its head ; but its great size, shaggy look of the
coat, and its being alone and so low down, convinced me that
it was a buck, and by the silent nod David gave me I saw he
was of the same opinion. As my ball struck its vitals, the
animal made a huge bound into the air, throwing up its head,
disclosing as it did so a pair of horns which, though of great
length—10 inches they proved to be—were, as the first
glance told one, those of a doe. This I saw ; but David saw
much more in that brief moment. " It's the blind and deaf
old barren doe from the Uberschall," he exclaimed, a few
strong epithets introducing the dire news. And, sure enough,
a glance at the white film that covered both eyes disclosed,
as we stepped up to the dying animal, the truth of at least
one part of David's comment, while the fact that she had not
heard our sufficiently noisy approach, left but little doubt as
to the fact of the old lady being also deaf. She was a well-
known old beast, but she usually frequented a distant region
—the one, in fact, where we had come across the bear's tracks.
Why she had emigrated suddenly to these parts was a
puzzle, for the rutting time, when chamois roam from their
usual haunts in a most wild manner, had not yet commenced.
The only conclusion we could arrive at was that she had
been frightened from her old ground by a whiff of the bear's
scent. That we both devoutly wished Bruin had made a
meal of her gaunt old carcase need hardly be added, for a
more unsatisfactory billet for that thirteenth bullet it would
have been impossible to find.

CHAPTER VIII

NOTHING that the Alps offer in the way of physical pleasure during the sultry summer, or during the usually more or less uncertain autumn, approaches the zest of an excursion in the Alps, on one of those superb sunny winter days which follow each other often for weeks at a stretch. The air is keen, the blood tingles, the pulse beats vigorously, and one feels fit and strong as at no other season of the year. Exertion becomes a luxury, and to overcome difficulties seems the zest of life. The severe frost has crusted the snow so that it bears one's weight, and the "bite" of the nail-studded sole ensures a firm footing, while on the steeps the sharp spikes of the crampons serve the same end. The cold is just intense enough to counteract the effect of the sun's brilliant rays upon the white pall which hides every unevenness of the ground. Look wherever one will the same undulating lines, the same absence of obstacles, permits one to wander whither one pleases. The rushing brook, the uprooted giant of the forest, the bare ugly boulders that strew the sloping pasture, and which, interesting as they may be to the geologist for ever seeking to discover the paternity of these straying orphans, are nevertheless hardly things of beauty, nay, even the crevasses on yonder glacier, have one and all disappeared under billowy masses many feet deep. One can walk where one dare not venture at other seasons, and a good footing is obtainable where in summer the ice-axe would have to be called into requisition.   On such a day life seems a glorious gift, and for once existence appears as free from obstacles and worries, as is the face of Nature free from the numerous stumbling-blocks which the nakedness of summer reveals to the wanderer's foot.

The coming of winter and the going of winter are alike seasons of dishevelled transition when it is well to be away, but the depth of winter is to the man really fond of mountain life the pleasantest season of the year.   The weather remains settled far longer than is the rule in summer, and the weeks of gloriously sunny days seem each more enjoyable than the other.   Neither depressing rain nor crowds of tourists in the more visited districts mar one's mountain walks or break the solitude which one is seeking, for the mountains are now one's own, and the great solemn stillness of those upper regions is broken by no other sound than by the roar of the descending avalanche.

That the sunny spots in the Alps are not oftener visited by the more robust seekers after change of scene, is but another proof of the blind obedience with which the world follows fashion.   To the native of the Alps, who all summer long has dinned into his ear exaggerated admiration for the patches of snow and ice which mantle his mountains, it shows that city folk's logic is rather at fault.   Some years ago, while resting on the top of a minor pass leading from Tyrol into Switzerland, I overheard some rapturous remarks made by an uncomfortably warm-looking tourist, as he surveyed the somewhat summer-stained and patchy remains of the previous winter's snow, which occupied the northern slope of an impending height.   A good-natured smile puckered up the weather-seamed face of a peasant standing at the tourist's side.   "All you folks who come here from

the great cities to look at the mountains and to gape at the
heel-taps of last winter's snow say the same thing," quoth
the peasant; "why don't you come here in winter when all
the slopes are one glistening snowfield, when the sky is blue,
the air is sharp, and it makes your blood feel young again,
when the sun shines brighter than it ever does in summer?"
"What, come here in winter? Why, nobody thinks of doing
that!" replied the tourist. Far down below us, a band of
sheep were going homeward, following in a long string
behind the shepherd boy who was leading the way across a
bit of green pasture, singing snatches of a mountain song.
The animals were pushing and shouldering each other, each
appearing eager to crowd into the narrow path, though on
either side lay the open meadow. "Well, well, I don't
suppose there is much use puzzling my stupid head,"
soliloquised the peasant, "God no doubt used superior clay
when he baked you town-folk, than he used for us simple
peasants, or when he made those sheep down yonder; but,
asking your pardon, it does seem to the like of me that he
baked you city folk and those sheep in the same oven."

It is not every year that one can add the further attraction of sport to winter walks in the Alps, for with the
expiration of the open season for chamois in December, the
chance to combine the two, ends. In the majority of years
there will be fairly deep snow on chamois ground from the
middle of November onwards, but the weather is not settled.
Warm winds, bringing rain in their wake, will suddenly
intervene, and the really cold weather so essential to give the
snow a bearing crust, has not yet set in. Now and again,
however, things will fit themselves just as one wants them;
and this was the case in the winter of 1893, when an early
and heavy snowfall on the higher levels, followed by very
cold weather, made the outlook for the *Gamsbrunft* or
chamois-rutting season, a promising one.

By an inexplicable provision of Nature, the mating season of the very animal that is most exposed to the inclemencies and dire hardships of a long Alpine winter, occurs six weeks later than that of red-deer and four months later than that of the roe-deer. Both animals inhabit lower regions, and have therefore to fight a less protracted battle with famine, and, moreover, also enter the severe season in a less emaciated condition than does the male chamois. The latter, quite as insatiable as is the stag in the excesses of the season, is, by the time his instincts have been satisfied, nothing but a walking skeleton. And in this state of physical prostration, seeking solitude as if thoroughly ashamed of himself, the buck who two or three short weeks ago was as strong and vigorous as he was masterful, enters upon the hardships of four or five months of winter in the desolate timber-line regions of the Alps.

As a rule, the rutting season is the only time of year when adult males mingle with the females and young bucks. During the rest of the winter, the spring, summer and early autumn, these wily old stagers are always alone, occupying comparatively confined "Standplätze," or runs, in shady nooks on or about timber-line, from which, if left undisturbed, they do not stir; while the females, and the young kids, as well as the yearlings and two-year-olds, running together in small bands, frequent more elevated playgrounds, far above timber-line. These places, during the hot season, are always situated on the north side of the ridges where there is shade, and where the chamois pass most of the day lying about on snow patches, or in "taking the breeze," scrambling in single file along the knife-back ridges, clearly silhouetted against the sky. Here the young frisky kids get their first lessons in the art of stepping where no other four-footed animal of to-day can tread. As the weather gets cooler in autumn, the adult males issue from their summer hiding-places,

CHAMOIS BUCKS FIGHTING DURING THE RUT.

and take to higher ground, the highest they can get at
in their mountain home, still keeping away, however, from
the small fry, as if not deigning to be seen in such frivolous
company. The chamois drives, which are usually held
during the months of September and October, only too often
prove the uselessness of attempting to circumvent the old
bucks, which are, of course, the chief objects of pursuit.
Many a carefully planned and otherwise well-executed drive
is spoilt by their solitary habits and wariness. And as the
result of this unwelcome condition of things, many a drive
proves to be a doe drive with not a single buck. While
in other, though much rarer cases, only old bucks are brought
to the guns by the beaters. An instance of this, with which
I am personally acquainted, happened in a certain drive well
known for this peculiarity, in the Hinter-Riss, where the
late Duke of Coburg on one occasion shot twelve fine bucks
at one "stand" without seeing a single doe.

The altitudes frequented by chamois in November are
usually rendered yet more inhospitable, as well as inaccessible,
by more or less severe snowstorms, lasting two or three days,
which much exceed in severity the early forerunners that
weeks before shrouded the peaks in their first coat of white.
From that time onwards, snow to a depth of from 1 to 3 or
4 feet covers the ground, while the latter half of November
almost invariably brings heavier falls, which increase it to
5 feet and more. The first fall usually is not deep enough
to drive the chamois down from their favourite haunts, for
the fierce wind soon clears exposed slopes, thus enabling
them to get at their sparse food. But the second November
fall, as a rule, produces too deep a mantle, and the hardy
beasts have perforce to seek the upper confines of timber-
line, where the wide-spreading, densely-foliaged branches of
spruce, gnarled by the vicissitudes of existence in these
exposed regions, offer them not only shelter, but also food.

10

Chamois, when one has once learnt their habits, prove themselves unerring weather prophets—their instinct seemingly foretelling the approaching snowstorm far more infallibly than the best barometer. Be the wintry afternoon ever so fine, the sky unclouded, and the air still, one can be sure that, when the animals leave the more elevated runs and press downwards towards timber-line, a snowstorm will be raging before sunrise next morning.

The commencement of the rut varies slightly from year to year. An old proverb has it, that a late rut means a late spring. In the autumn of 1893 it was certainly a trifle late, and as the mountains which I was proposing to visit, and which formed part of the Salzburg Alps, were already in October covered with a couple of feet of snow, I was, when the middle of November came, anxiously awaiting news concerning the commencement of the rut; for now, in the ordinary course of climatic event, it was only a matter of days before the deep November fall would commence. Presumably it would result in making the mountains inaccessible; for they were situated at the end of a long narrow Alpine *cul de sac*, flanked on both sides by steep grassy slopes, which exposed one in many places to a cross-fire of avalanches. The keeper's telegram, suggesting that an attempt to get to the ground should not be put off any longer, as more snow was threatening, reached me early on the 16th, and everything being ready for an immediate start, the next train conveyed me a few hours afterwards to the starting-point— a small station on the railway between Innsbruck and Gastein —a region much frequented in summer, but so entirely unvisited in winter that, apart from half a dozen third-class passengers, I was the only traveller. When I speak of the keeper, I am giving him a title to which he really no longer deserved. He acted as such to a friend of mine, and when the latter gave up the lease of the ground, and no tenant turning up, a few peasants and the keeper clubbed together and leased the shoot as a speculation, the cheap rent, and a considerable head of game, promising to make it a good spec.[1]

When I arrived at the starting-point, a snowed-up little hamlet, the outlook was not very inviting; dull-looking snow clouds hung low in the valley, shrouding the peaks that enclosed it. Insisting on an immediate start with the keeper and a porter, we had a weary six hours' tramp along the narrow trough of the valley to the hut where we proposed to pass the night. At first over open meadow-land, then through sombre spruce forests, lying dark and silent under the deep covering of snow, we finally, as we gradually gained higher ground, left below us the forests, and continued skirting the bottom of the steep grass slopes, which it was easy to see were frequently swept by avalanches. Darkness had overtaken us when we were hardly more than half-way; for the porter, a man beyond his best years, and unaccustomed to snow work, "played out," and his load, consisting of the provisions, a few bottles of wine, etc., had to be divided between the keeper and myself. We took turns in the lead, the undesirable condition of the snow—semi-crusted—at first bearing one's step, but, as one's full weight began to rest on it, giving way and letting one down some 15 or 18 inches—making occasional changes in the leadership (which, of course, entails the hardest work) quite necessary.

Following the course of the ice-bound stream, which in the summer is a likely-looking trout water, we finally reached our destination, a small log hut used in summer as a spirit distillery, where, with the most primitive appliances, the favourite "Schnaps" is produced from the roots of the gentian and the moss berry. As is generally the

---

[1] Instances such as this one occur rarely.

case throughout the Alps, where this kind of distilling is in the hands of females, our hut was owned by a sturdy young woman, who annually passed the four or five summer months in this solitude—first collecting the material and then brewing the pungent cordial. But for the last month or so the place has been deserted.

Digging the key out of its hiding-place and shaking the snow from our clothes, we were soon in possession of the tiny room, the only space in the hut not cumbered by the implements of the owner's trade. A small stove of sheet-iron, about the size of a hat-box, was soon aglow, and a candle we had brought with us, placed in an improvised candlestick, and stuck in a crack between two logs forming the wall, enabled us to prepare our simple supper and hang up our clothes to dry. A coarse linen sack, the size of a small mattress, stuffed with hay, to lie upon, and the stove frequently replenished, enabled one to pass the night quite comfortably. We were up betimes, and had completed our breakfast, and were ready to start before the first tinge of dawn was showing on the horizon.

The weather had become quite clear during the night, and the air was decidedly cold; in fact so much so, that the water in the pail in the room was a block of ice. The condition of the snow was much more unfavourable than the weather; for not only was climbing the steep slopes exceedingly fatiguing, but, what was worse, it was impossible to approach game so long as every step in the semi-crusted snow made a noise audible for a considerable distance. We decided, therefore, to try and gain the level of chamois ground as expeditiously as possible, i.e. before the rays of the sun could strike the slope and change the current of the wind; and then, by keeping to the ridges, where we hoped the wind had cleared off the snow, to strike chamois where our approach could be managed more noiselessly than was possible where the snow lay deep.   It was not more than 1500 feet of sheer ascent to the top; but the first 500 already made the perspiration stream down our foreheads, and there was not a dry thread on our bodies when, after almost three hours of the hardest work, we gained the height.

It was a perfect winter's morning, hardly a breath stirring, the sky overhead one vast blue arch, and the sun's rays so warm that after a couple of hours the crust was perceptibly softer, and at noon one could move about quite noiselessly, sinking deep into the yielding mass.   We had seen half a dozen chamois during the latter part of our ascent, and quite a number of others must have winded us, for their whistle of alarm had betrayed their presence several times.   But of course it would have been worse than useless to attempt a stalk, for the snow had only got soft where the sun had shone upon it, while that in the gullies remained crusted. Chamois can of course be seen a great distance off on a background of snow; for their dun-coloured summer coats have by November become black and shaggy, and their movements during the rutting time are more rapid and less cautiously watchful than at any other season of the year.   In fact, they seem to feel far securer from molestation in their wintry surroundings, where the solitude is hardly ever broken by the sight or scent of humanity.   On reaching the top we divided, the keeper taking one side of the ridge and I the other, but it was useless.   Since the last snowfall there had evidently been no wind, for the ridges, which we hoped to find almost clear of snow, were quite as heavy going as the lower levels.

If the day's hunt proved unsuccessful it was not, at any rate, quite useless, for it enabled us to shape plans for the morrow, which, as the sequel will show, led to very satisfactory results.   We got back to our hut with empty *Rücksäcke* some time after dusk, having been out eleven hours; and the comfortably warm room and substantial supper the porter had prepared, were enjoyed to the full.

Our start next morning was purposely a little later, for we wanted to await the effects of the first rays of the sun upon the air-current, before tackling the slope up which we had decided to try our luck in quest of a small band of chamois, lorded over, as we could easily see, by a very large buck. When, after another tiring three hours of snow wading, we finally breasted the height, we found that the chamois, in the course of their morning's ramble, had moved yet farther up, and were now scrambling about on the very top of an isolated peak, some 700 or 800 feet above us. Clearly silhouetted against the sky, now one then another member of the band could be closely scrutinised with the glass. When the old buck, the last one of all, stood forth on a crag, his great size made one's breath come quicker, and caused the hand to clutch the rifle which, to allow full freedom to both arms and hands for climbing, was still slung over one's back. So clear was the air, and so blue the sky against which he was outlined, that with the glass I could plainly see the breeze play with the " beard."

To get at the buck, where he then was, would have been an impossibility; for the ground that lay between him and us was an entirely open and steep sweep of immaculate whiteness, on which even a mouse would have been a conspicuous object. There was nothing to be done but exercise patience, and console one's self with the knowledge that at any rate the chamois could not get higher; for within a wide radius their retreat was the highest attainable point. At other seasons of the year one might have waited all day in vain for the chamois to come down, for just such breezy points of outlook are their favourite abode; but during the rut the usual caution is forgotten, and the buck's heated instincts lead him occasionally into trouble. As it probably would be hours before they would stir down, the keeper, who knew of another favourite ridge, went to have a look at it, while I remained where I was to keep a watchful eye on the chamois.

Crouching behind a sheltering snowbank, upon which the sun presently shone with grateful warmth, the glass left my eyes only when the strain became too painful. I had been watching them for an hour or so, when suddenly a violent commotion among them became noticeable. There was trouble of some sort or other in the camp. My first thought was that they had winded me, but a glance at the smoke of my pipe showed me that it was drawing steadily down the slope from me. The true cause became visible very shortly. Unperceived by me there appeared on the ridge leading up to the band another buck, a so-called *Sucher* (*i.e.* searcher), that is a solitary buck seeking does. The chamois during the rut is less constant to its mate than are either the red-deer or the roe-deer, and one can, therefore, frequently observe these love-lorn searchers rambling from mountain chain to mountain chain in quest of unprotected females. Like the stag, the chamois buck during the rut is up and doing all day and all night. He hardly feeds at all, so that his paunch is usually found empty, while the membrane surrounding the latter, instead of being white in colour, is of an angry red. On several occasions when I gralloched chamois myself, or they were opened before my eyes, the only contents of the paunch was a small handful of gravelly sand. The searcher evidently meant business; he had come to conquer the band and drive off one of the does for his own pleasure. Though not so large as the other buck, his efforts, one must remember, were assisted by the fickleness of the females, who one after the other made attempts to join him by darting towards him, but they were successively driven back by their lord, who, with astonishingly rapid movements, headed off each

attempt. Presently the old buck got tired of these moles-
tations, and he made for the intruder, who, however, did
not await his coming but darted to one side, but, instead of
taking himself off, circumvented his elder, and by a series of
immense leaps was in the middle of the band before the
other had time to regain his post. This exasperating
manœuvre was, however, too much for the equanimity of the
patriarch, who, with lowered head, now made a determined
rush at his rival. The latter took to his heels, and there
being no other avenue of escape open to him, he went down
the slope towards me at headlong pace followed by his enemy.
The snow on the slope was at least 3 feet deep, and, as the
sun had been shining on it for some time, it was soft, so that
often only the heads of the animals were visible when they
landed after their stupendous leaps down the steep declivity.
This latter, beginning, as I have said, at a point some 800
feet above me, continued for about the same distance below
my hiding-place, and it was about 600 or 700 yards wide.
On this slope, about on a level with me, there was a slight
ridge running parallel with the direction of the slope, and
dividing the lower half into two separate hollows. The
chamois were making for the one farthest away from me,
and their lightning-like movements were so sudden and so
unexpected, that they had almost reached and disappeared
behind the ridge before I had recovered from my surprise.

If the chamois continued their mad career, a few minutes
would take them, I knew, far down the slope, into the region
of the *Latchen*, or dwarf-pine, and there, of course, they
were quite out of my reach. If, on the other hand, it should
happen that they stopped behind the ridge, possibly because
the lord of the manor would not want to leave his band too
long unprotected, a quick advance on my part to the ridge
might yet lead to success. All this flashed through my mind,
and throwing off my coat to enable me to run faster across

the open, I was wallowing in the deep soft snow up to my waist, a few seconds after the two chamois had disappeared behind the ridge. But my progress was lamentably slow; the distance was not more than 350 yards or so; in fact, had the chamois halted while yet in sight, I do not know that I would not have risked a shot. Even 350 yards can, under circumstances, test one's endurance, and that obstacle race certainly did test mine. While floundering across the open towards the ridge, I was, of course, in full view of the band of does, who had remained on the peak jumping about uneasily from crag to crag, and I now heard their whistles of alarm very plainly. The ridge was not higher than 20 feet, but where I breasted it there was an almost vertical bank of drifted snow into which I sank up to my chest. It was only on the third attempt that I succeeded in gaining the top. Taking off my hat and cautiously raising my head over the crest of the snow-bank, my heart stood still, for there, actually not 5 feet off, his horns on a level with my eyes, stood the big buck, evidently doing from his side of the ridge the very same thing I was doing from mine—trying to see what was on the other side. Fortunately I had got to the top first, but he, on the other hand, was far less impeded by snow, of which there was only a thin film on the rocks forming the off-side, where wind and sun had full play. I must have succeeded in remaining perfectly motionless, staring the animal straight in the face, for a good many seconds seemed to pass before the unexpected interview was as abruptly closed as it had commenced, by the chamois suddenly pivoting round, and with an audible snort dashing off with huge bounds down the slope. Three lengths of my *Bergstock* (or 18 feet), as I afterwards measured, intervened between some of the marks in the snow.

Not an instant was to be lost! I do not know how I managed to gain a firm footing on the ever-yielding snow,

snatch the rifle from my back, remove the short leather
sheath from the muzzle, without which the barrel would have
been full of snow, brush from the sights the snow which had
caked round lock, stock, and barrel, and finally, with heart
and lungs fiercely palpitating from the preceding exertions,
to shoot with sufficient steadiness to roll over that old veteran
with a bullet through his shoulders, as he landed after one of
his immense leaps.   How I did all this, I say, I do not know,
and I certainly would not have achieved it without a very
considerable share of good luck and the excellent shooting
qualities of my Holland and Holland ·450.   Quite a new
rifle, it was the third shot I made with it at game, the two
previous ones having laid low two stags going equally fast,
but at longer range.   The impetus of the buck was so great
that, with his heart split in pieces, his legs supported his
weight for quite 100 yards before he collapsed.   I had
not been mistaken when I sized him up as a buck above the
average, for he turned out to be the heaviest shot that year
in the district, weighing when gralloched 67 Austrian pounds,
or nearly 74 pounds avoirdupois.   His horns were, however,
nothing particular, following in this respect the general rule
that chamois found in the crystalline rock formation of the
Alps have smaller horns than those frequenting regions
where the dolomite or limestone formations prevail.   A buck
of the great weight mentioned would in the latter regions
have carried horns 1½ or 2 inches longer.

In looking for an explanation of the singularly sudden
stoppage of the two bucks behind the ridge, which proved to
be such an important factor in bringing about my success,
it must be ascribed, there is little doubt, to the whistle of the
does, which, great as the distance was, instantly arrested the
pursuing buck, and caused him to climb the ridge from which
to ascertain the cause of the alarm.

The male chamois during the rut exhibits great curiosity;

it is a quality which, one knows, is shared at the same season by the bighorn, the antelope-goat of the Rocky Mountains, and to an even greater degree by the antelope of the plains, or prong buck. In the case of the chamois its curiosity seems to be chiefly aroused by anything resembling its own form without being quite like it. Thus I have seen a keeper with a black *Wettermantel* (a sort of cloak) thrown over his body, and moving about on his hands and knees, gradually beguile a three-year-old buck close up to him—the wind, of course, being in his favour.

Letting the keeper take the buck down to the hut, I spent the afternoon in ascending the peak from which my victim had been lured, and in a stalk along the ridge, hitherto invisible to me, from which the "searcher" had first come. The latter, it must be mentioned, made a big circuit after my shot, and was seen to return to the band of does, over which he would for the rest of the rut probably assume the duties of the dead champion. From the top I had a splendid view, but the only chamois I saw were too far off, and were making for lower ground. Far to the south of me, on about the same level as where I was, I could see the snow-covered surface of a small tarn of piscatory interest. Lying at a height of about 8000 feet, at the north base of cliffs forming the last elevation of the highest mountain for miles around, the rays of the sun rarely reach it, so that it remains frozen over until July, and freezes again in September. Twenty years ago it was stocked with a few trout, which a keeper brought from a distant stream in a large glass bottle. Now the lake, in spite of the briefness of the open season, is full of the finest trout, but of somewhat peculiar characteristics. When the ice first disappears in July, the fish are excessively poor, consisting, so to speak, of nothing but a head and a pre-ternaturally long tail. Within a fortnight after the disappearance of the ice, so men who have been there at the time assure me, the fish have regained their usual plumpness, a large supply of flies and insects bringing this about. But, strange to say, their movements remain of unusual slowness, as if they had entirely lost the use of the propelling power during their long imprisonment. Thus, on casting in August an artificial fly, half a dozen large sleek trout will make a rush for it; but this rush is most ludicrously slow, and, while one can see that the fish are straining their utmost to get at the bait, it will take them seconds to accomplish what other trout would have obtained with the rapidity of a flash of lightning. I am no fisherman, so unfortunately do not know whether this loss of locomotive power is the invariable result of similar circumstances; if this is the case, the incident would not be worth mentioning.

Sunset found me still on the heights, and though the air was still clear the breeze began to veer about, and the sky assume that leaden tinge which foretells snow. In this one was not wrong, for by the time I reached the hut strong gusts were coming down the glen, and long before morning a good old snowstorm was upon us, blocking the door of the hut with drifts 3 feet high before daylight broke. Fortunately, the small windows—less than 18 inches square—of our tiny chamber looked out on the lee-side of the house, or we would have had them blocked too; an exigency, to meet which our slim stock of candles was by no means adequate. For two days the snow came down thick and fast, entirely obscuring the opposite slopes of the glen not more than 300 yards off. Slowly, inch by inch, our hut seemed to sink lower and lower in the white billows, and darker and darker got our prison; where time, notwithstanding some papers I had taken with me, began to hang somewhat heavy on one's hands.

On the third day, a start was made though the storm was not yet over. The snow was now quite high, but it was dry, and one sank no farther than the crust of the previous fall. Our destination was not more than a couple of miles off, with quite a gentle rise, for chamois had been driven down by the snow, and numerous indistinct tracts within a few hundred yards of the hut showed how close the game had been, and what good chances the storm had spoilt.

The place we were trying to reach was a certain dense grove of spruce trees, which for some reason or other grew there at considerably higher altitude than elsewhere in the glen. Here the keeper was sure we would find chamois congregated for the sake of shelter, but a new difficulty arose—the shiftiness of the wind. Blowing for ten minutes from the one, the next quarter of an hour from the opposite, direction, it of course betrayed our approach half a mile off. What, had the wind been less tricky, would have been simply a perfect day for our purpose, was by that one blemish turned into as unsuccessful a one as the first had been.

On getting into the forest, where the branches of every tree swept the ground and thus afforded shelter, almost impervious to the fiercest snowstorm, we found numerous signs of the late presence of chamois, which probably left the wood on the upper side as we floundered up to its lower approaches. A long day spent in wading up and down rises, always tempted onwards by fresh signs of chamois, but invariably betrayed by the shifting breeze, we finally had to confess that further attempts under such unfavourable conditions of snow and weather would be useless, and that it was about time to return to civilisation—a decision to which our depleted stock of provisions pointed with equal force. That morning I had boiled up my last tea for the third time, and, as it would have to be used for a fourth boil for breakfast, I reluctantly had to yield to force of circumstances, and next morning saw us trudging through the deep snow homewards. Had the weather been propitious—an overcast sky, so as

not to give the sun a chance to produce that fatal semi-crust
—and had the snowstorm not come on just when it did, I
am convinced the bag would have been a different one.

In some years, when no heavy snowfalls occur in November,
such as was the case in 1894 and 1895, the sport assumes
a somewhat more dangerous aspect than when deep snow
covers the slopes. For then all the declivities are frozen
hard and, in consequence of the warm sun during daytime,
coated with ice, transforming it into a sort of imitation glacier,
more dangerous than the real thing on account of its deceptive
appearance. On such occasions the *Steigeisen*, or crampons,
remain buckled to your boots from start to finish. Without
them it would be impossible to stir out, and even with these
trusty, much-maligned friends, to help you, the risks are often
considerable, for when the ground is quite bare it is of such
iron hardness that if the foot is not planted on it with a
certain amount of force, one is apt, in spite of the six or eight
sharp spikes, to slip. And what that means if there is a
precipice at your side, and nothing but ground of this nature
whereon to regain the lost footing, need not be told.

In some parts of the Alps, particularly in Styria, owners
of good chamois preserves have drives in December for *Bart
Gams, i.e.* to secure old bucks with the longest possible "beard."
As the condition of the ground is thus very different to what
it is in September or October, when driving chamois is the
easiest possible sport, it is much more of a sporting undertaking than the latter. Let me briefly describe such a winter
drive in a first-class Styrian preserve.

The Wild-Alpe is the name of the shoot, and, next to
those of the Emperor of Austria, it enjoys the reputation of
being among the best in the Alps of Styria. It is very
extensive, embracing a huge tract of mountain country, consisting of numerous glens, favourite retreats of the red-deer,
as well as of some barren ranges, the playground of chamois.

A mere glance at it fills the heart of the sportsman with delight. Its owner, the noted Austrian *Jäger* and explorer, Count Wilczek, is a sportsman of rare mettle, reminding one in many particulars of the doughty Nimrods of old, whose minds knew as little of fear as their bodies did of fatigue and exposure.

A roomy, delightfully picturesque, shooting lodge occupies a central position in the preserve, and from here the Count and his guests usually start when stalking stags or chamois, while the more outlying ground is taken quite early or quite late in the season, when driving no longer militates against the stalker's chances by disturbing the game where perfect quiet is a primary condition for success. Owing to this circumstance our headquarters are not in the shooting lodge, but in a roomy old-fashioned inn of an Alpine village situated in the centre of the outlying district which it is proposed to drive. The beaters, forty or fifty in number, are sturdy-looking fellows from the vicinity, born to the climbing work before them. To them the good pay they get is on this occasion of less consideration than usual, for they love sport and follow the fortunes of the day with the greatest interest. They are mostly young men, and, were the keepers not such vigilant guardians, more than one of the former would turn to good account his knowledge of the ground, and be tempted to try poaching, for the love for chamois-stalking is inbred in these people.

In the judicious arrangement of the drives lies the secret of success, provided unfavourable weather does not mar at the last moment the carefully matured plans. As a rule, only one drive is made each day, and as much ground taken in as the lay of the land will permit. To prevent the chamois escaping across the top, *Lappen* are used.

The beaters have to be on the ridge very early, so that often they have to leave the night before, in order that they

can surround the game as soon as possible after sunrise. The
guns, on the other hand, need not bestir themselves, for three
sleighs take the party to the bottom of the range which is
to be the scene of that day's drive. Time passes only too
pleasantly during the seven or eight miles' drive, for my
host is not only one of the most agreeable and best-informed
sportsman imaginable, but his knowledge of every minute
detail relating to the day's sport is great, and he is ready to
explain them. One sees that the planning of the drives is
not left, as it generally is, to the head-keeper, but has been
thought out by the master himself.

When the sleighs stop, after having passed for the last
mile or so over a narrow and very rough mountain road, a
group of keepers, all dressed in their national costume,
headed by the genial head-keeper, await the arrival of their
master and his guests. A list of the six or seven guests who
are present, is rapidly marked by the host, each post having
a certain number, and thus he designates each guest's " stand."
Long experience has shown what under ordinary circumstances can be expected at each. As a rule, the lower guns
will get fewer shots, but have a better chance of getting big
bucks, while those stationed higher up on the mountain,
where the chamois usually come in bands, consisting of the
younger bucks and females, will be able to fire oftener. If
number rather than quality is the sportsman's desire, it is, as
a rule, easy to gratify his whim, always provided that he
does not follow the example of the old gentleman who got
the post under me, and who, though he was an experienced
chamois hunter, managed to miss four bucks at easy range.
Sly old dogs these veteran bucks prove themselves. They
have been through the wars too often not to know what all
this unusual hubbub means, and as soon as the reports of the
rifles warn them that danger lurks ahead, they try to steal
through the line of guns as stealthily as possible. On such

occasions the younger generation of chamois fall easy victims to panic, generally rushing in wild fright along the whole line of guns; the old stagers, on the other hand, will first betake themselves to some point from which they can overlook as much of the ground as possible. There they will stand for half an hour, or even more, taking in the scene. On one side the breeze tells them there are human beings in numbers; above them, on the sky-line of the jagged knife-back ridge, they see countless blue and red handkerchiefs fluttering in the air, and in front of them, as well as below, occasional white puffs of smoke go up here and there. And strangest of all, though the sky is clear and the sun shines, there is constant thunder in the air. Whither is escape possible ? Why not try the favourite *Wechsel* (run way) through the uppermost fringe of trees, where it will be possible to sneak through like a roe-deer that won't break cover ? No puff of smoke has gone up yet from that direction, and no angry peal of thunder has issued from that corner ! So he takes himself off to it, cautiously spying ahead, and watchfully peering over the top of each of the numerous ridges he has to cross. If the gun posted on this run way is at all fidgety, and does not sit as motionless as a statue, nine out of ten chances are against his getting a shot at all, for the buck will have seen him long before the unconscious sportsman is aware that he is under observation. Often have I had a chance of observing these tactics of old bucks from "stands" where I could overlook not only the approaches to the other posts, but also the men themselves, and much amusement these proceedings afford. With one's glasses one can almost see the old fellow shake his head and wink his left eye as he inspects his would-be slayer from behind a bush scarce 100 yards off, as the latter fidgets about on his camp-stool—for such conveniences are by no means unheard of on such occasions—or as he raises his rifle, taking aim at some

11

imaginary chamois, or looks at his watch, or does any one of
the hundred and one things one should not do when watching
for chamois. An hour and more have I known bucks stand
with gaze rigidly fixed upon the unconscious enemy, and
then slowly turn and make their way quite leisurely to some
recess in the rocks, or hide under the overhanging boughs of
a *Latchen*, where they remain until the beaters have passed
them, often only a few yards off; and then, when they are
once behind the line of the latter, they jump up and rush off
at their best pace in the direction from which the beaters
came, as if they instinctively knew that danger no longer
lurks there.

But now to the drive and its incidents. Quality rather
than number having the chief attraction for us, the old
gentleman I have already referred to, and I, got the two
stands for old bucks, mine being the upper one of the two,
some 600 yards of impassable rock separating us. Each guest
gets, in this instance, a keeper to accompany him, and, where
quick shooting is necessary, the latter acts also as loader; but
his services as such are rarely needed. His presence is,
however, welcome to many a sportsman for other reasons,
viz. to settle any doubt regarding the sex of the approaching
game. Sitting close at the side of his *Herr* the keen-eyed
keeper will, when he has assured himself, with the assistance
of his glass, of the sex of the quarry, answer the anxious
interrogatory glance of the sportsman with a quiet shake of
the head or a nod, as the case may be. In other shoots,
again, where the rules of venery are not so strictly observed
as in Count Wilczek's, the novice is allowed to wreak his
sweet will; and, notwithstanding the best intentions on his
part, ghastly results are now and again the consequence.
For ghastly it must be called when such a novice, filled with
feverish impatience, opens fire at the first beast he sees, and
by dint of a regular fusillade succeeds in bringing down a

doe or two, whose helpless progeny is, of course, doomed to succumb to the next snowstorm.

As the rest of the guns, the host included, occupied much higher posts, some of which it will take two hours to reach, for the snow is deep, a long wait was my lot, but it gave me a chance of having a good chat with the keeper, Ferdl Mühlbacher by name, who is quite a celebrity in his way. As favourite gilly and personal attendant of the Count, he has seen a good bit of the world, from the North Pole, whither his master inaugurated the Austrian North Pole Expedition a score of years ago, to the Sierras of Spain and the peaks of Aosta. Born in a little châlet in the Styrian Alps, this child of the mountains had not lost a whit of his quaint simple - mindedness, and his remarks about the countries and people he had seen were most diverting, for when once the innate shyness of all mountain-bred people was overcome, it was easy to get him to talk. Rarely have two hours of waiting at one's post passed so quickly and agreeably as on this occasion, and I could hardly believe my ears when the far - away sound of a shot notified the commencement of the drive, and obliged us to break off conversation.

My post was a typical " old-buck " ambush. Immediately in the foreground was a strip of snow-covered moraine of loose stones and boulders at a steep angle; opposite were a few bushes of dwarf-pine, hiding from my view the base of a high cliff a couple of hundred feet in altitude. About half-way up the perpendicular face of it, a tiny ledge, inches in width, ran almost horizontally across. This, and a favourite run right at the base of the cliff, were the two approaches which the game would probably use. Both routes would force the beasts to cross the strip of moraine which would give me a safe shot, so that the keeper was right in calling it " ein sehr schüssiger Stand." Three hundred yards higher up, where the moraine ended and the cliff commenced, was stationed an *Abwehrer*, lest the game should try to take to the rocks at that point. "Any chamois you see on the top of the cliff must sooner or later come here," were the last words spoken by my companion before absolute silence had to be observed. An hour or more passed, and though the echo of numerous shots come rolling back from a grand tier of mountains on the far side of the valley we overlooked, nothing living came our way, and the nape of my neck began to pain me from the constant scanning of the sky-line far overhead. I was just in the act of lifting my left hand to give it a rub, when I saw Ferdl's left eye close slowly and his face assume a rigid look. It was turned upwards, spying the sky-line. He had seen a chamois—that I knew instinctively—and, as the first precaution to be observed under such circumstances is to avoid any rapid movement, I slowly, very slowly, began to lift my eyes in the direction he was looking. Sure enough, there, right on the top of the cliff, I could see the head of the animal as it stood peering with craning neck down in our direction. Had the animal seen us? We were sitting with our backs against a big boulder, a trunk of a prostrate tree hiding all but the upper part of our bodies. The gray and green of our clothes matched so completely the tint of our surroundings that we escaped observation, and after a few minutes' inspection, the chamois, followed, to my surprise, by two others—for old bucks usually come singly—picked their steps quite slowly down a sort of gully leading to the upper ledge. When they were all three safely on it, I saw that the last one carried the best head. There, to that corner yonder, I would let him pick his way, where I would have him broadside on. But I had reckoned without the man who was guarding the upper escape, who at this moment, instead of following his instructions to keep under cover till they were quite close, showed himself and began to wave his arms frantically. It is needless to say that there wasn't much repose left about those three animals after that. They came bounding down the almost perpendicular face of the cliff in a way that was truly wonderful. Down and down they leaped, taking advantage of every minute crack or protrusion; now one ahead, then again another, so that it was quite hard to keep my eye upon the one I had selected as the best. When they reached the moraine at the foot of the cliff, it was time to shoot. Rising from my seat, and aiming well forward at the buck, now not more than 90 yards off, I let him have it. He turned head over heels and went rolling down the slope, fetching up against a big boulder at the foot with a heavy thud. Had I been armed with a double-barrelled rifle I might possibly have made a right and left; as it was, I had not time to reload before the two other bucks had turned a corner and were out of sight.

Half an hour later I got another chance at a good buck flying down the slope, at the head of which he had almost run down the *Abwehrer*, who this time kept quiet until the buck was quite close to him. His pace was terrific, and as the distance was quite 150 yards, I had to aim 2 feet in front of the animal, and even then the ball was a trifle too far back, and really it was a good deal of a fluke that I hit the fellow at all. Two good bucks with two cartridges was my record for the day. It was, however, an average which I failed to keep up on the following days.

CHAPTER IX

THE subject with which the chapter on chamois-shooting in the past dealt, was one that lent itself more advantageously to treatment within the narrow confines of a chapter, than does the matter of the present one. For, unlike the chamois, to the chase of which in the olden days only a very few prominent sportsmen devoted their energies, the stag was pre-eminently the foremost beast with which venery concerned itself. There is, therefore, a vast mass of material at the disposal of the student, or of those to whom the close of the shooting season is the signal to commence stalking of another kind. This latter has for its quarry old manuscripts and tomes thick with the dust of centuries, wherein are inscribed, in the crabbed handwriting of an age that witnessed the invention of printing, prodigious deeds of venery and records of bags such as we know not in modern times.

A nearer acquaintance with the literature of the chase of England, France, and Austria-Germany, brings home to one the fact, that each of these countries claimed to be the most sport-loving, and to be the home of the best and keenest sportsmen. It does not lie within the province of these pages to examine into the respective merits of these claims, further than to repeat the well-known fact, that in the late Middle Ages France had certainly a much richer literature on sport than either of the other countries. Almost every one of the English works on sport were copies or adaptations of French books, and the Germans were not much more conscientious cribbers. The latter, we must remember, had, on the other hand, created the richest vocabulary of sport, as might be expected from the academic national character. And while they cared little and knew less, till a later period, of the pursuit of deer on horseback or the use of running hounds, they were far and away the first in stalking the big game which overran their great forests, and for which sport neither of the other countries held out so many opportunities. Indeed, at the very period when the chase had reached its highest pitch in Germany, James I. of England, when writing his instructions for "the nurture and conduct" of the Prince of Wales, says: "I cannot omit heare the hunting, namely, with running hounds, which is the most honourable and noblest sort thereof; for it is a theivish forme of hunting to shoote with gunnes and bowes; and greyhound hunting is not so martial a game."

That King James's sentiments were not shared by the Scottish chiefs, we know from Taylor the Water Poet's account (1618) of the *Tinkhell* or *Tainchel*, a great annual drive at the Brea of Mar, where a hundred couple of Irish greyhounds were let loose on herds of deer, which were slaughtered with harquebusses, arrows, dirks, and daggers in a somewhat indiscriminate manner.

France, entirely in consequence of the momentous social changes wrought by the great revolution, has for the last hundred years dropped out of the van as a sport-loving country. In Great Britain a vastly increased population has worked another kind of revolution, and King James's "most honourable and noblest sport" is no longer what it was, while "the theivish forme of shooting with gunnes" is coming more and more to the front, in fact so much so that game has to be artificially produced, or is imported in ever-increasing quantities from foreign countries.

In Austria and Germany sport has not undergone any such radical changes as in France and England; indeed, in the Alps the chase is conducted to-day, in some respects, in almost precisely the same manner in which we know the sportsmen of the Middle Ages obtained their quarry.

French and German archives afford ample proof of the extraordinary pitch to which the love for sport was driven, a pitch for which no parallel is to be found in our history. Great Britain never produced a Landgrave of Hesse who, to the dismay of his clerics, insisted on substituting in the Lord's Prayer an entreaty to "Give us our daily hart in the pride of grease," "for," said this irreverent old sportsman, "'tis the fare the *Jäger* can least afford to miss." Nor do our annals of olden sport disclose a prototype of the whimsical old duke who, whenever he passed certain great heads killed by himself, that hung in the corridors of his Schloss, doffed his hat "with ceremony and esteem," the gentlemen of his suite having, of course, to pay similar homage to what their master never grew tired to declare was " God's noblest creation." The great hunters of those days only found time to enter into their diaries the events relating to the chase; nothing else was worth noting. In France the chase remained the all-absorbing subjects of men's thoughts until the actual outbreak of the great upheaval. Louis XVI.'s diary, under the fatal date of the 14th July 1789, which witnessed the storming of the Bastille, contains nought but the laconic :- " Killed nothing." While on the 5th of the following October, the day the maddened hordes of the "Great Unwashed" threw themselves upon Versailles, his diary contains but the following: "Shot at the gate of Chatillon, killed 81 head, interrupted by events; went and returned on horseback." Nothing more, nothing less. That it was destined to be his last hunt he knew not, or assuredly he would have ended his diary with the grand total of all he had slain in his lifetime, as representing that summary of his career most worthy of perpetuation.

Upon two important facts historical research throws a strong light, viz. upon the great diminution in the number, and an almost equally great deterioration in the size of stags, that have taken place within the last 250 years. Perhaps nothing will bring this startling retrogression more convincingly home to the reader, than a brief comparison of the game lists of two representative sportsmen of the seventeenth and of the nineteenth centuries. That the two sportsmen belonged to the same dynasty, and the bags were obtained in what geographically speaking is practically the same country, though the extent of the ground reserved for sport has of course become much contracted in the interval by an immensely increased population, adds interest to the comparison. The proposed parallel to which I have in another place once before had occasion to refer,[1] relates to the old Wettin dynasty that has ruled for nearly 1000 years over Saxony. For a great part of the seventeenth century a father and son occupied the throne, and killed the game of Saxony by the hundreds of thousands.[2] Elector John George the First, who reigned from 1611 to 1656, and Elector John George the Second (1656-1680), were probably the greatest slaughterers of game known in modern history. In the seventy years of father and son's reign, they bagged a total of 110,530 deer.[3] As the details of their stupendous bags

[1] Badminton Library, *Big Game*, vol. ii.

[2] According to Schreber's *Inventarium* there were bagged during the reign of John George I. a total of 795,403 head of game. *Vide* Von Schimpff.

[3] It may be mentioned that the historical details here given were obtained in the course of researches in the private library of the King of Saxony, and in the archives of the Duke of Saxe-Coburg, which contain MS. shooting diaries and other interesting original matter, as well as from more accessible material in the State libraries of Vienna, Dresden, Munich, Gotha, Stuttgart,

are of interest, I have in the following list given a general summary taken from reliable sources:—

	Elector John George I. reigned 1611-1656.	Elector John George II. reigned 1656-1680.	Total of both.
Red-deer	35,421	43,649	79,070
Fallow-deer	1,045	2,062	3,107
Roe-deer	11,489	16,864	28,353
Total of deer . .	47,955	62,575	110,530
Wild boar	31,902	22,298	54,200
Bear	238	239	477
Wolves	3,872	2,195	6,067
Lynx	217	191	408
Hares	12,047	16,966	29,013
Foxes	19,015	2,740	21,755
Beavers	37	597	634
Badgers	930	1,045	1,975
Otters	81	180	261
Wild cats	149	292	441

The finest antlers obtained by	John George I.	John George II.	John George III.	John George IV.
Head of 30 points .	1	...	...	...
,, 28 ,, .	1	...	...	...
,, 26 ,, .	1	...	...	1
,, 24 ,, .	3	...	1	...
,, 22 ,, .	9	6	2	...
,, 20 ,, .	25	26	9	20
,, 18 ,, .	133	54	?	?
,, 16 ,, .	374	295	?	?
,, 14 ,, .	1202	985	?	?
,, 12 ,, .	3147	2108	?	?

It must be remembered, too, that during the reign of the elder Elector, the whole Continent was in the throes of the Thirty Years' War, during which Tilly invaded his territories, while the Swedes, in revenge for his making peace with the Emperor, wrought for ten years terrible havoc throughout Saxony. What his bag would have been

and others of lesser importance. The measures and weights are carefully converted and checked by Woolhouse's and other Tables.

in time of continued peace it is impossible even to conjecture; of startling size it was in any case. If we now, to carry out the comparison,[1] skip two centuries, we find a kinsman, *i.e.* the late Duke Earnest II. of Saxe-Coburg-Gotha, ruler of what was once an integral part of the old Saxon dukedom, leaves his mark as an equally distinguished and devoted sportsman. But what a vast difference in the quantity of game! In forty-nine years of his life (1837-1886) he shot in his own duchies 3283 red-deer. Amongst them there were:

1 stag of	24	points.
2 „	22	„
4 „	20	„
8 „	18	„
36 „	16	„
128 „	14	„

Much more considerable is the shrinkage in the weights of the stags. The heaviest animal killed by the two old Electors is said to have tipped the scales at 9 Nürnberg cwt., but this does not appear to be such an authenticated instance as that of a 12 point stag killed by John George I. on the 17th August 1646, which weighed, presumably as he stood, 61 stone 11 lbs. avoirdupois. Though this is more than 3 stones less than the above not so well-authenticated instance, it is perhaps best in the absence of particulars relating to the 9 cwt. stag, to consider the stag of 1646 as

---

[1] In Elector John George I.'s own MS. Hunting Diary, two gorgeously bound volumes, in part illuminated, preserved in the Dresden Royal Library, there is a complete list of all game caught, shot, and chased by this great hunter. It gives the total of deer at 47,239 head, while Sylvanus, from whom the above lists are taken, gives a total of 47,955 head. How this discrepancy arose it would be difficult to say. There is another and more serious discrepancy in the number of bears and wolves. The former state that the father killed only 102 bears and 818 wolves, while Sylvanus gives the figures as 238 bears and 3872 wolves. This probably arises from the fact that the former is the number killed by the Elector with his own hands, the latter those that were killed by the whole court *personage*. Tänzer, who wrote about the beginning of the following century, is very particular in saying that the deer were killed by the Elector John George I. himself.

top weight. Of the elder Elector's harts, 59 animals exceeded 56 stone, 651 exceeded 48 stone, 2679 exceeded 40 stone, and 4139 exceeded 32 stone. It is a sad proof of the enormous deterioration to have to state that not a single stag of modern times, killed by the late Duke of Coburg, in what is one of the best German forests of to-day, viz. the Thuringian forest, scaled 32 stone.

Nothing like such physical degeneration has occurred in the Austrian, or rather in the Hungarian sub-Alpine, hill-country, where, as we shall presently hear, stags weighing clean 44 stone are shot to-day.

In old days the stags were always weighed just as they fell, which is, after all, the most sensible, though not the most convenient, manner, the comparatively quite modern manner of first brittling the animal being much more open to mistakes. On the occasion of all larger hunts, big scales, able to weigh a 60-stone monster, were always included in the vast paraphernalia that accompanied the *chasse* to the woods. At the conclusion of each drive the larger harts were placed upon the scales and accurately weighed. Most accounts of drives, after mentioning the weights of the largest stags, state the number of animals that were found worthy of being weighed, and which amounted occasionally to 300.

The illustration (Plate XII.) shows the process of weighing; it is taken from the *Coburg Chronicle*, an illuminated work, painted more than 250 years ago by the Coburg Court painter, Wolff Pirkner. It consists of a number of large size water-colour pictures. They graphically represent the various methods of hunting employed by the Duke Casimir of Coburg (born 1564, died 1633), and, as such, are an unique record of the period.[1] Duke Casimir is represented standing near the

---

[1] Eleven of these pictures, in a reduced size, were published by me last year in *Land and Water* and in the *Field*, but it is my intention to republish, very shortly, facsimiles of the whole series of twenty-one plates, of which I have secured photographic copies, a good deal of interest having been taken in those already known to the public.

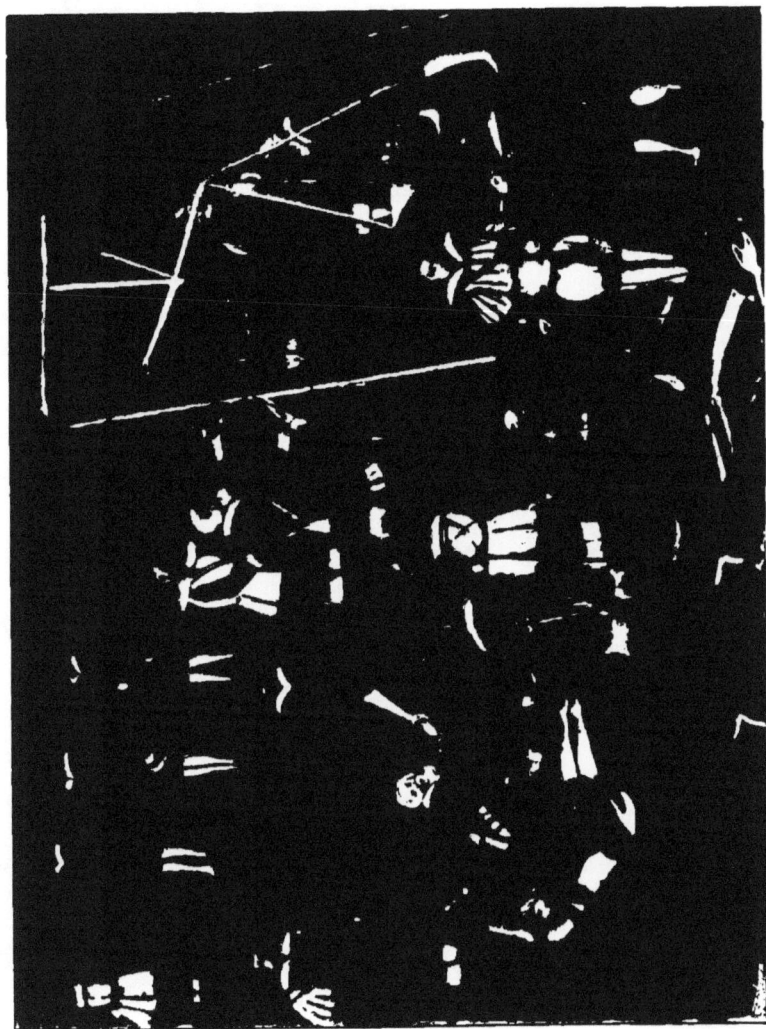

Inflicting the Punishment of "Blading" for a Breach of the Laws of Venery, and also showing how Stags were weighed in the Forest where they were killed.

(From the Coburg Chronicle of Duke Casimir of Coburg, 1564-1633.)

scales superintending this important function, a large hart
having just been placed on the weighing machine. He is
surrounded by his Master of the Game, the Court dwarfs, and
a number of personages in attendance upon him, who, hat in
hand, watch the proceedings. Also of another and amusing
ceremony does this picture enable us to gather some details,
viz. of the so-called *blading*. This punishment was inflicted upon all who had contravened any of the numerous
usages, ceremonies, or laws of the chase, or who had failed
to use the correct technical term in describing events connected with the chase. This *blading* gave endless amusement.
The culprit had to kneel down between the front and hind
legs of the largest stag killed that day. The Master of the
Game, or other high dignitary, who acted as executioner—
the duke taking this duty upon himself only if the culprit
was of princely rank—then laid the victim across the carcase,
and administered, as the picture shows, in old-fashioned
schoolmaster's manner, three strokes with the flat part of the
Waidblatt, which was a broad-bladed hunting-knife used for
cutting up the deer. Each blow was accompanied by a
quaint rhyme, which, roughly translated, ran thus :—

Jo, ha, ho ! this for the king, princes, and lords,
Jo, ha, ho ! this for the knights, huntsmen, and serving-men,
Jo, ha, ho ! and this by the good old law of noble venery !

While the punishment was administered, the assembled company doffed their hats, raised their bared hangers, and a squad
of trumpeters blew a loud fanfare ; after which the punished
one had to thank the prince or king for his merciful punishment. Then only could he slink away in the laughing
crowd.

This curious old custom, which dates back to the days of
Charlemagne, is, it is said, being revived by the present
German Emperor. In the last century, at some of the

gay Frenchified Courts of Germany, even fair huntresses, we
are told, had to submit to the ceremony of *blading*, the person
of highest rank having the privilege to act as *blader !*

Before we proceed to other considerations, let me quote
a few more instances concerning famous bags of red-deer, as
well as some details, illustrating the exceeding estimation in
which the chase of this the first favourite of venery was held.

Deer-shooting was in those days as much the principal
topic of conversation among the ruling classes, as it was one
of the chief subjects of the limited correspondence that
passed between crowned heads. Of this ample proof is to
be found in the letters of the period preserved in the
principal Continental archives. But not only this, the
antlers of stags that were in any way remarkable for size,
number of points, or on account of abnormal formation, were
the most valued presents exchanged by potentates, who, we
may take it, understood a good deal more about deer and
antlers than most men do to-day. These trophies were conveyed by ambassadors very much in the same way as
monarchs now send their portraits or the highest order of
their dynastic family, by special envoys of high rank with
all the pomp and dignity of a state ceremony. There are
extant several interesting accounts of how these ambassa-
dorial bearers of antlers were received at the recipient's
court, and as most of these august old hunters were collectors
of antlers, we can well believe that these offerings of friend-
ship were a good deal more appreciated than are now the
portraits or diamond-set orders which are the modern
tokens of esteem. One of the most interesting series of letters
concerning the chase of the deer, was written by our royal
sportsman John George I. to the Emperor Ferdinand. They
are preserved in the private archives of the Imperial family
at Vienna. Thousands of stags are enumerated therein; the
exact date and place where the heaviest were shot, what

they weighed, and in the case of many of the larger ones the Elector even gives, by a line drawn on the margin of the paper, the so-called " line of pride," representing the actual thickness of the layer of fat on the stag's haunches, and, now and again, also a second line indicating the thickness of the fat on the beast's brisket. Some of the former obtained from stags killed in the " pride of grease," *i.e.* in the month preceding the rut, when the animals are in the best condition, measure over 4 inches.[1]

I know of nothing that so convincingly carries one back to those heydays of the chase, as the perusal of these characteristic folio epistles, penned in the cramped hand of the time, on paper that has grown brown during the centuries

[1] If the royal sportsmen had not the heart to part with the antlers themselves, they sent each other pictures of these trophies, to paint which the most skilled artists of the day were called into requisition. In the preceding centuries we know that the presents royalties were in the habit of exchanging consisted usually of falcons and hounds. The latter never lost their popularity, but wild beasts of a larger sort took the place of the former when falconry went out of fashion. Thus we read of John George I. receiving from the Duke of Holstein and from Prince Radziwill a number of bears, from the Elector of Prussia some Arctic bears, from Maurice of Orange a lion, lioness, and a tiger, while Prince Christian of Denmark, a suitor to the hand of the Elector's daughter, opened his correspondence by a similar gift. White roes, black foxes, specimens of the rare sheep of Barbary, reindeer from Norway, camels and monkeys from Africa, chamois from the Alps, aurochs from Russia, and other rare beasts, were either solicited by the sporting Elector from foreign potentates and made the object of special envoys' missions, or were spontaneously offered gifts from friendly courts. Not a few of the animals, we are told, were conveyed from the most distant corners of Europe in sedan chair-like litters on men's backs ! The final destination of most of these beasts was the baiting arena, where, according to the fashion of the day, they were baited—lions pitted against bears, wild boars against wolves, aurochs against wild bulls, stags against vicious horses, and tigers against panthers. The greater the royal personage in whose honour these fights were held, the more varied was the selection and the greater the number of baited beasts. Less unnatural and more amusing must have been the ordinary bear-baiting. Huge tubs, open at the top and filled with water, were placed in the arena, and, when hard pressed by the hounds, Bruin had succeeded in scrambling into one of these receptacles, he was a formidable foe for any number of hounds. Striking out right merrily, his fore-paws, of long reach, distributed blows that bowled the hounds over in grand style, amid the laughter and cheers of the crowd.

it has lain undisturbed on the shelves of gloomy vaulted
archives. In many cases, I daresay, my hand was the first
that turned them over since the lifetime of the recipient,
in days when in an another country Queen Bess or James I.
evinced a similar attachment to the noble craft of venery,
though, perhaps, not to the same exaggerated pitch. Placing
the neat modern ivory measuring ruler along those carefully
drawn "lines of pride," penned by an old-fashioned goose-
quill, in many cases more than 300 years ago, is indeed
applying a modern scale to ancient institutions. That the
result should prove such an appalling deterioration just in
that species of *ferae naturae*, most prized by the sportsmen
of all ages, does not redound to the praise of the new age!

The communications bear the Elector's signature, "Johann
Georg, Churfurst," and the sand, which the old sportsman
strewed on the ink to prevent blotting, still sticks to the
quaintly-formed letters of the great hunter's sign-manual.

The custom of ascertaining the "line of pride" seems to
have prevailed, until recent times, also in the Scotch Highlands, as well as that of quoting the weight of antlers, for
even such a modern author as Scrope gives both, when
extolling the great size of a certain famous stag killed about
a century ago by the Duke of Atholl in the woods of Dunkeld.[1]

Considering the clumsiness of firearms in the sixteenth
century, the performance of another great sportsman, of a
generation preceding that of the last-named hunter, viz. the
Landgrave John George of Brandenburg, merits mention in
this place. When writing to the Landgrave of Hesse, a
scion of a dynasty also famous for its sportsmen, he gives

---

[1] This stag weighed 36 stone 6 lbs. as he stood. His horns weighed
13 lbs. 2 oz., and the fat on his haunches was 4½ inches thick. Scrope
accounts for the extraordinary size of this Highland stag by his having
abandoned the mountains, and had been feeding for four seasons in the woods
of Dunkeld, when the superior shelter and better food caused this striking
improvement.

him the details of his bag for the past year (1581) as consisting of 677 stags, 968 hinds, and 501 wild boar. According to
the game book of Duke William IV. of Bavaria, 817 stags was
the bag for 1545. That the passion for the chase remained
the ruling one under circumstances which one would have
thought would extinguish it, is shown by the fact that
when Landgrave Philip of Hesse lay imprisoned in the
dungeon of his enemy (1565), all his letters home breathe
his extreme solicitude for his beloved game. " Take thought
for the forest and the deer; see that the hounds are kept
in constant exercise; feed the game in winter, hunt out the
poachers," etc., recur constantly throughout that correspondence.

The Dukes of Würtemberg were also great deer-hunters;
thus Eberhard III. of that ilk stalked during the rut of
1655 in eight days in a single forest, that of Urach, one stag
of twenty points, one of eighteen points, seven of sixteen and
fourteen points, and six of twelve and ten points; while his
successor, Duke Eberhard Louis, in the same period bagged
one stag of twenty-two points, one of eighteen points, eight
of sixteen points, and sixteen of fourteen points, not to
mention the stags of lesser heads, of which in both instances
a number were killed.

A predecessor of the former, Duke John Frederick, in
the nine years of his reign, killed 4885 stags, although, as
he plaintively recites in his diary, " illness and wars often
unkindly prevented " his well-beloved chase. The largest
head was, however, only a twenty-point stag, the forests of
Würtemberg not being so famous for producing large heads
as those of Saxony. It was nothing rare to kill at a single
court *battue* 500 stags, and on one such occasion, in 1613,
672 stags were shot.

Empresses and duchesses were often as keen in the
pursuit of the hart as their husbands and fathers. The wife

of the Emperor Ferdinand II. was noted for her marksmanship, while Princess Sophia of Hesse-Darmstadt, Duchess Magdalen of Saxony, and Princess Frederica of Eisenach were all noted for their skill in deer-stalking during the "mault" or rutting season. The last-named shot on 21st August 1693, in the Pillnitz Forest, a stag of twenty-six points, which scaled what even then was a remarkable weight, *i.e.* 60 stone 10 lbs. The famous sixty-six point stag, killed 18th September 1696, near Biegen, the head of which is preserved in Moritzburg by the Elector Frederick III. of Brandenburg, scaled 15 lbs. less.

Maria, Governess of the Netherlands, was another royal lady who not only could track her stag and bring him down with her cross-bow, but in the end could also gralloch the hart her arrow had felled; for fair and royal hands a somewhat butcher - like performance. Princess Eleonore of Schwarzenberg, another famous huntress, but of a later century, shot on one day (27th September 1732) twelve warrantable stags, one of them being an eighteen pointer. These deer she stalked during the rut.

Great heads were still obtained in the last century. Duke Casimir of Saxe-Coburg shot in 1746 a forty-six point hart, and the skin of this animal is still preserved at the "Festung" in Coburg. I measured it lately and found it within a few inches of the size of a good wapiti's skin of my own, the animal, when I shot it, scaling, I am very sure, between 650 and 700 lbs. Another formidable stag of 670 lbs. avoirdupois was hunted in the then fashionable "French" manner, *i.e.* on horseback with hounds, by King Frederick August II. of Saxony on 19th August 1737, at Stauchitz, in Saxony.

An examination of the records and diaries in which these indefatigable sportsmen chronicled most minutely, generally in their own handwriting, their doings in the forest, shows plainly that matters of the chase took precedence of affairs of

State. Ministers and councillors had to wait upon their royal masters in the depth of the forest, or in some remote shooting-lodge, to transact the most important business. Thus we read that, when the crown of the kingdom of Bohemia was offered to the Elector John George, the deputation of nobles had to repair to a remote "forst," where the Elector was stalking, and that the real reason of his refusal to accept the proffered honour was not one of State or policy, but (as a contemporary states) the inferiority in number, as well as size, of the Bohemian stags.[1]

While the nobles attending the Court of their sovereign lord participated to a certain, though limited, extent in the pleasures of the chase, none but personages of princely rank could aspire to slay what might be termed record stags. Even the highest nobles of the land, on becoming aware of the presence of an unusually large stag in their forests, hastened to give their sovereign an opportunity to hunt and kill it. This would be contrived by dint of the most extraordinary exertions and elaborate arrangements. Miles of stout palisades of poles and canvas, or "stake and binder" fences 8 feet high,[2] upon which hundreds of peasants laboured for weeks, would be erected so as to enclose that part of the forest to which the great hart had been tracked, and on the day of the royal *chasse* he would be forced to pass the sovereign's *stand*. The death of such a notable hart was followed by State carousals and festivities that lasted often

---

[1] The Electors of Saxony, owing to their ancient hereditary dignity of "Lord High Masters of the Chase" to the Holy Roman Empire, enjoyed since 1350 exceptional opportunities to hunt, for this dignity gave them the right to exercise the rights of the chase in districts outside the confines of Saxony, which were *Reichsunmittelbar*, viz. which owed allegiance directly and only to the Emperor of Germany. In 1665 John George II. rebuilt at vast cost a high palisade fence along the whole boundary between Saxony and Bohemia, so that his stags could not stray. The Elector Augustus had in the preceding century erected this immense fence, but it had fallen into disrepair.

[2] For boar hunts these fences were only half that height.

for a week, and very often seriously impaired the fortune of the host. Marble monuments, some of which are still extant, were erected to mark the spot where the cumbersome firelock or the air-gun, which was then a favourite weapon, particularly for stalking, had brought down the great hart. Many a cloister or monastery, as well as church, owed its origin to the death of a great hart having made the spot famous. Gold and silver medals were struck in commemoration; and foresters were rewarded for tracking a stag, and enabling their master to kill it, with the gift of ducats, bearing on one side the imprint of a hart, on the other the words, " By this golden ducat I was betrayed."

In the eighteenth century, the same violation of art and taste which led to the monstrous productions of the rococo period, made itself apparent in venery. The chase became a mere pageant of stage effect and ludicrous mummery. Princes tried to outrival each other in the invention of the most bizarre *coup de théâtre*, as well as the most extravagant pageantry, which made it a travesty of sport. On such occasions, to give a few instances, huge temples, with great flights of steps, in one instance 240 feet high, leading up to galleries, were erected, and the driven stags and wild boars, by means of hundreds of hounds, would be forced to ascend these flights of stairs, to be shot from the galleries by the invited royal guests and their lords and ladies, amid the blast of trumpets and fanfares of hunting-horns. The preparations for such a *chasse* would literally occupy thousands of men and horses for months; and, notwithstanding the unfortunate peasants were compelled to give their services gratuitously, and that often just at harvest time, the cost of such an entertainment was enormous. In the Munich Museum there is an interesting picture of such a great Court *chasse*, held 170 years ago, on the Starnberg lake in Bavaria, by the Elector Charles Albert of Bavaria.

Covering the surface of the lake, one sees a great number of beflagged galleys and boats, decked out in the most brilliant colours. By far the most prominent is the Elector's *Bucentaur*, a huge galley built expressly for this occasion, and being an exact copy of the Doge's State vessel. Upon it one sees grouped a great assemblage of persons in the fantastic costume of that period, while personages of lesser importance occupy the other galleys. Swimming towards this great triumphal ark, one perceives the great twenty-point hart which had been specially selected for this important occasion. Followed by a great number of swimming hounds, the wide semicircle of galleys of course made escape quite impossible to the hart, which, as one reads in a grandiloquent description penned by a contemporary, had finally to succumb to the hounds, amid the great rejoicings of the august company, the firing of cannon, and the blasts of the hunting-horns. His body being dragged on board the *Bucentaur*, the right fore-leg was cut off at the knee-joint, and the master of the chase (one of the highest Court dignitaries) presented it kneeling to his mistress the Duchess. Other potentates, again, caused the driven stags to pass through great tunnels and grotto-like caves, where more than life-size statues of Diana in the fantastic costume of the day—perukes and Watteau gowns—held garlands of roses, over which the deer had to leap. While other royal Nimrods, equally bedizened in the fashion of the period, forced all harts carrying great heads to pass through triumphal arches, where rosaries were thrown over their antlers, and, thus "adorned," they were shot down.

In the seventeenth and eighteenth centuries Saxony, Bavaria, Würtemberg, and many of the smaller Duchies were practically one vast preserve wholly given up to game —principally red-deer and wild boars—which preyed upon the crops of the unfortunate peasants to an extent that can with difficulty be realised in these days when the rights of the subject are so carefully protected. Almost more dreaded than the often wholesale destruction of their crops by game was the oppressive " service of the chase," to which allusion has already been made. Poaching was in those days very literally a deadly crime; branding on the face, cutting off the right hand, plucking out the right eye, or getting flogged out of the country, being the usual punishment for a first offence, while hanging or decapitation for a repetition, and other even more inhuman punishments, were occasionally resorted to. Thus, in 1537, one Archbishop of Salzburg, a great Nimrod, as these church dignitaries almost invariably were, caused a wretched peasant, who had killed a stag that was nightly ravaging his crops, to be sewn up in the fresh skin of the stag, and be torn to pieces in the market square of the town by the archiepiscopal hounds.[1]

Enough has now been said concerning the chase of the stag in the old days, and we can pass to the subject of antlers, past and present. Close examination of a mass of statistical matter shows that in the 250 years following the general introduction of gunpowder for purposes of the chase, a very marked decrease in the weight of the stags and of their heads, as well as in the frequency of great heads, took place throughout Germany. After what has been said respecting the remarkable extremes to which the pursuit of hunting was carried, it cannot surprise one that the consequences of inbreeding, overstocking, and of other unnatural means employed to keep up the needed supply of deer, were more to be blamed than gunpowder for this rapid falling off in weight and number. In the middle of the sixteenth century the proportion of adult stags to hinds appears to

---

[1] Boner in his *Forest Creatures* states that the peasant only " took possession of a stag which he found dead in his own cornfield," but the authority from which I quote is probably nearer the truth.

have been still a perfectly natural one. Thus, to give the instance of a famous Würtemberg forest, the proportion in 1558 was one stag to three hinds; in 1578 it had reached the ratio of one to four; and in 1618 we hear that the proportion was one to nine hinds!

Let us take a glance at the most noteworthy collections of old antlers that have survived war, conflagration, and pillage during the last two or three hundred years. For antler lore was for centuries a favourite hobby, and history busied itself with the fame of exceptionally fine heads as with something of great moment.

The following four collections are the principal ones:— (1) the King of Saxony's, in the castle of Moritzburg, near Dresden; (2) the late Duke of Saxe-Coburg's, in the castle of Reinhardsbrunn, near Gotha, and in the Fortress near Coburg, both of which have now passed into the possession of the Duke of Edinburgh; (3) the collection in the castle Erbach, belonging to the ancient reigning dynasty of the same name; and (4) Count Arco-Zinneberg's collection, in his palace in Munich, containing approximately 4000 heads;[1] the majority in the latter, however, are of modern origin. Besides these there are a great number of smaller collections throughout Germany — those in the Imperial palaces at Vienna and of the Kings of Würtemberg and Saxony being perhaps the most noteworthy. For old heads, the Moritzburg collection is the most important, and is without a rival, though it now contains only a small portion of those which

---

[1] The attendants showing strangers this collection know very little concerning the origin of even the most important heads. The only MS. catalogue that exists is unfortunately very inadequate. Count Max Arco-Zinneberg, son of the deceased collector, and uncle of the heir to the collection, has given me much valuable information concerning the heads in this famous collection, particularly with respect to the remarkably fine wapiti heads, which are those of stags imported by his father, who was the first sportsman on the Continent to experiment with that species. It is said that the sum spent upon this collection exceeded £60,000.

were once in Augustusburg—the famous hunting-seat of the
great Elector Maurice of Saxony—where, in the year 1576,
there were 640 heads of great record, probably forming the
most remarkable collection in the world. What are now,
with few exceptions, the chief heads in the Moritzburg collection, were weeded out from the former in 1725, shortly before
Augustusburg, with its contents, was destroyed by fire.

Moritzburg, as seen to-day, is a rambling old Schloss, with
about 200 rooms, and a moat; and, being within a short
drive from Dresden, it will, no doubt, be known to many
readers. The following great heads hang on the walls of
the dining-hall, a chamber 66 feet long, 34 feet wide, and 38
feet high :—Two heads of fifty points, three heads of thirty-
six points, two heads of thirty-four points, ten heads of
thirty-two points, five heads of thirty points, thirteen heads
of twenty-eight points, eighteen heads of twenty-six points,
and eighteen heads of twenty-four points.

In the adjoining audience hall there are forty-two abnormal heads, which many of the old collectors greatly
prized. Amongst them is the famous sixty-six point head.
It does not, however, show sixty-six well-defined tines. By
the old laws of venery any protuberance or, as it is techni-
cally termed, " offer," upon which the leathern thong of the
hunting-horn could be hung, might be counted as a tine,
and in Germany or Austria one never speaks of a head having
an uneven number of tines ; thus, one having eight on one
antler, and, say, only five on the other, would be called a
sixteen pointer, *i.e.* double the number on the side having
most tines. The sixty-six pointer (Fig. 10) has thirty-three
on the right, but only twenty-nine points (they can hardly
be called tines) on the left antler.

The stag that carried this historical pair of antlers was
shot in 1696 by the Elector Frederick III. of Brandenburg,
who subsequently became the first King of Prussia. His

successor, Frederick William, whose hobby for tall grenadiers is well known, found in the person of the Elector Frederick Augustus of Saxony such a keen collector of antlers, that in exchange for this head the King of Prussia obtained, so the story goes, a company of the tallest grenadiers to be found in Saxony.

Modern critics have attempted to cast doubt upon the truth of this tale, but considering that a contemporary

FIG. 10.—The celebrated sixty-six pointer in the King of Saxony's collection in Moritzburg (shot 1696), for which a company of tall Grenadiers was given.

Master of the Hunt (Vice - Jägermeister von Meyrink) certified over his signature to the correctness of above detail, one must regard modern scruples, raised after the lapse of nearly two centuries, with some suspicion.

The Moritzburg collection contains a pair of antlers which is of far greater interest than the last-named ones, for it enjoys the distinction of being without question the largest pair of red-deer antlers in the world. Though it has only

twenty-four points, it is of the enormous spread of 6 feet
$3\frac{6}{10}$ inches, and weighs with a very small fragment of the
skull-bone no less than 41½ lbs. avoirdupois (Fig. 11).
Unfortunately nothing is known concerning the origin of
these astonishingly large antlers.   In spite of many weeks'
researches in the King of Saxony's private library, to which
I obtained access some years ago, it was impossible to trace
its history farther back than others have done, *i.e.* to
1586, in which year this head is enumerated in an inventory

FIG. 11.—The largest Red-deer Antlers in existence.   Spread, 6 feet
$3\frac{6}{10}$ inches ; weight, 41½ lbs. avoirdupois.
(Preserved in the King of Saxony's collection at Moritzburg.)

of the Elector Augustus's heirlooms, without mentioning
whence it came.

Two celebrated fifty-point heads that adorn this collection
also deserve mentioning.   The finer of the two (Fig. 12) has
the twenty-five points only on the left antler, while the right
one has but twelve tines.   The cup-shaped formation of the
royals on this right antler (which in the eyes of Continental
sportsmen marks the perfection of the red-deer's trophy) forms
the main difference, as most readers will know, between the
antlers of the wapiti (which never have it) and those of the

red-deer of Europe. Among many thousands of wapiti heads which I have examined, in the course of fifteen visits to Western hunting-grounds, I have never discovered one showing this peculiarity of the red-deer; and those who have read Caton's interesting work upon the deer and antelope of America will no doubt remember that he quotes but a single instance of his having met with this cup formation, *i.e.* on the right antler of a wapiti head, of which his work contains an illustration. In the case of very large red-deer antlers

FIG. 12.—Red-deer Antlers with fifty points in Moritzburg.

this cup is often so perfectly formed as to hold a considerable amount of liquid. This fact is illustrated by the famous "loving cup antler" in the Moritzburg collection. It is a single antler with thirteen tines, and has been used as a "loving cup" since the year 1689, every guest partaking for the first time of the royal hospitality having to "drink the welcome" by draining the contents of the antler cup. A carefully kept register enumerates all the names of the drinkers, mostly of princely rank; and amusing tales are told of the difficulty that beset the princesses in the days when the hair was worn built up in high masses on their heads, which made the draining a matter of some difficulty.

The Reinhardsbrunn collection contains some old heads, notably a twenty-eight pointer killed in 1735, which in weight come close to those of the previous century, referred to in the preceding pages, though 'there is nothing in this collection to approach the famous twenty-four pointer in Moritzburg. To those interested in the acclimatisation of the wapiti in Europe, some splendid antlers of that species grown by animals bred by the late duke in his extensive game park of Mönchröden, will prove an attraction.

The Erbach collection, mainly the work of a famous sportsman of the beginning of the present century, Count Francis Erbach-Erbach (died 1823), contains some very fine ancient red-deer heads, one coming close in weight to the monster at Moritzburg, for it scales nearly (within a few ounces of) 35 lbs. avoirdupois. It contains three highly interesting historical antlers of Alpine stags, to which some nearer reference has to be made. The first is a twenty-two pointer, the length of the main beam being 46½ inches, measured in a straight line from the burr to the extreme end. This, measured along the curve in the usual way, would exceed 4 feet by several inches. The spread of this head is also extraordinary, being 5 ft. 2¼ inches in a straight line from tip to tip. The circumference round the thinnest part of the beam above the tray tine is 8⅜ inches. The second head is a twenty-eight pointer, slightly less in length and spread, but an inch more in circumference. These two heads once formed part of what, in the sixteenth century, was one of the most famous Natural History collections in all Europe, that of Castle Ambras in Tyrol, the creation of Archduke Ferdinand of Austria. After the partial conquest of Tyrol by the Bavarian and French troops in the first

decade of the present century, the two heads were looted
by the then King of Bavaria, and were presented to the
Count Erbach, whom we have already mentioned as the
founder of the collection.   Though it is not positively
known that these two heads were of Tyrolese or even Alpine
origin, the whole type, particularly of the first, is that of an
Alpine stag.   Chevalier Dombrowski, a well-known authority
in antler lore, declares that there can be no doubt at all
that the former once graced a mountain stag.   The third
pair is one of the very few existing relics proving that
Switzerland once harboured red-deer.   The head in question
is a twenty-two pointer of very fine proportions, and the
animal that carried it was found, in 1687, in the Lake of
Lucerne, killed by four lynxes, who had evidently attacked it
simultaneously.   The antlers were acquired soon afterwards
by John Elias Ridinger, the famous delineator of the big
game frequenting Continental woods, whose copperplates and
woodcuts, upwards of 1000 in number, forms such an interesting subject for study, and are much prized by all collectors.
They are far too little known in British sporting circles, one
of the few collectors who possess a considerable number of
early impressions being Lord Powerscourt.

Castle Ambras, once a very treasure-house, though still
worth a visit, has not only been looted by the enemies of the
country, but the main part of the great art collection, which
during the Napoleonic wars was removed to Vienna for
safety's sake, unfortunately never found its way back to the
country of its birth, but is yet in Vienna forming part of the
Imperial collections.   One interesting piece Ambras still
contains.   It is a magnificent pair of stag's antlers of
twenty-two points, round the skull-bone of which a large
oak tree has grown.   A section of the tree, bearing in its
centre this singular relic, has been carefully preserved, and
as it has formed part of the old Ambras collection since the

time of Emperor Ferdinand I., it has puzzled generations
upon generations to account for this play of Nature. Though
it is not the single instance of its kind known, it is certainly
the most curious, by reason of the great size of the antlers.
The build of the latter indicates an Alpine origin, but the
fact that it is an oak tree with which it has formed such a
singular union of substances, would point to sub-Alpine

Fig. 13.—Ancient pair of Stag's Antlers round which an oak tree has grown.
(Preserved in Castle Ambras, Tyrol.)

origin. Possibly it came from Hungary, in the days when
the great Ambras collection was the receptacle of so much
that was interesting (Fig. 13).

Of one old Tyrolese castle it is still necessary to speak as
containing some interesting relics of the Alpine red-deer.
It is Castle Tratzberg, near Jenbach, the family seat of the
writer's neighbours, the brothers Counts Enzenberg, scions

ANCIENT STAG'S ANTLERS IN CASTLE TRATZBERG IN TYROL.

(They are fastened on the wall, the stag's body is painted, and acts as "supporter" to the Hapsburgh family pedigree in fresco above. *Temp.* 1500.)

of an old Austrian family. This castle was a favourite resort of Emperor Maximilian I., of whose prowess as a hunter I have so repeatedly spoken. During the latter's lifetime the walls of one of the large halls in Castle Tratzberg—a chamber 52 feet long by 26 feet broad—were adorned with an interesting tempora painting. It represents the genealogical pedigree of the Hapsburgh dynasty, and consists of 147 semi-life size figures of the various members of the family since the time of Rudolf, the founder of the dynasty. This strip of fresco work, in all some 153 feet long, begins some 5 feet from the floor and reaches up to the ceiling. At various parts of the room stags of a gigantic size, either standing or couchant, are painted as if supporting on their antlers the band of fresco work above them. Real antlers, fastened by strong iron stays into the wall, in a natural position over the animals' heads, give them a life-like appearance. These antlers are remarkably fine old sets, some of twenty and twenty-two points ; of their age there cannot be the slightest doubt, nor is there any reason to question the correctness of the general belief that the animals that once carried these noble trophies were killed four centuries ago by the great sportsman in the neighbourhood.

Before quitting the subject of old antlers I would like to revert briefly to engraved antlers, for they afford us another proof of the great esteem in which the stag's trophy was held. Perfect specimens of engraved antlers are very rare, only three sets are known to me. The one for which probably the highest price of modern days was paid, is in the possession of Baron Nathaniel Rothschild of Vienna, the well-known collector of medieval antiquities, and owner of what is undoubtedly one of the finest private collections of the kind in the world.

The antlers are of very regular growth and fair size, bearing fourteen points ; they are attached to a piece of the skull-bone. With the exception of about 4 or 5 inches at the extreme tips of the tines, the designs, which are engraved in black lines, cover every inch of the antlers. From the burrs, which the artist left in their natural state of pearly roughness, upwards the antlers have been smoothed and polished to look like white bone, so that at a distance they look more like antlers made of ivory than the genuine article. Upon this white background, slightly tinged yellow with age, the designs of various armorial bearings, surrounded by fantastic arabesques and masks such as distinguish the Renaissance art period, stand forth with great clearness, and form a whole the artistic elegance of which it is hard to describe. Unfortunately the large size (15 inches by 12 inches) of the photograph of this jewel of Renaissance workmanship, which the owner gave me and which is now before me, does not lend itself for reproduction in reduced size. On the right antler, occupying, as it were, the place of honour close above the brow tine, are the arms of Count Oswald Trab (the name is now written Trap), a Tyrolese family of great antiquity, for a member of which this rare and curious work of art was probably executed. Above it, and also on the left antler, are the arms and national emblems of Italy, Spain, Portugal, etc. The artist's initials, " G. H.," are to be seen close to the Trab crest, and next to it is the date 1563. I am informed on good authority that Baron Rothschild paid 6000 florins, or nearly £600, for these antlers.

The second specimen is in the possession of Lord Tweedmouth at Guisachan, near Beauly, in Scotland. It is a fine wide pair of antlers of over 40 inches, with thirteen points. The date upon this specimen, curiously enough, is the same as the one on Baron Rothschild's set. Lord Tweedmouth informs me that it is said to have been engraved by a pupil of Albrecht Dürer, the style of engraving being quite in character with that of that well-known master. The principal subjects engraved, the owner tells me, are figures representing the different countries of Europe, together with some grotesque and sporting subjects.

The third pair of engraved antlers has, by a piece of great good luck, lately come into my possession, and, being almost half a century older than either of the other specimens, it is not the least interesting of the three sets, the more so as the subjects of the pictorial representations are of greater interest to the sportsman than those that adorn the specimens already described. In my specimen the antlers are not on the skull, but are separate, so that they are either shed ones or some vandal hand has in past ages cut them from the skull. Their length (39 inches) is nothing out of the way, but their shape is more remarkable, for the beam between second and third tine is unusually flat, thus offering large comparatively level spaces for the designs. The treatment of the exterior surface of the antlers has been the same as already noticed in the case of the Rothschild head. They are white and smooth like old ivory, and show up the designs, which are jet black, remarkably well. The burrs are in their natural state. Unlike the Rothschild specimen, the tips of the tines are not left bare, the entire surface, from the burrs to the extreme ends of the points, being covered with the skilful handiwork of some master of the early part of the sixteenth century. The date, which is on the left antler, is 1520—a period when the Gothic element was still to the fore, and the engraver had not yet surrendered his art to the teachings of the Italian school of the Renaissance, with its architectural designs overladen with grotesque masks and wreaths of fruit and flowers, such as are on the Rothschild antlers.

These designs are either of a sporting character or relate to the history of that adventurous traveller of olden times, St. Korbinian, whose picture—not from life, of course, for he lived in the eighth century—adorns the right antler. He is

represented wearing the usual attribute of saintliness, *i.e.*
a halo of superior magnitude. By a cord held in his right
hand he leads his famous bear, of whom a legend tells us the
following gratifying story of a bear's susceptibility to the
influences of religion. Korbinian, then an unknown young
monk of the ancient monastery of Freising, in Bavaria, was
travelling one winter's day towards Rome. While crossing
the dreary solitudes of the Brenner Pass, which leads from
North Tyrol to the sunny plains of Italy, a huge bear
suddenly swept down upon him from its cave and killed,
before Korbinian's eyes, his faithful old donkey, on the back
of which were packed some choice offerings which the young
monk was conveying from his monastery to the Holy Father
at Rome. Irate at this sacrilegious conduct of the bear, the
monk directed such useful invectives at Bruin's head that
the latter forthwith offered his own broad back as a means
of transporting the sacred gifts to their destination. Thus
it came to pass that Korbinian, entered Rome driving his
sumpter bear in front of him—a feat which, we are told, was
the first step towards saintly rank.

The sporting scenes are full of life, and comprise 'representations of the chase of the aurochs, the stag, the bear, the
boar, the wolf, and the ibex, while numerous animals of every
imaginable real and allegorical kind, from sea serpents to
gigantic butterflies, from badgers and tortoises to spiders at
home in the centre of most artistically constructed webs,
lend animation to the details of the Gothic scroll-work. The
latter covers the antlers, where not occupied with pictorial
designs, from top to bottom in endless variety without a
single repetition of subject or of pattern. Several camp
scenes represent the happenings of a hunter's life in the
woods. Thus we see a fox stealing a big trout from a heap
of fish behind the back of the owner, who is stretched out on
the grass staring into the flames of the camp fire, over which

hangs a big kettle, which is in the act of being stirred by a burly underling, while a dog of some long-forgotten Gothic breed follows his master's example, and while gazing into the blaze also fails to notice the capture of the trout by Master Reynard. The figures and animals are, without exception, capitally drawn, the costumes of the former being quite a study in itself, so correct is every detail, so realistic are the scenes depicted by the master's tool. On the left antler occupying the same position that St. Korbinian does on the other horn, is depicted St. Hubert, with his inevitable stag crouching familiarly at his feet. Underneath this picture are the bust portraits of a man and woman in the quaint head-dress of the period, and near them, occupying the broad part of the antler, where the tray-tine branches off, is a shield with a coat-of-arms, presumably that of the couple for whom the curious relic was executed.

The style of the whole workmanship is that of the Augsburg or Nuremberg school in Dürer's time, when one of his most famous pupils, Burgkmair, was a leading exponent of his master's art as applied by the engraver.

CHAPTER X

MUCH that has been said in the previous chapter related to
the red-deer of Germany. In now turning to the stag of the
Alps of our own day, a distinction has to be made between
the stag of the Alps proper and the Carpathian stag. Taking
the latter first, it appears that too little is known of its past
history to enable one to compare the Carpathian red-deer of
to-day with its progenitors of the sixteenth and seventeenth
centuries. This field for research is lamentably barren. No
great historical collections, no carefully kept sportsmen's
diaries, such as are to be found in the archives of German
dukes, no State chronicles narrating with punctilious care
all the details of the *chasse*, with a minuteness that even
noted the slightest malformation of a stag's antlers, or a
peculiarity of colour of a deer's coat, reward the sportsman's
researches in Hungary. That country, with its dependencies,
was, in past ages, an exceedingly wild region, periodically
invaded by barbaric hosts of Mahomedan savages. At the
present day the Carpathian red-deer are by far the heaviest
and finest in the whole of Europe. Stags have been shot
there in the present generation with a clean weight that
equals all but the largest beasts the lucky old Saxon Electors
used to slay.

A few details concerning some record mountain stags of Hungary will not be out of place. The heaviest of which I have authoritative knowledge, was a stag scaling clean 44 stone 4 lbs. avoirdupois.[1] The longest antlers I know of were of a stag killed in 1894 in Zemplen by Count G. Andrassy; along the curve this truly magnificent trophy taped a trifle over 53½ inches! The heaviest pair of antlers of the present generation was, I believe, shot by Prince Rohan in Radauc; it weighs an ounce or two over 31 lbs.! This is a tremendous weight, beaten nowadays only by good wapiti. One of the widest heads was obtained by the present Duke of Ratibor in the Pillis Mountains, measuring from tip to tip no less than $55\frac{9}{10}$ inches! These may be considered the records of the last decade or two, and as such will suffice most sportsmen. For those who take a scientific interest in the weights and dimensions of modern antlers, I add in the Appendix[2] a table with some further instructive details. Concerning the origin of this table the following may be mentioned here. Nine years ago the representative sportsmen of Hungary, who, as every one knows, are among the very keenest in Europe, formed an association among themselves with the object of annually exhibiting in the capital of Hungary all the good heads obtained by them that season. Three of the members are elected to act as judges, and these pick, out of the sixty or seventy choice heads sent in, the best ten. These are carefully measured, weighed, etc., and from the ten the best three are then selected, their owners being rewarded with sporting prizes. The dimensions of the ten are then published. With the whole series of these tables before me, I took the three prize-winners of each year, and after changing the metrical weights and measures into

---

[1] Mentioned by E. von Dombrowski as being that of the heaviest stag shot at Munkacs.

[2] See Appendix, Note 2.

their English equivalents, constructed the table, a glance at which will demonstrate the great size of the Hungarian stags. Most of those enumerated came from the Carpathians, but in justice to the *Tiefland*, or Lowland of Hungary, along the banks of the Danube, it must be mentioned that there, too, great stags are to be found.

The Emperor of Austria's favourite forests at Gödöllo, not very far from the capital of Hungary, is famous for its heavy red-deer, animals of 36 stone being shot there every year. In one season there were killed four stags of eighteen points, five stags of sixteen points, fifteen stags of fourteen points, and forty-three stags of twelve points. The nine stags of sixteen and eighteen points averaged over 33 stone, the others 27 stone less 3 lbs. clean.

Very heavy stags are also killed at Bellye, the magnificent preserves of the late Archduke Albrecht of Austria, a renowned sportsman.

The Hungarian sporting estates are often of great size ; of *Herrschaften*, covering 500 square miles, there are quite a number along the slopes of the Carpathians, and several of the men whose names figure among the prize-takers are lords of even larger territories. As a rule, they are remote from railways, for those whose natural resources—timber, minerals, etc.—have been opened up by better means of communications than is the average Hungarian country road, have also lost their pre-eminence for sport of the kind I am alluding to. The great stags to which reference has been made, are not the denizens of semi-civilised woods, touched by the axe or traversed by roads. The first inroad of man sends them to forests where they can continue the perfectly wild existence to which they have been accustomed, and where the sight of a human being is as unusual an event as were they wapiti roaming some Wyoming or Montana upland. We have to go back to the last century to find social conditions similar to those still prevailing on great Hungarian estates. The pages of Scrope, where that charming author describes the olden manner of hunting in the great Scotch forest of Atholl, remind one of conditions as they are to-day in the Carpathians, always remembering the radical contrast between the two countries consequent upon the absence of those great woods which are such a prominent feature in the latter country.

In the Alps the conditions are very much less favourable to the well-being of the hart. There the winter commences earlier, which naturally has a most prejudicial effect upon animals that have not had time to recover from the exhaustion consequent upon the rut. The latter leaves them at the close mere walking skeletons, wrecks of the vigorous beasts they were a few weeks back. Shelter, too, is less abundant and effective in the spruce and pine forests of the Alps than in the dense thickets and deep gorges of the Carpathians. And, lastly, the food is vastly inferior in the Alps. No beech or oak mast underlies there the crust of snow, upon which to recuperate the wasted strength. While the lateness of spring in the Alps keeps them, for several weeks longer, on shorter commons than their Hungarian kinsmen. In most Alpine deer forests the owners resort to artificial feeding. About the lasting benefit of this measure in districts subject to severe winters, there can be but one opinion. It must be remarked, however, that artificial feeding, when once commenced, must be carried through to the very end of winter, and continue year after year, or the losses will be very much greater than if no feeding had occurred, for it has been shown over and over again that the animals get so accustomed to the comforting presence of the hay-rack, that if the supply from one cause or another comes suddenly to an end, they still hang round the spot for days upon days till from utter weakness they are unable in the deep snow to appease the craving for food in the manner natural to their kind.

Some suggestive facts are learnt by comparing the weight of antlers with the weight of the whole deer, and extending this comparison to countries where the food and the shelter obtainable by the stags are acknowledged to differ to a considerable extent. A careful analysis of the table containing the two respective weights of over 700 Continental stags of ten points and upwards, proves that an exceedingly wide range exists between the extremes in these proportions. In other words, I found that in one of the two extremes (in the case of a fourteen-point stag killed in Silesia in 1879) the antlers weighed $26\frac{4}{10}$ lbs. and the stag only 277 lbs., or a proportion of 1 to $10\frac{1}{2}$; while the other extreme is represented in the case of a ten-point stag killed in the same year in the Harz Mountains, the horns being $3\frac{4}{10}$ lbs., and the whole stag 275 lbs., or only 2 lbs. lighter than the last-mentioned animal, carrying antlers eight times as heavy; the exact proportion being 1 to 83. To arrive at the general average proportion, some care has to be exercised to take an equal number of instances from each locality, for there is a wide range, though nothing like the extremes spoken of between the respective averages of each separate locality. Thus, in the Harz Mountains the average proportion is something like 1 to 45, while in Silesia the average proportion is 1 to 23. Generally speaking, without taking up further space by the intricate details which have to be considered in these calculations, the weight of antlers is about one-thirtieth of that of the entire animal in stags of ten points and upwards— the older the stag the smaller the difference. Quite a number of instances of sixteen and eighteen point stags, all over the Continent, appear in my records, where the proportion is 1 to 20.

Another important point to be considered in these calculations is the time of the year when the stag was killed; for, of course, the rut decreases the weight of a hart considerably—the loss amounting to 4 or 5 stone in the case of a master stag, while antlers increase in weight as they become solid.

In Austria great attention is paid to the management of deer forests, no expense being spared to improve the strain by infusing fresh blood from other parts of the empire, as well as experimenting with stags of foreign breed, and even of different species. Constant care is exercised during hard weather to keep ample supplies of fodder where the deer can get at it; and, where oaks do not grow, acorns or horse-chestnuts, to the extent of about 4 lbs. per head per day, are fed out, particularly to the stags, for this food contains good horn-producing properties. Till similar and continuous care is bestowed upon the deer in Scotch forests, the antlers in that country are likely to remain of the same small proportions exhibited by the deer themselves, in comparison with those of the Continent. I well remember the astonishment with which an ardent Austrian sportsman, owner of scores of square miles of superb woods, read a letter which appeared in the *Field* some years ago upon Scottish red-deer, and the good management of a certain forest in Ross-shire. The manifold improvements the owner of the forest had inaugurated, led the writer of the letter to hold up the forest as a model, and as illustrating the great benefits accruing from cross-breeding his deer with three English stags, the writer remarked that " the effect of their sojourn is visible to this day in the improved heads of the native deer." It was the reason given for killing off these valuable sires after a very limited period of usefulness, which surprised my Austrian friend. They were shot, as the writer of the letter naively admitted, " on account of the damage they caused to the woods near A—— House," the owner's country mansion, a reason wholly incomprehensible to the Austrian sportsman, in whose mind an injury to a few trees in a plantation

(presumably left quite unprotected) was of utter insignificance
in comparison with the paramount considerations of sport. ′
From his point of view, woods only existed in order to shelter
deer; and my explanation, that the so-called forests of
Scotland are usually destitute of trees, and that existing
woods are accordingly valuable possessions, did not justify
in his eyes the Scottish laird's action.

Last year there was a lengthy correspondence in the
Field concerning the influence of food, climate, and shelter
upon the growth of antlers. It showed how divergent were
the views of those capable of forming correct opinions
concerning these points. That some of these should deny
that the poor heads of modern Highland deer are not the
direct result of the changed conditions now prevailing in
Scotland, seems to me almost inexplicable. All authorities,
so far as I am aware, from the days of Twici—who, as Edward
II.'s Master of the Hunt, wrote: "The head grows according
to the pasture, good or otherwise"—to those of Scrope, have
dwelt upon the importance of these influences. It has been
suggested to me that a republication of the above correspondence would be of interest to many. This, on account
of its great length, I cannot unfortunately do, but in the
Appendix will be found two letters embodying my own views
upon the question.[1]

Let us now turn to the chase itself. From what has
been said, it is easy to infer that the surroundings of the
stalker in the Alps and Carpathians are very different from
those familiar to all who have once visited the Highlands,
or better, have trodden rifle in hand a Scotch deer forest,
misleading, as I confess, the latter term has always seemed
to me, considering the general absence of trees which in the
ordinary sense of the word forms its chief feature.

One can safely say that an Austrian stalker who has never

[1] See Appendix, Note 3.

before been out of his home surroundings, if suddenly trans-
planted to the Highlands and ordered to stalk a band of
deer lying out in the centre of an open stretch of moor, far
from what he would call covert, would be more puzzled
and be less likely to succeed, than would a good Scotch
stalker on being for the first time turned loose in a typical
Alpine forest. For I consider that a really good Highland
stalker cannot be beaten in the manœuvres of approach.
On the other hand, to be just to both countries, I believe
that there is a far larger number of fair amateur stalkers in
Austria than there are in Scotland, where the popularity of
this sport is of comparatively recent origin.

That the stalker's tactics in the Alps are very different
from those in use in the Highlands, is chiefly caused by the
physical differences in the two regions. The more or less
dense woods, which are the home of the Continental stags,
make it impossible to spy them at great distances, in fact
the glass plays a very secondary *rôle* on the Continent, and
for the same reason, it is impossible to approach the wily
beasts in the stealthy manner by which the skilled Highlander
knows so well how to outwit the muckle hart. With few
isolated exceptions, the Alpine stag is invariably shot during
the rut, when his loud roar betrays his whereabouts in the
woods, and be these of the densest. For other obvious
reasons, too, good judges maintain that the rutting time is
the proper period for deer-stalking, and it is rather singular
that this has not been earlier recognised by the owners of
Highland forests anxious to improve the quality of their
deer-heads. The Continental system, unlike the Scotch,
spares the master stags till they have had a chance to
propagate, if not to the full time-limit for which Nature
has made provision, yet to an important extent. In the
Highlands the good as well as the bad stags are shot before
the former have had a chance of mating and leaving their

impress upon the future generation. In consequence of this, propagation is left to the small or immature—a policy which reverses the doctrine of the selection of the fittest, which is so closely observed by all breeders. That it should be thus negatived in the case of the very species appealing most of all to the sportsman's proclivities, does not do honour to the Highlanders' acumen. It is true, to give both sides of the question, that venison, from the first day of the rut, deteriorates very fast, and soon becomes unfit for food, except as smoked winter provender for the natives; but this commercially utilitarian consideration should not be taken into account by those who are really anxious to stock their forests with deer carrying the best possible antlers. The game dealer may perhaps be indirectly a sufferer, but that person is about the last who needs consideration by sportsmen. On the Continent everything is sacrificed to the one end: what will produce the finest heads? In past centuries, even up to the year 1848, the welfare of hundreds of human beings was as nothing in comparison to the welfare of a lesser number of antlered beasts. The former have now learnt to take care of themselves, and they are reversing the old order of things, and it is the turn of the deer to claim the protection of man.

Thinking it best to leave untrammelled the matter of the preceding chapters, I have deferred till now the consideration of an extraneous subject, viz. a comparison between Austria and Britain regarding the spirit and the manner of conducting sport in the respective countries. A few reflections on this head may perhaps fitly be included in the present attempt to make English sportsmen acquainted with a country and a race of *Jäger* that in my humble opinion deserve nearer acquaintance. In doing so I claim the privilege of freely criticising both people. Equally at home in the two countries, I have enjoyed good sport in both; in the mountains of

Austria off and on from my early youth; in Britain, the Greater Britain I mean, in a variety of places from my schoolboy days to very recent years. The only premise I desire to make in this place is that when alluding to my German-speaking *confrères* I refer exclusively to those of Austria and Hungary, for between the English representative sportsman and the one "made in Germany" there is less kinship of spirit and sympathetic fellow-feeling, than between the former and the Austrian or Hungarian.

Taking the latter class first, it has to be remarked that, with the exception of half-a-dozen great magnates, the Austrian aristocracy, which is the class from which nine out of ten sportsmen are recruited, is not as wealthy as are most of the British sportsmen who go in for deer forests in Scotland. In Austria, fortunately for the tone of sport, the chase is still to a great extent in the hands of the old families whose ancestors for generation after generation, back for four or five hundred years, hunted their stags in the same forests in which their descendants now enjoy the sport. Still living up to the traditions of their old race, the Austrian aristocracy is to-day, as is well known, the most exclusive nobility in the world.

Brought up from early youth amid sporting surroundings, with sporting topics as the general, if not sole subject of country-side conversation, the ancestral hall, if bare of showy luxury, is adorned with the trophies of the chase brought down by the youth's great grandsires in the same woods where he has perhaps just managed to kill his first "royal." His wants are administered to by servants and keepers that have grown gray in the service of the family, as their fathers have, and who know but its interests. Is it surprising that under these patriarchal circumstances of life, the young hunter should have instilled into him a deep-seated love for the pastime proper to his class since history was written? His old-

fashioned conception—class prejudices the radical will call
it—invests sport in the country with ideal qualities long
stripped from it by our English ultra-practical turn of
mind.   Pecuniary questions are tabooed by him as much
as possible from the realm of sport.   The vulgar boast of
our own *nouveaux riches*, "My stags cost me a fifty-pound
note apiece," would be hailed with the same polite smile
of contempt that greets the Continental Mr. Moneybags
when attempting to follow the example of his socially
ambitious *confrère* of the Scotch Highlands, who, by leasing
a great sporting estate, wants to pose as a *Jäger*.   Unlike the former, he never, however, succeeds by these means
to force his way into the charmed circle.   He is left severely
alone, and men smile at the *parvenu's* failure.   For these
reasons sport is taken up by the genuine sportsman in a far
more frugal and healthy spirit, and it is not regarded as a
means of displaying the power of money, or as a stalking-
horse, by the aid of which to get into Society.

The lodges and shooting-boxes up in the recesses of the
Austrian mountains are all of the simplest description; one
sits on hard deal chairs, the walls are plainly whitewashed or
wainscoted in unvarnished pine, the floors are uncarpeted,
and the beds are of anything but eider-down.   Beer or cheap
country wine is the beverage.   Many a Scotch head-keeper's
lodge is a little palace, in the way of furnishings, in comparison
to most Austrian shooting-boxes.   To introduce into these
retired nooks and corners of the Alps, the luxuries of town-life,
is deemed in bad taste, as not in keeping with the surroundings.
Long may it remain so, for in consequence of it the native has
been kept unsophisticated and unspoilt.   Men brought up in
this school evince warm attachment to the quaint little lodge
and the wide-spreading woods that have afforded them, from
their youth upwards, shelter and sport.   When necessity
compels them to retrench, for the landed classes of Austria

have suffered almost as much as those of England, they will not dispose of their shoot to the first comer who can afford to pay the rent. The idea of seeing what is near and dear to them, pass into the hands of a stranger, is repugnant, and if they cannot find a friend, as good a sportsman as themselves, to take it off their hands, expenses will be cut down wherever possible, but the shoot will not be passed over like a worn-out coat to the first bidder. Sport is placed by them on too high a plane to make the thing that provided it, the object of barter, as were it a commercial commodity, the value of which can be solely expressed by £ s. d.

To those who in these ultra-money-grubbing days put the latter scale upon everything in life, these considerations will no doubt smack of rubbishy sentimentality. I will not quarrel with them, for sport is a term that bears widely differing construction, and no detail can with such difficulty be brought down to rote and rule, as the fundamental question : when does sport cease to be manly, and when does it become, if not exactly effeminate, at any rate too luxury-loving and pampered, to harmonise with the good old meaning of the word ?

It is now and again useful to see ourselves as others see us. Fashion and vastly increased wealth have of late years wrought so many momentous changes in England, that the foreigner's old byeword of the British being a nation of shop-keepers, has long lost its sting; nay, more, in the ear of the nation at large, it has become a compliment, for what else has placed England on the high pinnacle of prosperity, one which no other European nation can at all approach ? But it does not follow that what is good for trade and commerce and general prosperity, is good for all and everything that life offers. In that department of sport to which this little book is devoted, our shopkeepers' spirit has certainly worked harm. It has introduced principles which, like the " New

Woman " who seeks to pose as a man, and yet remains naught
but a woman, claim to be those of sport of a high order, but
which, after all, are nothing but those of shopkeeping. For
what else but a long purse is to-day the essential requisite
of the sportsman of the class I refer to ?   Who but a very
rich man can to-day exercise the ancient craft of deer-stalking
in the Highlands ?   Who are, one feels inclined to ask, these
modern deer kings ?   What has been their training ?   What
experience have most of them had in the hunter's vocation
till middle age brought them the means and the leisure to
take up that *rôle ?*   The query which I know will arise in the
minds of some who read this : "And pray why should not
these successful business men take their pleasure at deer-
stalking in the Highlands if they so choose ? " brings me to
the substantiation of my previous remark anent the harm
these new-fledged sportsmen are doing to Highland sport.

Old sportsmen who knew the Highlands before the
"Southron's hamesucken," are at one upon the deplorable
degeneration which has manifested itself in the red-deer of   .
Scotland in the last thirty or forty years.   The deer, taking
the average in a forest, are to-day several stones lighter than
they were a generation or two ago, and their antlers, once a
trophy of which any sportsman could well be proud, have
shrunk even to a greater extent than has done their bearers'
avoirdupois.   Of this there can be no doubt ; correspondents
out of number have filled columns with their wails, but only
a few appear to realise the true cause of the deterioration.
Put briefly, it is none other than the result of fashion causing
a demand so great, that to supply it, quality, in good shop-
keepers' fashion, has to be sacrificed to quantity.   To
accomplish this the course of nature is interfered with ;
ground which fifty years ago sustained 100 deer, is now
stocked with three times that number ; wire fences criss-
cross some Highland districts into vast paddocks, nicely

fenced in, but bare of that essential, good shelter, which the deer can no longer seek elsewhere. To make up for the deficiency of natural food, artificial feeding is resorted to, but in many cases only partially carried out, and hence, as experience in other countries has amply shown, it is far worse than none at all. For it teaches animals to rely upon a supply which fails them at the critical time. Graver than any of the above causes, is the one where our commercial instincts come most patently to the fore. I am alluding to the pernicious system of yearly leases, which now prevails to such a great extent, and than which no more egregiously foolish system can be imagined, provided the speediest possible deterioration of deer be not its special object.

Yearly leases have worked great harm, for they put a premium upon the breeding from the weaklings of their race. Human nature remains human even in the inspiring scenery of the Highlands, and decidedly human it is to try one's utmost to include in the limit which the lessor of the forest has prescribed, the very best that can be got. To make use of an expressive vulgarism, "You pay your money and you takes your choice." Very different are the feelings of the lessee if he has leased the forest for a longer term. Well enough he knows that the good stag he spared this season will next year (up to certain well-known limits, of course) carry a better head, and in the interval the spared one has been granted the chance to leave the impress of his mature vigour and strength upon posterity. How the pernicious principles which stare one in the face when examining this system of yearly leases, could ever have received the even passive consent of sportsmen, is one of those things which pass one's poor understanding.

It is hardly necessary, I think, to follow the tracks of a "deer king" on his royal road to that social distinction which it is supposed the possession of a good Highland forest

14

confers upon the happy lessee. It is not a far cry from his club in St. James Street or Pall Mall to the Shooting Agency round the corner, where his cheque-book can purchase the precise number of stags he desires to provide for his fashionable friends. The transaction is as simple and as quickly concluded as is the purchase, by those moving in a lowlier walk in life, of a herd of "beasties" or Southdowns. I remember once being present when a certain forest was offered to a sportsman with the usual laudatory comment. The answer was as brief as it was to the point: "Why, my good fellow, I had that forest myself last year!" It told its tale very plainly: Take a forest, indeed, in which in the preceding season he did his level best to kill every good stag that was on it!

I trust, for the sake of the good old cause of sport, that my fault-finding will be taken in the same friendly spirit which prompted these criticisms.

I have so often been asked by friends at home whether they could rent chamois shoots in Austria, and what difficulties, if any, stand in the way of their getting what they want, that I have gained some practical knowledge on this point, and am induced to make a few general remarks concerning the upshot of my experience.

Foreigners are not prevented in any way from leasing preserves from private persons. Crown leases used formerly also to be granted to foreigners; of late years, however, the Emperor, who takes a personal interest in matters appertaining to mountain sport in his realm, has caused an old byelaw, which prohibits foreigners holding Crown leases, to be enforced, for North Germans have been acquiring quite a number of good shoots from the Crown, paying higher prices than were formerly the rule. To this invasion by northern sportsmen the authorities have therefore put a stop, so far as possible. I do not think that the same difficulty would meet English sportsmen of the right sort, who, I have always found, are most popular in Austria and in Hungary, and, even were they debarred by the Government, private shoots are not infrequently to be had, though hardly ever for such short periods as English sportsmen desire. Yearly leases are quite unheard of, and the very shortest I have ever known a forest let, was for three years, for which period, I may incidentally mention, I was able to lease a Styrian chamois preserve last year for an English friend, special family reasons inducing the owner of it to part with it for that unusually short term.

The rents for Austrian chamois and deer ground are low in comparison with those asked in the Highlands. For £500 per annum, lodge and keepers included, one can get quite good chamois and red-deer ground. Now and again one hears of shoots, well worth having, coming on the market, owing to death or illness, but as the demand is far greater than the supply they are quickly snapped up.

CHAPTER XI

IT will be with relief that the reader, weary of the discursive and argumentative generalisations that occupied so much of the preceding chapter, will turn to the following more "business-like" account of actual experiences while stalking the mountain stag in the Austrian Alps.

Time: the 5th of October, the height of the rutting season in average years. Locality, a fairly good preserve, in which I had shot several good stags before, and with the topography of which I was fairly well acquainted.

A long day's tramp from the nearest railway station had brought me on the preceding afternoon to the starting-point, a log-hut, which I proposed to make my headquarters.

Well acquainted with the ground, I began my stalking early next morning without further loss of time; and having no occasion to use the keeper, I left him at the hut to collect a fresh layer of mountain hay for the bunks, and afterwards to undertake certain necessary repairs of the shingle roof, where several black patches in the thin layer of last night's snow, no less than corresponding damp spots on the floor of the hut, proved that covering of this kind, even when weighed down with hundredweights of stones, can ill withstand the fury of an early October snowstorm.

In the morning the sky had been overcast, a dense

leaden-hued bank hanging persistently over the eastern horizon—an ominous sign, indicating, if the wind did not change to a more favourable quarter, an early repetition of autumnal snowstorms. The breeze, too, was up to all kinds of tricks. Now from the east, then shifting to the south, then · backing to a north-easterly direction, or dying out entirely for a few minutes—it was about as unfavourable a state of things for stalking as well could be, and made me long for the steady westerly wind, which, during summer and autumn, makes "still hunting" in the Rocky Mountains so very easy in comparison to Alpine sport. There you can form your plans days ahead, with positive certainty that the wind, till the first snowstorm, will continue from the same direction. In connection with the influence of the south wind upon the calling of stags, a somewhat strange circumstance must not be omitted. As long as this wind, here called the "warm wind," continues, stags either do not call at all, or do so only at rare intervals, and with but little energy. All old Alpine stalkers know this as a fact; indeed, I find it mentioned in a seventeenth-century *Guide to Stalking*, and one has often occasion to speak with anything but pleasure of the southerly breeze.

About noon, however, a long lull occurred; and a quarter of an hour later, just as I was debating with myself what course I had best pursue, the first puff of smoke from my pipe blew right into my face. It was the good wind, and if it did not change its mind, fine weather was sure to follow; and so it happened. Two hours later, it was as fine an autumn afternoon as one could wish. The leaden-coloured clouds had vanished, and the grand landscape was bathed in glorious sunshine.

Though perhaps unnecessary, it may yet be of use to those who have not had the opportunity to study the interesting provisions of Nature upon which the existence of the deer specie is based, to say a few words concerning the rutting season. During the time the new antlers are forming the stag retires to the thickest woods, and there he stays practically invisible to human eye, for he comes out to feed only at night. He is at this period not only an exceedingly indolent Sybarite, but also a high feeder, for he has to lay up a goodly stock of fat for the exhausting excesses in which Nature insists he shall indulge soon after his antlers have reached their full growth. When this occurs, and the last shred of " velvet," through the innumerable blood-vessels of which the growing horn received part of its nutriment, has been tossed aside or rubbed off, the animal's proud trophy is said to be " clean," and it is ready for use as a formidable weapon of defence or attack. The middle of September has come round by the time the lordly beast, now sleeker and fatter than at any other season of the year, feels stirring within him the first warm impulses of love and war. These very soon become the predominant instincts, nay, one might almost say the exclusive ones, for so filled is his whole being with them that he forgets to feed, and hunger and thirst are cravings unknown to him at the height of this period of excessive passion.

It is not my intention to add another to the innumerable attempts of writers and artists to describe the lordly monarch of the forest, as with distended neck he takes upon himself the duties of mastership over the herd. Only the sportsman can really appreciate the stirring beauty and charm of the reality, and neither the pen nor the pencil can possibly do justice to the scenes of mortal combat between lusty champions of the forest whose virile passions, to the utmost inflamed, cause them to do battle with a sturdy vehemence betrayed by no other wild creature in the wide realm of nature. To those who have never seen it, I would say, Go and see for yourselves.

To the stalker, the call of the stag is the essential part of the rut; for by it, at first faintly, then gradually nearer and nearer, he is guided towards the spot where the champion of the forest is roaming through his demesne, bent on love and war. If the locality is his usual home, or he has already beaten off all rivals and is the undisputed master of the herd, he is preceded by the hinds that form his harem. If, on the other hand, he is an interloper, who on his own ground has been beaten off by a stronger rival, and not much injured in the combat, he is alone, and the frequency and force of his "call" will soon betray this to practised ears. With the exception of a couple of days at the very height of the rut, stags only call at night and during the early hours of morning, and the late ones of evening. In good years—that is, when the rutting season is short, but very intensive —stags will call also in the middle of the day, but this is decidedly the exception; and in bad seasons, as was the one I am writing about, when stray stags commenced to *brunft* or rut before the middle of September, one could spend days in the mountains without hearing a single call, except at or after dusk. There are also localities which are special favourites with stags during the rutting season. These *Brunftplätze* (rut places) are elevated spots, generally not far from timber-line, where the ground, if possible, is a little marshy, and expanses of Alpine meadow-land, dotted with copses of pine, afford them open space for their nocturnal rambles, and good covert during daytime. My steps were bent towards such a place, a favourite spot of mine, where in past years, sitting in the evening in front of my hut, I have heard as many as nine good stags "call." Indeed, on one occasion, the autumn of 1874, that number was eclipsed by two. But, poor fellows! of those eleven only the minority saw springtide, for the ensuing winter was one of the most destructive known in the Alps for generations.

The distance from the hut was insignificant; so I took
my time, enjoying to the full the grand solitude of timber-
line scenery.

With my telescope I could see a small band of chamois
grazing on a tiny slope of grass, one of the solitary patches
of vegetation visible on the forbidding crest of a peak close
by. Welcome as such a sight would have been at another
time, it now failed to quicken my pulse, for the rutting
season is too short to lose any chance.   The afternoon
waned, and not a single call had I heard.   As the sun tinted
with rosy blushes the stupendous barren cliffs overhead, I had
reached and was occupying a favourite place of outlook—a
gigantic pulpit of rock, overlooking the amphitheatre-shaped
expanse of forest and cliff spread out at my feet.   Here I
could hear every call for miles round; and, what is of importance, the elevated nature of my post gave me the desired
opportunity of distinguishing the exact locality from whence
the sound came—a matter not as easy as one might think, for
the echo in Alpine regions is most misleading.   ＊

Of course my chances of getting a shot that evening were
nil; for, although the moon was very nearly full, and a keen
sportsman can now and again, by a happy fluke, bag his stag
by moonlight, it is most difficult to accomplish.   I have shot
some stags in this manner; but the odds are twenty to one
that you will either miss him, or be spotted by the sentinel
hinds before you get near enough.   On the whole, it is therefore better to abstain from the attempt, and to get one's shot
about dusk or early morning, the latter being preferable.

Experience has proved that, as a rule, a stag will call the
last time in the morning, close to or in precisely the same
spot where he first betrayed his presence the preceding
evening; for rutting stags, if not disturbed, generally seek
the same covert during daytime.   My intention was, therefore, to discover such a locality, then return to my hut for

a few hours' sleep, and start before dawn with a good chance of "making meat." Red-deer, as everybody knows, can, similar to the moose, be called by using artificial means to imitate either the male's roar or the female's bleat. It is, however, a knack not easy to acquire; and, though I have shot some by using it, I have spoilt sport rather oftener. The best call is made of a large sea-shell, known to conchologists as the "ammon's horn," a shell the size of a child's head, with spiral channels. The sound you strive to imitate with it is the male's roar.

Night was fast closing in, and the pink shimmer of the rising moon was already tinting the horizon in a gap between two peaks, when the first call, as yet very distant, was brought to my ear on the tranquil evening air. Twice it was repeated, a few minutes' interval between the sounds, then a stag, much closer to me than the first, gave voice in long-drawn tones. The guttural bellow was unmistakably that of a good stag. Though many a thorough *Jäger* pretends to be able to tell approximately the age of the animal by the higher or deeper basso of the call, I have often found myself at fault; but an ear the reverse of musical may have something to do with my inability to make any finer distinction. What I can do, is what anybody, by dint of a little practice, can acquire, viz. to be able to tell the roar of a "good" stag of ten or more tines from that of a stripling too fond of hearing his own voice.

Well, the notes I heard were, so far as my judgment went, those of a good stag. Far less easy was it to tell the exact locality from whence the tones issued. Around, below, and also partially above me, great green billows of forest stretched away, broken, here by a patch of barrenness, where rocks of fantastic shapes rose far beyond the surrounding ocean of tree-tops, there by sylvan glades that seemed to penetrate into the very heart of the forest. Right at my feet, a quarter of a mile off, lay a bigger glade, its peculiar bright green colour betraying the marshy nature of the ground. Thereabouts, or a little beyond, I concluded, the stag was calling. But increasing darkness precluded all chance of catching sight of him. For the present nothing more was to be done. By the waning daylight I had "located" the spot, by easily distinguishable landmarks mapped out in my memory. This, for the kind of work I had in hand, is often more than half the battle. An hour's walk through the dark woods, where the air was heavy with the fresh fragrance of pines drawn from the trees by the afternoon's sun—across peaceful glades, some already lit up with the silvery sheen of the bright moon—brought me back to my hut, where a bright fire was blazing on the open hearth, and Jokel, the keeper, was busy with the preparations of a primitive but savoury supper.

The trained Alpine sportsman is supposed to be recognisable by the facility he evinces of awakening at any given time — let it even be such an unseasonable hour as 2 o'clock A.M. Long practice, especially in spring, when capercaillie and blackcock oblige one to be on foot at hours when other people go to bed, make it, after a while, an easy task to many. I am not able, with any regard to truth, to claim to be one of the many, so I deputed the duty of wakening at the right time to Jokel. As I had to be on the ground before the first tint of day, and allowed myself double time for getting there, the latter had me up soon after three. A steaming jorum of tea, the last drops with a dash of Kirsch—the genuine stuff, not the vile concoction palmed off on tourists—brightens one up in double quick time. With a hearty *Waidman's Heil, Euer Gnaden* (The best of sportsman's fortune, Gracious Master), from Jokel, who, I well saw, was burning to accompany me, I stepped through the low doorway out into the cold, bright October night. The warm sun of yesterday afternoon had melted the last vestige of snow; but the atmosphere, several degrees below freezing-point, had during the night again cast a crystal veil, this time of glittering rime, over all vegetation. The keen frost-laden air made my cheeks tingle, as I pursued my way across the forest-girt opening, where the hut stood, past giant conifers, stragglers from the near pine forest, where, standing in more dense masses, but yet leaving ample space between the trunks, one saw trees of great age and size. They were glorious old Alpine pines, and as I continued my walk right through the heart of the sombre forest, I had ample opportunity to note anew the wealth of curve, the beauty of outline, exhibited by their branches—some sweeping the smooth short Alpine sward, others, higher up, clearly contoured against the heavens, while the coating of hoar-frost that covered every needle, and bent low each blade of grass, glittered and gleamed in the mellow light of the moon.

Crossing an insignificant ridge, I presently reached the declivity of the mountain, leading to the spot I was steering for. The moon was sinking low on the horizon, and I was well on my way down the slope, when the first call reverberated through the air. A second and third from different directions following in quick succession, made me quicken my strides. Consulting the face of my watch, illuminated by the glow of my pipe, I found it was not yet five—rather earlier than I expected, and explaining the frequency of the calls. I sat down on a handy trunk, but my impatience, augmented by the calling in comparatively close proximity, would not let me rest long. As I have already said, it is no easy matter to guess correctly the whereabouts of calling stags, and, indeed, it is next to impossible if the listener is himself in the forest, and not on an elevated point. In Alpine regions, such as I am speaking of, the air appears as though it were full of

echoes, which, although they may not be distinguishable, yet
combine to create a misleading resonance of the original sound.
In the forest each tree acts as an acoustic reflector, while
the cliffs add their share to the *tout ensemble* of reverberating
sound.

While the rutting stag, full of his passions, is singularly
heedless of danger, and hence easy of approach, the hinds
exhibit at this time redoubled vigilance; and it is no easy
matter even for trained stalkers to get at a stag surrounded
by his female court. A minute's deliberation showed me
that, instead of trying for the stag I was now listening to,
and perhaps losing him as he moved on, it would be wiser
to continue my way to the place selected by me last night,
and upon this, as being a far surer course on the whole, I
decided. My progress now became slow and of the proverbial
"stalking" aspect. In former times, when youthful ardour
was wont to overrule other considerations, I used to stalk
barefooted, that being by far the most noiseless way of
approaching game; for the naked foot instinctively feels
its way more cautiously—also in the dark—than when
protected from injury by ever so thin a covering. But
of late years the hoar-frost on the grass has somehow
grown much chillier, and the sharp points of stones appear
to be much more jagged than they used to be, so that now
I ordinarily use on such' occasions either Indian moccasins
or lawn-tennis shoes. In the damp climate of Europe the
latter are preferable, and are decidedly the most practical of
the several makeshifts employed by stalkers to render their
approach noiseless. Substituting these invaluable "stalker's
friends" for my heavy iron-shod shooting boots, and slipping the latter into my *Rücksack*, I was soon creeping along,
with the cautiousness rendered imperative by the vicinity of
the calling stag. To guard my scent I was obliged to make
a slight detour, but finally reached the selected spot. Not

knowing from whence my victim would approach, it was essential to be most careful regarding the wind. Four stags were now calling in different directions, one close to my left, the rest farther off. From my post I could overlook the marshy opening already described, most parts of which would be covered by my ·500 Express as soon as it was sufficiently light. My supposition, that the stag to whom I had allowed a wide berth was the very one I was in search of, proved correct, for gradually the calling came closer and closer, and there could be little doubt left that he was the one I had spotted last night. I was beginning to feel very sure of his antlers, and was already selecting in my mind their future resting-place, when my hopes were rudely dispersed by one of those unexpected *contretemps* to which the stalker is so often exposed during the rutting season.

Day was dawning, and I had just slipped my two cartridges into the chambers, when suddenly, without the slightest warning, a fifth stag began to call right behind me, not 50 yards off, and a second later I heard a crashing of branches, and the beast, alarmed, I suppose, by a tainted whiff of air (for he could not help getting wind of me), broke at a full run across the opening. It was far too dark to shoot, and, moreover, I felt sure he did not carry a good head. The most alarming feature was the fact that he made off in the very direction from which I was expecting the big stag presently to appear. I had not heard the latter for five minutes or so, but I was soon to learn, that he and his suite were closer to me than I could have wished; for hardly had the fugitive stag disappeared in the covert that skirted the opening, when I heard the clashing of antlers and the dull thud of stamping feet. The fugitive had got into unpleasant quarters, and evidently he was a much smaller stag than the other, for the combat was over the next instant, and he, pursued by the master-stag, was making the best of time

across the glade. At one moment they were not 100 yards
off, and I was sorely tempted to chance the shot; but in
the treacherous gloaming it would have been next to madness
thus to spoil my still good chance. The pursuer did not
chase the intruder very long or very far, but, alas ! far enough
to get my wind. Had the hinds been there, I should not
have seen the deer again that day ; but with the stag it
was different. Wheeling sharply round, as if shot, his first
instinct was to be off; but his animal passions, then at their
very height, overruled his native caution, and his first headlong start gradually changed into a curve, back to the spot
where the hinds, mere shadowy outlines, were lying about, or
grazing on the brink of the opening. Here evidently the
family would have gone to covert, and the stag, a quarter of
an hour later, would probably have been mine, had not the
event just described occurred. Unsettled by the scent, but
yet loath to leave the hinds, he had them on their legs and
was driving them before him in less time than it takes me to
write it. There was now no time to lose, for they were going
away at a trot. Daylight was fast gaining upon dusk, and
with my noiseless stalking-shoes I could make good speed
after the band, tracking being rendered easy by the thick hoar-
frost on the grass. Soon, however, I came to the unpleasant
conclusion that the stag was making for a bare ridge, and, by
crossing it, was evidently intending to put a good deal of ground
between him and that noxious whiff of humanity. Up and
up they went, and in ten minutes or a quarter of an hour the
forest grew gradually more open, and the trees began to betray,
by their gnarled trunks and weather-beaten look, that timber-
line was close at hand. I had stalked over the ground many
a time, so knew that I could no longer overtake them before
they would reach the bare ground, where an approach was
next to impossible.

Close to the top of the ridge, but quite a mile to the

right, there was a tarn surrounded by a few scattered patriarchal mountain arves, a favourite pass for red-deer changing
from one slope of the mountain to the other. If the deer
took this pass, and if, by making a detour, I could reach the
covert of the trees near the lake before they hove in sight
—two significant ifs,—I could yet bag my stag. Deciding
upon this plan, execution followed very speedily. The slope
was a very steep and treeless mountain-side, covered in most
places with small beds of stunted *Latchen*, investing my
run with the essential features of a hurdle race. The
distance was about a mile and a half, by the line I had to
take to escape observation. Needless to say, before I had
done the third, my run up the slope had subsided to a trot,
and finally to a fast walk. Coat, *Rücksack*, and finally waist-
coat, were abandoned—flung aside, here one, there the other.
As my Rocky Mountain trapper once remarked, after watching me (from a safe place) making the best of time towards a
handy tree, with a crippled bear after me, "I was all legs,
with elbows for handles." My object, however, was gained,
and I reached covert behind the first tree near the tarn, a
couple of minutes before the craning neck and pricked-up
ears of the leading hind topped the rising ground. I had
guessed correctly; the deer, after reaching the top of the
ridge much to my left, had followed it to where the lake and
their usual pass over the mountains lay. With the wind
dead in my teeth, I remained glued to the pitchy trunk;
there was no fear that a fluttering garment would betray me,
for the only things about me that could flutter were heaving
lungs and throbbing heart, for the race up that slope had
taken it out of me. Intensely exciting minutes followed.
For there, with the noble beast in full view and not
100 yards off, crouched the hunter, so exasperatingly
pumped that he dared not even raise the rifle lest the
wobbling barrel be detected by the ever-watchful hinds, who

were tip-toeing over the short sward down towards the tarn. Love happily is blind, and fortunately the tree behind which I was hidden was a giant, of a girth amply affording shelter to half-a-dozen such trembling wretches as I was. There was, therefore, no immediate cause for despair. The stag, whose attention was now directed to more congenial matters, was evidently thinking himself perfectly safe, for was there not a long bare slope behind him, and had not one of the faithful hinds posted herself on the brow so that she could overlook the whole declivity? It was fortunate I had reached the height ahead of the deer, for now, with that sentinel there, I could not possibly have gained the brow.

The stag's attention to the fair ones, presently made a dip in the limpid waters of the little pool appear acceptable, and one or two of the hinds, with their half-grown progeny of the previous spring, followed their master into the shallow tarn, but did not venture in deeper than their knees. It was a strikingly beautiful picture, the equal of which I have rarely seen, at least not in European forests. The sun was just peeping over the crags at my back, and while I was still in the shade the rosy rays of morning were resting full upon the animals grouped along the shore of the loch. From the surface of the latter rose a gossamer veil of mist that presently half hid the graceful forms. As the stag left the water and shook his head he was shrouded by a semi-transparent cloud of sparkling mist, such as would have delighted a painter's eye.

The dozen or so of Alpine arves, the typical and perhaps most picturesque of coniferous trees, growing only at the highest altitudes attained by arborial vegetation, were all veterans who had weathered for many generations, nay, centuries, the wintry gales that sweep over these exposed uplands. Their gnarled branches and weather-beaten trunks bore evidence of the hardships of life above timber-line.

Two or three of them had succumbed to them—one, evidently not many months before, had been struck by lightning and was lying where the bolt had felled him, half of his riven trunk immersed in the water. To the branches, twisted and full of rugosities, clung long tresses of the picturesque beard of the Alps, that grizzly moss growing often to the length of a couple of yards, and reminding one of the beard of some giant mountain goblin such as we see in old-fashioned fairy-tale books. Some of these festoons were floating on the clear water, still attached to their parent stems, and were moving gently to and fro, as the tiny wavelets lapped against the stricken trunk.

But I would be stretching truth were I to state that I noticed all these details while, still breathless, I waited behind that tree. They burst on my eyes when my work was done, when I sat on a boulder close to the water's edge, smoking a well-earned pipe, before me stretched out on the beach, with his hind legs half immersed in the water, the dead stag. How he came to his end a few words will tell. Whether a distant challenging roar, inaudible as it was to the human ear, had struck his finer organ, or whether it was in the mere pride of virile strength, I do not know, but the stag, just as he leisurely planted his front legs on the pebbly beach, halted, and with inflated neck, gave one grand roar. The graceful hinds, who had been idly roaming about on the short sward, nibbling at stray blades, or licking the coats of their young, while awaiting the pleasure of their lord and master, raised their heads and looked about as-if expecting the rush of a rival. But a secreted foe they knew not of was closer at hand, and just as the great hart, with his antlered head well thrown back, his almost black neck distended to double the ordinary size, was in the act of repeating the battle-cry, and his hot breath issued from his nostrils and open mouth like puffs of steam, one of his forefeet angrily pawing the ground, I was putting my finger to the trigger. "A good stag deserves a good shot," says an old hunter's proverb; so I did my best. When the smoke, that hung heavy over the frost-laden grass, cleared off, all but one of the actors in that still life scene had vanished. He that was left was stretched out on the shore of the tarn, in the last throes of death, his hind legs churning the water. What better death could he have wished himself?

CHAPTER XII

STALKING RED-DEER IN HUNGARY

THE red-deer inhabiting the Carpathian Mountains, that much too little known " tail " of the main Alps, are, as I have so repeatedly said, the largest representatives of their species to be found in Europe. In the same way that the forest in which they roam, is in many places as primeval as any to be found farther east in Asia, they also deserve to be called primeval. And practically they are that, for they live in much the same condition of wild freedom in which they existed at the time the Huns overwhelmed Eastern Europe 1000 years ago. In those rugged, densely-wooded hills, for mountains they hardly deserve to be called, at least not in the same sense as those constituting the Alps proper, the deer are born, grow to maturity, and get old without coming in contact with man. The forests are as yet far too remote from great centres of population to make the beech, oak, and coniferous trees of marketable value, and the wretchedly poor native population of Ruthenians, completely in the hands of Jew harpies, belie the usual influences exercised by a mountain home, and show none of the manly characteristics one usually finds in a mountain-bred people.

Though as a matter of fact feudal institutions throughout Austro-Hungary came to an end by the brief if violent upheaval of 1848, the country is still in much the same condition as it was in for centuries preceding the Revolution. There are now as there were then only two classes, the peasants or tillers of the soil, a class who a generation ago were absolute serfs, and the aristocracy. Of a middle class there is hardly a trace in any but large towns of Hungary. The contrast between the lower and the upper classes is the greatest imaginable, and the abject servility of the peasant as he humbly, almost with bended knee, approaches any member or even guest of the ruling class, and kisses the seam of the dress or sleeve of the coat, carries one back to social conditions that have not prevailed in Western Europe since the Middle Ages.

Conditions such as these are, it is needless to point out, most favourable for the chase, and as has already been remarked when speaking of the Alpine stag, the climate and the food are equally superior in the Carpathians.

On the occasion I am about to describe, I visited one of the wildest forests to be found on the southern slopes of the Carpathians as the guest of Baron Schönberg, who is the owner of some 70 square miles of primeval woods in that region.

Previous engagements prevented my reaching Hungary in time for the height of the rut, and by the time I got there (27th September) the master-stags were, with the exception of a brief renewal, already silent. That renewal sufficed, however, to show me what it must be like at the height of the rut. But of this anon.

Fourteen hours' railway journey from the beautifully situated and flourishing capital of Hungary, at first across broad, productive-looking plains, then skirting for many miles the rich bottom lands of the river Theiss, which a well-engineered system of reclamation has added to Hungary's already vast wheatfields, landed me at my destination, at least so far as railways were concerned, viz. Szolyva-

Harsfalva. A dozen miles beyond the historical Munkacs on the Pest Lemberg line, Harsfalva is not far from the Galician frontier.

Hungary, as everybody who has once travelled there knows, is a land of contrasts—contrasts that suggest the fact that one is in the borderland where European civilisation and Asiatic dirt and squalor shake hands. I had not been in Hungary for more than twenty-five years, and while the country has in almost every respect experienced a truly wonderful progress since its emancipation from the apron-strings of a too paternal government, these contrasts, as well as the chief drawback against travelling in the interior of the country, are still quite to the fore. The latter is the almost total absence of country-side inns, forcing the traveller to have recourse to the good old Hungarian custom, easier of adoption to the native than to a stranger, particularly if he be troubled with shyness, of claiming hospitality from the chief personage in the neighbourhood, be it a prince in his château or an humble Greek pope in his exceedingly dirty ramshackle habitation. With such contrasts I was to become acquainted as soon as I stepped from the train at Harsfalva. My host had written to me that a pony, a mounted guide, and a cart for my luggage, would await me at the station, and that a ride of five or six hours would bring me to the central shooting lodge where he would await me. In the train I was seated in a luxurious Pullman dining car, with all that refinement can suggest; when I left it I was in another world. The village, near the station, consisted of miserable mud-plastered hovels, with one or two windows the size of a sheet of notepaper, tenanted by swarthy, half-naked Ruthenians, together with their generally perfectly nude children, and droves of quarrelsome pigs or flocks of noisy geese.

It being wet weather, the road leading away from the station was a perfect sea of deep mud, and, as I was still in

my town clothes, it became necessary for me to change my
garb. The question where I could do so was therefore one
of the first which I addressed to the guide. The latter was
a soldierly, well set-up Magyar; his moustaches turned up
fiercely, and his round Hungarian hat sat jauntily on his
head. He fortunately knew some words of German, and
took me to the only place in what was really quite a populous
village, corresponding to an auberge of the humblest imaginable type. The sole living room it appeared to contain was
filled by a crowd of exceedingly dirty, jabbering Jews, in
greasy caftans that reached to their heels. On their heads
they had black skull-caps and broad-brimmed hats, while
two corkscrew curls hung down in front of their ears. They
presented a typical picture of native Shylocks, for this they
are in deed as well as in appearance, the wretchedly ignorant
native Ruthenian population in this part of the country
being entirely in their cruel grasp.

My change of dress had to be performed in the presence
of these chattering Semites, who cast admiring business
glances at the contents of my kit-bag, while my riding rig
appeared to give occasion for general surprise. After various
attempts by the grovelling Jew innkeeper and his progeny
to kiss my hand in return for the trifling gratuity " the
gracious lord" had bestowed for the use of the somewhat
public dressing-room, and, seeing my luggage snugly stowed
away in the country cart, which, as I was told, would, on
account of the state in which the roads were, take three
hours longer than I should to reach the shooting lodge, we
started for my unknown goal.

At first we followed a sort of high road, supplied with
occasional bridges, where rivers of larger size had to be
crossed, but by and by we rode in the bed of the streams,
which formed the only road, showing how the strong arm of
Government lost force with distance.

It was a rolling hill country, only sparsely timbered; every mile or two we would pass through villages, consisting of straggling rows of mud‐plastered hovels, the walls of which were not more than 4 or 5 feet high, with a huge roof of thatch overtopping them like big extinguishers. The slightly larger houses one noticed here and there, with glass in their windows, were those of the village Jews, chief among them being the money‐lenders, store-keepers, and cattle dealers. The Ruthenian natives we saw working in the fields or met on the road seemed a hardy race, for in spite of the bitterly cold drizzle they had naught on but a "shirt," reaching from the neck to a little below the armpits—leaving the lower part of the chest exposed—and a nether garment of coarse linen. Both men and women were mostly barefoot, or at best had only moccasin-like shoes, which of course afforded little protection against the wet. When the road and stream occupied the same bed, the women I happened to meet simply tucked up their short nether garment, and though the water reached often above their knees, they waded along as if that were the normal condition of things. My pony was a famous little beast, surefooted and nimble, as only animals accustomed to mountain work can be. He took me along at a good pace, and as the distance before me was an unknown quantity, and my Hungarian guide's German was not up to a description of distances, I made rather better time than was necessary. As we rode on, taking short cuts over hills, I obtained good views over the country, un-interrupted towards the south, but hemmed in on the north by the Carpathians along the foot of the southern flanks of which we were riding. From one of these points of view we saw at our feet a broad cultivated valley, occupied by two or three villages, great stretches of maize fields separating the settlements. On the other side of the valley, occupying a beautifully timbered terrace, lay my host's country-house.

Just now he was living at the central shooting lodge, situated a couple of hours' ride up a narrow valley that led into the heart of the mountains. As we followed this latter glen, we entered the timbered region of the main range, and though we rose but gently, cultivated fields soon gave way to ever-narrowing slips of pasture land, till finally, as we neared the lodge, the glen had narrowed to a couple of hundred yards. This central lodge turned out to be a commodious and most picturesque house, consisting of timbered walls resting on masonry, with broad-eaved roof, in style somewhat resembling that of a Tyrolese châlet on a large scale. It stood at the point of juncture of four or five smaller glens, down each of which coursed the headwaters of the stream along which we had been riding for some time. Situated at an elevation of some 1800 feet, the hills which rose on every side to what appeared an even level, reached in their highest altitude 6000 feet. Timber-line was very clearly defined, the forest stopping very suddenly at about 4500 feet, while the upper-most portion of the hills were unbroken, perfectly treeless Alpine pastures, which in summer are the home of many thousands of semi-wild oxen and sheep, and in the autumn (after 1st August) that of the deer. During the rut the latter stay, however, chiefly in the dense forest.

From prominent points one gained a good view of the whole region, which, as far as the eye could stretch, was a sea of hills clothed with magnificent beech forests and inter-sected by steep gullies. These primeval woods were genuine *Urwald*, for not a tree, so to speak, had ever been felled in the whole expanse, the remoteness of the spot from railways having hitherto made the exploitation of this future source of wealth unremunerative. In this respect the forests of Csonok, as the estate of my host was called, form, I under-stand, an exception, for the properties of Count Schönborn and of Count Teleky, on either side of Csonok, have railways

and ironworks near at hand, and more or less extensive
clearings are annually made in the course of a systematic
exploitation of these magnificent hardwood forests. As these
clearings, beloved by game, facilitate stalking to a considerable extent, my host's warning, that his was the hardest
stalking ground in this part of Hungary, was perfectly
warranted by facts.

The shooting is managed by distributing the sportsmen—
there were three other guests beside myself—in different
parts of the forest, each gun having a district quite to himself. In the centre of it, and pretty well up, stands his hut,
to which a trail leads. Most of the eight huts (two for each
guest) my host possesses are within a two hours' ride from
the central lodge, from which provisions, post, etc., are daily
sent up. These huts are delightful little log buildings containing two rooms—one for the sportsman, the other for the
keeper and for the native "boy," while another native and a
pony is also at the sportsman's disposal, should he wish to
reach distant points and riding be possible. The huts are
quite simply furnished; they have a wide, old-fashioned
fireplace in the chief room, in which the Ruthenian boy keeps
up a permanent fire of huge beech logs, in front of which
the tired sportsman, after his long day, can pass pleasant
evening hours in the comfortable armchair. That the days
are long can be imagined from the fact that it is necessary
to rise at half-past three or four o'clock at latest, so as to
be on the nearest ridge or elevated point before dawn, to
shape one's plans according to the direction from which the
best stag is calling. Dawn is, here as elsewhere, almost
invariably the time of day when, during the rut, stags can
best be *verhört*, *i.e.* spotted. On the day of my arrival it
was of course too late to get up to the hut destined for me,
and though every hour was now of importance, the season
being so advanced, and stags having roared already since the

7th or 8th of September, I only started for my hut next day
at noon, the interval passing most pleasantly under the
Baron's hospitable roof.

Two of the other men had shot great stags, one weighing, brittled, 275 kilos, or 605 lbs. avoirdupois (43 stone
1 lb.), and his head, measured in my presence, taped along
the curve, a trifle over 46½ inches, which brought it close
to the dimensions of a moderately large wapiti head. Speaking of weights reminds me to give the official return of thirty
stags shot in one rutting season on the adjoining estate of
Munkacs, showing that there the heaviest stag weighed even
more, viz. just 44 stone (clean), and the average of the lot
was 415 lbs. avoirdupois, or 29 stone 9 lbs. So far as I
know no European shoot beats this record.

The sportsmen reported very indifferent weather; snow
had fallen and the stags were roaring very intermittently.
The rut was therefore supposed to have a day or two's
life yet.

By 4 P.M. on 28th September I was snugly housed in my
hut with my keeper, a Hungarian, who knew German, and a
pleasant-faced Ruthenian youth, who certainly was the most
willing and observant native servant one could desire. The
evening stalk is rarely as successful as the morning or
forenoon one, for in the regular course of things one has not
time to get near to the roaring stag before twilight robs one,
under the bower of trees, of the precious sight of the "bead."
Full moon, which, in the Alps, can now and again be made
use of for creeping up near enough to shoot with a fair chance
of success, is, on account of the density of the forest and the
absence of open glades or clearings, of less importance here
than elsewhere. Of the many stags killed here by my host,
not a single one, he told me, was bagged by moonlight, in
fact, he had never heard of a moonlight stalk being carried
out with success.

We (that is the keeper and I) did not go far the first evening; our goal was a knoll close to the hut, from which we could overhear a great part of the district which I was to shoot. Seated on a convenient stone at the foot of a giant beech, the keeper a few paces behind me, we sat listening for the first roar within approachable distance. As it did not come till it was almost dark, I had ample time to take in the sylvan beauties of my surroundings. Of forests quite untouched by the hand of man there are not too many in Europe, and I do not remember ever seeing one in any part of the world in which there were so few traces of decay in the shape of fallen trunks prostrated by gales, lightning, or old age. The rising generation, on the other hand, as I soon found out on penetrating into the underbrush, was of lusty growth, so that most of the time I was stalking under a double canopy of boughs, those of the tangled undergrowth, reaching to a height of 8 or 10 feet, and above that again the wide-reaching branches of the great beech-trees, whose silvery gray trunks, reaching, in the larger specimens, a diameter of 5 feet and more, were of a correspondingly great height. They soared upwards in stately beauty. Just then autumn colours lent an additional charm to this unbroken vista of forest, and while I did not see a single coniferous' tree during my entire stay, patches of variegated tints proved the presence of occasional groves of maples, ash, and elms.

It was past five o'clock, and dusk was already gathering under our leafy bower, when the sharp ear of the keeper heard the first preliminary grunts which a stag is apt to make as he rises from his couch where, if the season is at all advanced, he has probably enjoyed a nap, and is now about to get on his legs to collect round him his straying hinds. Then it is that the scent or sight of another stag who has been attempting to poach on his ground will rouse the master's ire, and the next sound will be the deep, long-drawn roar by which the lord of the soil betokens his presence, calls his family to order, and challenges his foe. If it be one worthy of him the two champions will meet by and by; if it is but a giddy youngster who has sneaked in to play the gallant while the master is nodding, that one roar will send the interloper very speedily into hiding.

It was, of course, much too late to do anything that day, and even with another hour of daylight I should have hesitated to start stalking, the risk of not getting at the beast and only spoiling the ground for the morrow being too great. The stag was roaring in a wide glen—densely timbered, of course—somewhat below us, and by the deep, sonorous notes I judged he was a big fellow. But the keeper, to whose judgment I was very ready to bow, thought it was only an unattached *Bei-Hirsch*—adjutant-stag it might be translated—a beast of minor head, such as nearly always attaches himself to a master-stag's herd, following in its train often for the whole of the rut, and commencing to roar when his lord has wearied of the excitements of the season. In this the keeper was probably right, for the really good stags have, as I subsequently discovered, still deeper-toned voices, which an acute ear can hear at an incredible distance.

After a comfortable night in the snug hut, I was sitting at breakfast before 4 A.M.; but a pelting rain and gusts of wind, that occasionally made the forest ring with the crash of falling trees, made the prospect somewhat hopeless. Out into the deluge, however, we went, at first by the light of a lantern; but defeat in that miserable weather was an almost foregone conclusion, for even had stags been calling, the wind—that arch-enemy of the stalker in Hungarian forests—would have drowned the sound for all but short distances. Not a grunt, much less roar, did we hear, and drenched to the skin we returned to the hut about noon. In the afternoon it cleared up a bit, and we resumed stalking in another direction, winding up at the head of the glen we had visited in the morning. We were walking along rather dejectedly, now following a game trail, then with noiseless tread stealing along the twists and turns of a regular *Bürschsteig* or stalking-path the Baron had caused to be cut through the most promising corries, when suddenly, apparently not 200 yards off, and ahead of us on the path, a stag roared. Grander sound I had never heard, the whole forest seemed to vibrate with it. Only a giant among giants could emit such volume of sound. A glance at the keeper behind me showed me that this time I had before me one of the masters of the forest, for the man's face was blanched, and when he approached me closely to whisper into my ears the advice to stay where we were, he was trembling with excitement. "It's the great stag the Count missed" (alluding to an incident he had previously told me of, which had occurred to my predecessor in the district), he whispered as we cowered down behind the nearest tree to await the next call and thus learn whether he was stationary, and if not in which direction he was travelling. If he was coming in our direction we were as favourably placed as we possibly could be, for when shifting ground in the leisurely manner usually observed by a band of deer lorded by a real master-stag, the hinds would be ahead, slowly grazing along, eyes and ears keenly on the watch, while his majesty would stalk some paces behind, heedless of danger, now angrily crushing down a sapling, then throwing up his head and sniffing the air, or with outstretched neck sounding his guttural challenge, the *timbre* of which is of such astonishing force. But of such scenes, though enacted but a few dozen paces off, one sees precious little in these impenetrable forests. My host's warning that one shoots not at stags, but in nine cases out of ten merely at brown patches momentarily visible between trees that hide the rest of the animal's body, was, as I soon found out, strikingly correct. For, though the band was coming my way not more than 40 yards above the trail at the side of which we were crouching, I saw but occasional glimpses of the hinds as they slowly filed past our ambush. Of the stag himself I saw but the upper half of the right antler, but it made my heart beat hard ; it was a double royal, five massive points forming the crown, so that it was at the very least a head of fourteen points. The fallen trunk of a beech of great size, behind which the stag passed when I caught the only glimpse I did of his antlers, was a bulwark that effectually shielded the animal, and prevented my taking the random shot which I would probably have been tempted to risk, had merely a bush intervened between the prize and my ·450 rifle. Some supremely anxious moments were thus passed, hoping against hope that some fairy hand would turn the herd downwards, and thus lead them to cross the path where there would have been a rare chance for the old rifle to give tongue, but, alas ! such would have been too good luck. Two minutes later the advanced guard had got my wind, and, with an angry snort amid loud crashing of dry sticks, the deer took flight, some strong language, in Hungarian and English, tainting the breeze for the next minute or two.

Much the same fate overtook me a second time after a tedious stalk across the next ravine, when, by dint of great care, I got again to within 100 yards of deer feeding along under the mastership of a stag, who apparently had reached that stage of surfeit when he emits only occasional grunts rather than regular roars. This time I did not even see his antlers, dense brush intervening between us, and, before I had time to get their wind from a slightly more open side, the breeze shifted, and we were again alluding to the sylvan surroundings in uncomplimentary terms.

The only two stags that roared in the whole district had both escaped us! This was hard luck, but worse was to follow, for on the following day not a sound, not a single grunt, much less roar, broke the often oppressive stillness in those vast forests as we tramped through them, making occasional halts to listen. Some hours of driving rain and heavy dropping, where the leafy canopy was too dense to let us feel the force of the wind, did not increase our good humour.

The following day was the 1st of October. What sportsman is not just a bit superstitious, at least to the extent of believing in good and bad days? Who does not experience a certain inward confidence when following up one's luck on the former, or the reverse when fickle fortune has settled that it shall be one of the latter? Now for the last quarter of a century the 1st and 5th of October have invariably been lucky days with me. Many of my best trophies, some of my best bags in the Alps, in the Rocky Mountains, or in the Sierras on the Pacific Slope, were secured on those days. What wonder that I gave my old friend an extra rub up, looked to my cartridges with double care, and astonished the keeper, when he served me my early breakfast, by the confidence with which I predicted that a good stag would fall to my rifle that day!

The outlook next morning was anything but a promising one, for heavy rain was coming down in torrents when, somewhat later than usual, we stepped out of the hut into the dark forest. We began by ascending the slippery path that led to the top of the hill behind the hut from which a stag calling in any of the surrounding glens could easily be heard. This time we had not to wait long, for from a corrie right below us, where bad luck had hitherto so persistently dogged our steps, there came the impatiently awaited call. Threateningly ferocious it sounded in the great forest, still steeped in the mysterious half-light of early dawn, and from afar came an answering roar. They were the first notes of a concert in which presently four other great stags joined—a concert of master voices such as I have never heard before, and probably will never hear again, save in those matchless forests. But this was a thought to which at that moment I gave little heed. There, not half—nay, hardly more than a quarter—of a mile away the nearest beast called, and this one, after a few moments' consultation with the keeper, I decided to stalk in preference to any of the others, whose precise location it was less easy to guess. I have never been in a more puzzling country in which to determine the direction from which sound travelled, nor in one in which it was easier to get turned round and lose oneself in. Conspicuous landmarks there were none, and the dense foliage prevented one getting sight of the few lesser ones that did exist.

The wind being still unfavourable—*i.e.* drawing down the hillsides—two courses were left open to us. One was to make a great detour and approach the deer from below; the other was to wait patiently till the wind should veer, which, as the weather was brightening up, we presumed it would do as soon as the first rays of the rising sun would strike the slopes. I decided to follow the latter course, as being the safer of the two, and giving me more time. But the most careful plans are often upset by unforeseen trifles, and in this instance a couple of small stags sneaking silently through the forest, bent probably upon mischief, suddenly came upon us before we had covered half the distance to the big stag, and in their mad flight down the slope carried with them, of course, also the herd I was after. Balked again! But that 1st of October was still young, and my belief in the lucky day not a bit shaken. Returning again to the ridge from where we could best listen, it was not long before we had located another stag of lusty voice, and were making our way in his direction as fast as legs could carry one, for these early hours are precious ones. What we dreaded, of course, also happened, and, long before we had got up to the place where the stag had been roaring, he became mute, and not a grunt did he give to guide our steps. When we thought that we were within 300 or 400 yards from the spot, we sat down to await patiently his first growl. The spot we were on was a fairly steep slope, not so densely timbered as most others, so that one could absolutely see for 100 yards up and down the declivity. The wind permitting, I was just deliberating whether a pipe could not be indulged in with safety, when, glancing for a moment at the slope above where we were sitting, and which space of ground we had, of course, carefully scanned before we emerged from the cover that skirted it, my eyes fastened themselves upon an object on which they remained eagerly centred. An instant later the keeper's clutch at my leg told me that he, too, had discovered that a stag was actually quietly peering straight down at us not more than 90 or 100 yards off! The animal was couched in a small depression of the ground, and only his head and antlers were visible to me. The distance, as it afterwards proved, was ninety-six steps, but even at that number of yards the only mark I dared fire at — the stag's forehead — was a somewhat small one. It was a very awkward shot also for another reason, for I had to twist round slowly to the off-side, so as to bring the rifle to bear on my mark, and naturally the strain of doing so did not increase the steadiness of my aim. Yet, though at the moment of firing I could have sworn that the shot broke inches too high, I fluked it into the centre of the stag's forehead, and, without even springing to his feet, he simply dropped his head and was dead before the sound of the shot could have reached his ear.

"Well," remarked the somewhat astonished keeper, who had all along been anxiously whispering to me to wait till

16

the stag should rise, "that's a shot I wouldn't like all my gentlemen to risk!" Was it worth while explaining to him that the credit of that happy fluke was due to the day more than to the hand that gripped the rifle? The stag's antlers might have been a bit finer and larger, but it was a ten-pointer all the same. The "royals," which I had seen before I fired, were finely developed, and really should have adorned a hart of twelve points. His weight, clean, when we got him down to the central lodge in the evening, was found to be 191 kilos, or 30 stone 2 lbs. English weight.

That the stag was not a master-stag was amply proved by the absence of hinds. He was probably the "bei" stag of the big fellow I was stalking; but all the more remarkable was his behaviour.

After gralloching the beast, the keeper left me to go down to the lodge to fetch half a dozen natives to carry him to the nearest point to which a team of mountain-bred oxen with a sort of drag-sleigh could be got. He wanted me to return to the hut in his absence, for he warned me I would be certain to lose myself in the forest were I to continue to stalk alone. As four stags were roaring in the next glen I would not hear of this, but proceeded alone. The stags, for some reason or other, were all on the move, and the one I had selected led me a stern chase over ridge and dale, which obliged me to keep my bump of locality in working order, or the keeper's prediction might easily have come true. I was making my way along a ridge on the off-side of which I knew the deer were feeding, dense brush hiding them from my view at the time. On the side of the ridge I was on the forest was free of undergrowth, and the slope downwards could be overlooked for more than 150 yards. Not paying particular attention to this part of the ground, I suddenly came upon a band of deer feeding out on the slope. The hinds and I saw each other simultaneously, not so the two stags. The larger of the two, the lord of the soil, was a fine beast of at least twelve points, and as I came upon the herd, he was in the act of driving away a smaller animal—a brocket he turned out to be—who had ventured too close to the harem. The hinds, of course, were off downhill the instant they saw me; while the stags diverged to the left, keeping parallel with the ridge. It was a course which I saw would enable me, by running a couple of hundred yards, to get in a long shot when they turned the bend of the curving hillside. My anticipation in this respect was correct, and the chance for a long running shot presented itself as the stags emerged from a narrow strip of cover not more than 20 yards in width. When they entered this strip the brocket was ahead, the big stag a few yards behind him. I naturally expected that they would emerge in the same order, and, without taking much notice of the first one, as he emerged, I fired at the second one as he ran out. Both were going at a swinging trot: the light, as is almost always the case in these forests, was very indifferent for fine shooting, and the distance was some 150 or 160 yards. But the stag on that 1st October dropped to the shot, my bullet, placed rather high, having broken the animal's back above the shoulder. But this time luck had played me a nasty trick, for on getting up to the animal, what was my horror to find that I had slain the wrong stag, and that instead of the lordly royal a miserable brocket was lying dead at my feet!

The misadventure was, of course, caused by the stags reversing their position very unexpectedly while running through the narrow strip of cover, where they were out of my sight. That I was very disgusted with myself is but a mild way of describing my feelings, for here in the home of the giants of their race nobody ever thinks of shooting either brockets, spades, or even staggards of six, the least ever being killed being stags of eight points. It was rather singular that my second deer fell dead within 200 yards of the first one I had shot, though many miles of ground had been covered by me in the interval, the stag I was really following when I came upon my second victim having brought me back to the spot by a ringing course. It was too late to do anything more that day, and other engagements obliged me, unfortunately, to leave on the following one, so that I had no chance to make good my misdeed in my host's magnificent forests.

On getting down to the central lodge and comparing notes with the other guns, it was discovered that the glen in which the five stags had chimed that unique concert the morning before was the only spot in the whole preserve where a sound was heard. My host thought that the "music" was caused by the straying in of some strange hinds from some adjoining glen, giving fresh cause for rivalry among the several *Platz* stags (those holding the ground during the rut), which very probably was the correct solution of the incident.

Experienced old hands use in Hungary, as well as in the Alps, the artificial "call," which is, as I have already said, a large sea-shell of the Ammonite order wherewith one can imitate the stag's roar fairly accurately. This call is, as a rule, less successful in bringing the stag up to one, than it is to cause him to betray his whereabouts by an answering note of anger. If dry sticks are about, and the stag is not too near, the efficacy of the ruse is heightened by stamping about on the sticks, as a stag does when breaking cover or when getting ready for a rush. These are tactics which are also observed in Canada when moose-calling. Another ruse which, in the early part of the rut, when stags are still on the lookout for hinds, is often attended by success, is to imitate the squeaking grunt of the hind which she emits when hard pressed by a pursuing stag. I have known this to bring up the stag

MODERN HUNGARIAN ANTLERS OF TWENTY-TWO POINTS BELONGING TO
PRINCE MONTENUOVO, VIENNA.

with such an impetuous rush as to oblige one to shoot very quickly. Calling the stag with the shell so as to bring him up to one, is quite a knack which requires practice, for the stag's guardian angels at this season of the year, when his own senses are blunted, are for ever on the watch, and are not so easily deceived. If the sound lacks naturalness, the hinds are off and their lord follows them. When imitating the call of the stag it should be pitched half a tone or so higher than the roar of the beast one desires to bring up, so as to let it appear that a younger stag is replying to the challenge. Some men acquire a wonderful dexterity in "calling." A Count Türkheim once shot during one rutting season twelve stags he had called up.

Some interesting statistics from Count Schönborn's adjoining forests at Munkacs—a locality to which I have already referred—may be added. This estate, which is one of the largest in Hungary, extends over nearly 600 square miles, of which a good deal more than half is forest. During the last rutting season, that is, in less than four weeks, there were shot by the owner and his guests twenty-eight stags, all of first rank, consisting of one stag of eighteen points, three of sixteen, nine of fourteen, six of twelve, six of ten, and three of eight points. This is a record which nowadays would be hard to beat.

The head represented in Plate XIV. is one of the best Hungarian heads secured two years ago. It is remarkable, not only on account of the great size and number (twenty-two) of the tines, but also because of the treble points on each of the brow-tines. The weight of these antlers (without the shield on which they are mounted) was, at the time the stag was killed, $29\frac{7}{10}$ lbs. avoirdupois, as vouched for by the owner, Prince Montenuovo, at whose palace in Vienna I recently saw the head, and who gave me the photograph from which the accompanying illustration has been engraved.

CHAPTER XIII

OF the 68,000 or 69,000 roe-deer killed annually in Austria, exclusive of Hungary,[1] by far the larger proportion are bucks, for to kill does is considered a most unsportsmanlike proceeding, the shooting of the necessary number of the latter being left to keepers. It is safe to say, that nine out of every ten of these roebucks are shot with the rifle, the use of shot being considered as unsportsmanlike as is the killing of does, except in drives in perfectly level country, where rifles would be too dangerous. These two facts convey to one at once in what different estimation the roe is held on the Continent to that vouchsafed to it in Great Britain, where it is treated as a sort of nondescript game, unworthy even of being protected by a close time, and at which any charge, from No. 1 to No. 7, that happens to be in the 12-bore, when the game is sighted, can quite legitimately be loosened. Concerning the venison of roe, curiously enough, the same difference of opinion exists as does regarding the chase. About fifteen years ago a discussion respecting this very point occupied for several weeks the columns of the *Field*, and I recollect that several Scotch sportsmen, one of whom

---

[1] Counting Hungary, too, the annual bag of roe certainly exceeds 100,000 head. The province at the head of tho Austrian list is Bohemia, where in 1892—an average year—12,920 roes were shot, Lower Austria coming next with 11,683.

claimed to "have very great experience in roe-shooting, never having missed a season for fifty years," considered that in August, September, and October, the roe was little better than carrion! An opinion more contrary to that entertained in the countries which are the home of this deer it would be difficult to find in the wide realm of international sport. One of the correspondents introduced the subject by stating, that there was "much relating to the roe that is still a puzzle to naturalists," a remark which suggests to one that the writer's researches into the history of the roe were on a par with his gastronomic experiences. Those who have ever tasted the juicy and deliciously "gamey" *Rehbraten*, as prepared by a decent Continental cook, will, I am sure, bear out all that can be said in praise of roe venison.[1]

So far as I am aware of, there is nothing about the *habitus* of the roe that is either puzzling or less known to the naturalist than there is, for instance, in respect to the red-deer. For the one vexed question that puzzled our fathers, viz. at what period of the year occurs the rut of the roe, has long since—more than half a century ago—been definitely settled as taking place in the latter part of July and the commencement of August.[2] An old *Jäger* proverb designates Portunculus day (2nd August) as marking the height of the rutting season, when best can be enjoyed one phase of roe-buck-shooting, namely, "calling" them.

No other deer species exhibits in respect to its horns so many irregularities, abnormities, and monstrosities as does the roebuck. Likewise is the occurrence of does carrying horns, though not exactly frequent, by no means of such extraordinary rareness as is the case with the red-deer hind. In the regular course the young buck throws tiny knobs at the age of seven or eight months, before the first snow surprises him. The second winter finds him with longer

[1] See Appendix, Note 4.   [2] See Appendix, Note 5.

single spikes, the third with forked spikes, and the fourth with three prongs on each horn. Occasionally this last stage is reached a year sooner, and in more than one authentic instance did a nine months' old buck set up six pronged horns and continue to grow similar sets for a series of years. Horns with eight prongs or ten are occasionally heard of, but they are sufficiently rare to make them the object of the greatest ambition to Continental sportsmen. It seems to be a now well-ascertained fact, that the farther eastward the roebuck is found the larger is the growth of his horns. At the west end of the line of his geographical distribution, which is Great Britain, the horns are the smallest; at the other extreme, viz. Siberia, they are of such great size— 16 to 18 inches in height and frequently adorned with ten, twelve, and more points—that many modern naturalists are inclined to follow the lead of Pallas in creating a subdivision for the Siberian roe-deer.[1] In former centuries the roebucks of Central and Southern Europe grew somewhat larger horns than those met with there to-day, and collectors are wont to speak of these old German and Austrian heads as those of the *Urbock* or original buck. With this, naturalists, as a rule, do not agree, and many heated discussions have occurred

[1] This Russian naturalist was, I believe, the first who gave the Asiatic roe the distinctive name *C. pygargus*, and as he had ample opportunity to study this species, his classification should meet with general approval. There is a well-marked structural difference between these Siberian heads and the European. The burrs are much smaller in proportion to their height than those of large European horns, and in no specimen which I have seen do they approach so close together, or come into contact with each other, as is so often the case in large European horns. Brehm is among those who favour a subdivision, giving the roe-deer of Eastern Asia the name *C. pygargus mandschuricus*.

The discoveries in the lacustrine remains of Switzerland, so ably described by Dr. Rutimeyer, corroborate to an important extent the evidence of historical ages that in the Alpine regions the roebucks at no time grew very much larger horns than they do now, making in this respect an exception to other deer species. The same, Dr. Rutimeyer points out, is the case regarding the diluvial roe horns found in England, which, according to Owen's researches, are of precisely the same shape as those of the present day.

concerning this question. As these *soi-disant* ancient German roe-deer horns, of bygone centuries, have a considerable pecuniary value, collectors giving £20 or £30 for large specimens of what they believe to be ancient German ones, there presented itself a good opening to unscrupulous dealers to palm off Siberian roe horns in lieu of these much sought-after old German heads. The profits were so considerable that, I believe, quite a trade sprung up, and by putting these Siberian horns on old-fashioned carved heads, experienced collectors (English ones included) were victimised.[1]

Most of the great collections of ancient German roebuck horns containing, as some do, many scores of these gigantic *Urböcke*, must be regarded, therefore, with some caution, for there can be little doubt that this substituting of Siberian for European horns is not of quite recent origin. In one instance that I could name, a well-known collector, who paid enormous prices for these "ancient" roe horns, was probably taken in on many an occasion.

How I came upon the origin of this fraud may perhaps be told. For years I had always heard that two Tyrolese valleys were specially renowned as harbouring in castles, inns, and better class peasants' houses, these much prized ancient trophies. In neither of the valleys, it seemed to me, could roe-deer ever have flourished to such a marked degree, for the climate of Tyrol is too rough for the highest development of this most delicate of European deer species. This, more than anything else, raised doubts in my mind concerning

---

[1] Last year a well-known English collector and the writer visited together a Munich dealer in antlers, and there discovered a very fine roe-deer head, mounted on an old carved head, which the dealer was anxious to sell to us at a good round sum as that of a German *Urbock*. Its structure, however, betrayed its Asiatic origin at a glance. After letting the fellow exhaust his powers of invention and persuasion, the former of which enabled him to give a long account of the historical collection in a certain old castle of which this particular *Urbock* had formed part, we were amused by his discomfiture when he discovered that his visitors knew rather more than he thought they did about *C. pygargus*.

the local origin of these big heads. One inquiry led me to
another, and at last I had traced out the matter to the
following perfectly natural solution. From both valleys in
question, the Zillerthal and the Leutasch, there existed in
the last century, and up to the first half of the present one, a
large export trade to Russia of the famed Tyrolese dairy
cattle. The beasts were driven by natives of the two
valleys to the most remote parts of European and Asiatic
Russia, journeys that now and again lasted two years, the
winter being passed at some suitable intermediate point.
The cattle drivers, after remaining a year or two as in-
structors of the Tyrolese dairy system, then returned home,
probably to repeat the great journey a second and third
time. They were in the habit of bringing home with
them such easily transportable curiosities as struck their
fancy. The two things that many did bring home were
exactly such as one might expect would strike men of such
highly religious frame of mind, but who were withal keen
sportsmen.

The one consisted of pictures, crosses, and small church
ornaments of Byzantine workmanship that adorn Russian
house-altars and churches, the other the horns of the Asiatic
roebucks, which, by their extraordinary size, we can well fancy
captivated these primitive travellers. Curiously enough my
attention was first attracted to the possible Asiatic origin of
the roebuck horns, by the discovery of a take-in to which a
great art-connoisseur had fallen victim, and which at the
time made a stir in art circles on the Continent. This
expert finding in an out-of-the-way peasant's house in the
Zillerthal an ancient-looking Byzantine cross, thought he had
made a very valuable find, dating from the twelfth instead
of from the nineteenth century. The ornament was exhibited
as of the former period at a great European art centre, and,
of course, the fiasco, when more lynx-eyed experts proved it

to be of quite modern Russian origin, was great in comparison to the supposed value of the find.

A short time afterwards I discovered in the person of an old reformed poacher, an individual who forty years ago had been an emissary of one of the chief collectors of red-deer antlers and roebuck horns in Europe. As the latter's agent T—— travelled about the country, penetrating into the most remote valleys and buying up all good heads. Under gentle cross-examination, he told me that in the two above-named valleys he had made his best finds of *Urböcke*, though he professed ignorance concerning their foreign origin, which, considering that the man was a perfectly uneducated fellow, was not impossible. When next I visited the Zillerthal I made a point of interviewing the few old men there were then still

FIG. 14.—Rare *peruque* monstrosity of a Roebuck.

alive, who in their youth had been in Russia, and from one of them I learnt the facts I have mentioned as a likely solution of the *Urbock* puzzle.

Perhaps the most singular of all abnormal growths peculiar to the roe is the so-called *peruque* horn, or wig monstrosity. These, as can be seen from two sketches of such specimens, form huge, irregularly shaped, semi-hard clusters, sometimes covered with a hairy skin. Fig.

14 is a reproduction of · what is probably one of the largest of these monstrosities known to the naturalist.[1] It completely covered the left eye, and almost as completely obscured the vision of the other one. The bearer of this unsightly curiosity was killed by Prince Frederic Charles of Prussia on the 8th December 1872, near Potsdam. At the top the growth was quite hard, but farther down it became soft and slightly movable to the touch. Fig. 15 is a good specimen in the collection of Lord Powerscourt at Powerscourt, County Wicklow. Another and still larger *peruque* head is mentioned by Winckell, who states that it weighed 10 lbs., or about 11 lbs. ½ oz. avoirdupois. In this instance the spongy growth hung down on both sides of the head 2½ inches below the jaw, resembling locks of scale-covered hair more than anything else. In the last century these monstrosities were produced artificially, castration at a certain time of the year causing this peculiar form of abnormity.

FIG. 15.—*Peruque* monstrosity of Roebuck horns.
(In the collection of Lord Powerscourt.)

A similar case came under my notice last year, when a roebuck with fine *peruque* horns was shot near here. In spite of close examination no trace of any injury to his

[1] The original of the sketch is in Altum's *Forst Zoologie.*

ANCIENT ROEBUCK HORNS IN THE COLLECTION OF COUNT ERBACH.

generative organs could be detected; everything appeared to be in a perfectly normal condition. It was only when a medical man carefully opened and examined the testes that the presence of a small bird shot was discovered in one of the glands. Among the 2342 roebuck horns in Count Arco-Zinneberg's famous collection there are several of these monstrosities, interesting to the pathologist rather than to the sportsman. For one very curious, though quite small, malformed roebuck head this collector is said to have given 3000 florins, or close upon £300.

In Count Erbach's very fine collection there are also some remarkable old roe-deer heads, the German origin of some of which is unquestionable. Of others, whose origin, it is acknowledged, is unknown, it is, to judge by structural evidence I have alluded to, safe to assume that they are not European but Asiatic roe-deer heads. The larger of the two heads here represented (Plate XV.) is the longest pair of horns in the Erbach collection; it measures (in a straight line) a trifle over 15 inches; its origin is unknown. The other one has five beams, and a total of eleven points, and is of German origin. These two photographs are taken from Herr Ed. Störmer's interesting illustrated work on the Erbach collection.

The normal roebuck horns show, it is well known, different types in different localities, and heavy bucks by no means always carry the largest horns.

Neither the buck nor the doe are ever fat in the way that are red-deer in August, for they never put on external fat. Both the buck and the barren doe are in the primest condition from the middle of June until the commencement of the rut towards the end of the following month. The roebuck recovers from the excesses of the rut much sooner than the red-deer stag, no doubt in consequence of the warmer weather and the abundance of rich food then at the buck's service in the shape of bountiful crops of cereals. Under ordinary conditions the buck is his old self again by the end of August. That the recovery should be slower in the Highlands of Scotland is very possible, for there the absence or scarceness of agriculture deprives the animal of the chances to recuperate as quickly as he otherwise would. At the same time to call roe venison carrion at any time of the year, except when it is made to resemble it by the machinations of an incompetent cook, is to do grave injustice to this graceful and useful little deer.

On the Continent roebuck shooting is a popular sport. In the month or six weeks which precede the rut it is practically the only shootable beast. Those fond of quiet morning or evening rambles with the light ·360 or ·400 can obtain very fair sport, skirting along the glades and meadows, whither, just before dusk, the roes come out to feed. As they return to their thick covert shortly after break of day, there is only about half an hour at either period when under ordinary circumstances a shot can be got. Calling the buck during the rut is accomplished by imitating either the bleat of the doe or that of the young calf. In the latter case, if there is a doe near, she will come up, and almost certainly the amorous buck will presently follow the latter. In either case the sportsman must be prepared to shoot rather more quickly than is pleasant with the rifle. For the bucks have a way of stealthily sneaking up to the covert where the sportsman is hidden, and then rushing with great impetuosity towards the spot where they think the doe is, which tries the nerves of the steadiest shots; for as soon as the Jack-in-the-Box rush reveals the nature of the deceit the buck is off like a flash of lightning.

In forests where there are no red-deer to disturb, roes are often hunted with hounds or driven with beaters, the guns being posted on favourite run-ways or *Wechsel* well known to the keepers. But this is somewhat tame sport, in every way inferior to stalking or calling. Walking up roes with a *Dachshund* or other slow hound leads also to success. Curiously enough, if the buck gets away before one can fire it is the wisest policy to remain very quietly close to the spot where the roe was roused. In five cases out of six the buck, after circling round in the forest at a speed commensurate with that of the pursuing dog, will return to his couch, probably with the intention of foiling him.

Small as the animal is, it evinces an astonishing amount of pugnacious courage. In the rut the buck is constantly fighting with rivals,[1] and at all seasons of the year the sportsman should be careful how he finishes off a wounded buck, which he should do by severing the vertebrae of the neck, and not by cutting its throat. If he fail to take a good grip of the buck's horns, the animal is liable to give him an ugly thrust, and such injury is attended with danger. How strong such a thrust can be I had once cause to learn in a manner that was not at all pleasant. I had wounded a buck during a drive one very cold day in the first week of December. As the snow was quite 3 feet deep escape was practically impossible, and the bloodhound, that was put on the wounded beast's tracks as soon as the drive was over, brought the buck to bay in a few minutes in the bed of the

---

[1] That well-known Bavarian sportsman, F. von Kobell, describes in his *Wildanger* an incident showing the pugnaciousness of roebucks during the rut. While stalking, he came upon two fighting roebucks, who were butting each other across a small ditch. . . . He shot the larger one, and he fell in his tracks, but to Kobell's astonishment, the other one did not make off, but after a leap to one side at once resumed a fighting position, his venomous hatred to the dying foe getting the better of all other considerations. On another occasion Kobell shot a buck dashing out of a wood where he had evidently just been beaten off by another buck. Kobell had hardly shot him, when the pursuing roe came rushing out, and though the sportsman was standing on a clearing plainly visible, the pursuing buck was so intent upon following up his foe, that in spite of the shot and Kobell's presence he dashed up to within 100 paces of him before he turned off.

stream at the bottom of the narrow glen in which we were hunting. Hurrying down to the spot as fast as the snow and the clumsy snow-hoops on our feet allowed, we found that the buck was standing in the centre of the open part of the stream in very fast flowing water. Just below him was a deepish pool, and when the hound, obeying his master's word, entered the water to tackle the buck and make him leave the stream, the force of the water was such as to sweep him past the buck into the pool. A second and a third time did we try to dislodge the buck by this means, but the same result attended each attempt. Though the water was hardly more than 2 feet deep, it looked very uninviting that particularly cold December day, with the thermometer a good many degrees below zero, Fahrenheit. Being a peasants' shoot there were no keepers whom one could order to fetch the buck; while to shoot him dead would have made matters worse, for the body would then be swept into the pool, where it would have been much harder to recover it. None of the peasants seemed inclined to face the water, but the poor beast, shot too far back, standing hunched up in the middle of the dark rushing water, was a picture of misery I could not endure to watch any longer. Divesting myself of my coat and taking my open hunting knife between my teeth, I stepped from a protruding cake of ice into the swirling dark waters. The rush was of such force, that it was well I was provided with my long iron spiked *Alpenstock*, upon which I had to lean heavily at each step. The bed of the stream consisted of smooth, round boulders of irregular size, which were very slippery, and though the distance was not more than 15 or 20 feet, it took me several minutes to get across to the buck's level. The latter, curiously enough, had still his horns on his head, and stood on a slightly larger boulder, not more than a foot under water, which raised him higher out of the water than he otherwise would have been. As he

saw me coming he faced round, his head lowered as if ready
to receive an enemy's charge. The closer I got the less I
liked the look of things, for I dared not let go of the stick,
or I would have been swept off my feet, and consequently
had only one hand with which to tackle him.

He gave me no chance to use the knife in the orthodox
manner, so I finally decided to pull him from his stone and
dispatch him as best I could. Taking hold of one of his
horns, I hauled him into the deeper water where I stood,
but he was much too quick for me, and before I knew what
happened, he had given me a violent thrust with his horns.
It caught me with such force on the upper part of the thigh
that the sharp-pointed prong cut through the deerskin
breeches which I was wearing, and what was worse, caused
me to lose my balance, so that I was ignominiously flung into
the pool below.

Very fortunately for me, the stout leather broke the force
of the thrust, and I got off with a good bruise, and a rent in
my garment 4 inches in length, in which, when I got out,
I found the horn was sticking. The latter, I suppose, was
nearly coming off, the ordinary shedding time (November)
being past, so it got detached with a certain amount of ease,
though still sufficiently firm on the head to permit my
hauling him from his stone by it. He went into the
pool with me, for once the water caught him broadside he
was swept off his legs with the same unceremonious rapidity
that had come into play in my case. A stroke or two brought
me to the bank, where my knife soon finished the career of
the gallant little fellow. I had a desperately cold two hours'
walk home, for the cold was so great that in five minutes I
was a column of ice, and by the time I reached my quarters
the tight-fitting armour had rubbed the skin off my knees and
legs in a most unpleasant manner.

In bygone centuries the roe-deer were far less numerous

17

than they have become since the extermination of the bear, lynx, and wolf, all of whom were most dangerous foes of this comparatively small animal, which is far less able to defend itself than the red-deer. To-day, broadly speaking, the proportion of roes to red-deer in the Alps is about five or six to one. Three hundred years ago the proportion was, under the most favourable circumstances, exactly the reverse, and even much more to the roe's disadvantage in certain instances I shall enumerate. One of the earliest game registers known to me concerning Alpine districts is that of Duke William IV. of Bavaria. This sportsman killed in the one season of 1545, 1032 red-deer, 535 wild boar, 38 wolves, and 224 roe-deer. His son in twenty-five years (1555-1579) had very different success with roe, for to his 4783 head of red-deer he killed only 100 roe-deer. Tegern See, a rich and sport-loving monastery in the foothills of the Alps in the centre of a splendid game country, has left us similar evidence in its game registers; we find that in thirteen years (1568-1580) only 48 roes were sent to the buttery. Two centuries later, in the same number of years, there were delivered 575 roes. In the forests of Central and North Europe a similar preponderance of the red-deer in the sixteenth century, and gradual increase of roes in the following 200 years, manifests itself. Roe venison, it must be remembered, was the most prized of all game, and one can be sure that every roe was enumerated on the register, and that every carcase duly found its way to the kitchen of these great hunting lords. In 1560 over 300 carcases of red-deer went to the buttery at Kassel,[1] but only 49 roe-deer. On another occasion the proportion was 940 red-deer and 177 roe-deer. In 1582 there were killed by the ruler of that principality (Hesse) and his court, 652 red-deer and 85 roe-deer; nine years later, 883 red-deer and 96 roe-deer. In 1611 the proportion was 674 red-deer

[1] Landau.

and 53 roe-deer; 1669, 615 red-deer and 53 roe-deer. Much the same numerical relation seems to have existed in other parts of the Continent. In others the proportion showed even a greater preponderance of red-deer. In the Electorate of Saxony we know that in 1581, 1244 red-deer and only 119 roe-deer were bagged. The Count of Henneberg shot in his countship in the same year 1003 red-deer and 97 roe-deer. The Elector of Brandenburg two years later killed 1295 red-deer and 249 roe-deer, which latter is next to Duke William IV. of Bavaria's bag, the most favourable relative proportion for roe-deer I have come across in sixteenth-century annals.

I have already referred to the one exception to the rule observed by all Continental sportsmen, of shooting only roe-bucks, and those only with the rifle. In perfectly level country, when beaters and other guns are about, a rifle would be too dangerous. On the few occasions when placed in these circumstances I had to use the gun, the pleasure of bringing down one's game, or the shame of missing it, which has more than once happened to me, have been of a kind to make one forswear such hunts altogether.

As it is necessary in well-stocked preserves to thin out barren does, this is ordinarily left to the keepers or village dignitaries. In most of the provinces of Austria the game laws strictly prohibit the killing of does at any time of the year, so that when a superabundance of useless old females make it desirable to kill off a few, it is necessary to obtain the special sanction of the authorities to do so. At drives in very dense coverts it is often difficult to ascertain the sex of the roe in time to shoot, and many a doe is shot accidentally. In certain second-class preserves, where such " accidents " are of too frequent occurrence, a fine of five or ten florins is imposed for shooting a doe. Some years ago an aristocratic but very unpopular sportsman in Bohemia, Count X——, annoyed by

one or two does having been killed accidentally the previous
season, announced to his guests before starting out that he
had ordered his head-keeper to collect fifty florins for every
doe shot in his preserves. His guests were not of the sort
to require such a bourgeois hint, and took great offence
at it. The day's hunt was to consist of a series of drives,
but the shoot, so the story goes, terminated with the
first, for at its conclusion more than a score of does lay
dead on the ground, and the keepers were chuckling at a
handful of bank-notes, which the delinquents had promptly
handed to them before bidding polite adieu to their mortified
host.

I have seen it stated by more than one English writer,
that when the rut commences, roe-deer pair off without any
contest between the males, and that, when once paired, the
buck remains true for life to the doe. Were there not several
good reasons why the habits of roe-deer in England and Scotland can never be so closely watched as on the Continent,
one could make less excuses for such incorrect opinions as the
above. The "true-for-life" theory is, on the face of it,
impossible, for in a country where generally only the bucks
are shot, the females naturally preponderate in the proportion
of from four to six does to one buck. How could this, without speedily bringing about extermination, be possible, considering the great mortality among young roes, which is
undoubtedly greater than with most other species of *ferae
naturae*, for not only is the calf a very delicate little thing,
but it is the ready prey of numerous beasts and birds of prey?
Actual experiments prove the incorrectness of this theory;
thus, according to one experiment made in Vienna in July
1862, one buck covered seven does, every one of which gave
birth to two calves the following May.

Besides, most sportsmen acquainted with the habits of the
roe, have time and again observed strong old roebucks, after

driving one doe round and round with such persistency as to deeply score the ground, creating what are known as " rutting rings," which remain visible for months, go off and presently drive up some younger doe that has taken his fancy, with which this performance is repeated.

CHAPTER XIV

IT is safe to say that neither the naturalist nor the sportsman know of a single other instance where the complete extinction of a species of *ferae naturae* so entirely depended upon the will of one man, as has to be recorded in the case of the ibex of the Alps. Nobody at all acquainted with the circumstances can for a moment doubt, that had the late King of Italy, just forty years ago, not taken the measures he did to establish in the mountains of Cogne a sanctuary for bouquetin, this animal would to-day be extinct.

According to such excellent authorities as Dr. Girtanner of St. Gallen, and the late naturalist Brehm, there were not fifty head left in the whole of the Alps when Victor Emanuel visited for the first time what afterwards became his favourite retreat in the recesses of the Piedmont Alps. In Switzerland proper the ibex has been extinct for a couple of centuries, though isolated specimens that strayed over the frontier from the Aosta and Cogne peaks were occasionally waylaid by Swiss chamois hunters—one of the last instances, I believe, having occurred in the first decade of the present century.

One is often asked why the bouquetin should have become so much rarer than the chamois which inhabits lower regions, and the chase of which is less arduous. Nature and man joined forces to bring this about. The one by avalanches, which even the sharp-witted ibex fails to avoid—as many as eighteen head having been found destroyed by a single snow slide—the other by waging for many centuries a relentless war against this most prized of mountain game. Its massive horns were of great value, and they were much used in the late Middle Ages by gold and silversmiths in making goblets, for, according to an ancient belief, certain poisons betrayed their presence in these ibex-horn cups. While the medicinal qualities of the horn substance, as well as that of other parts of the ibex's anatomy, gave the carcase high intrinsic value, and led to a far more persistent persecution on the part of man than would otherwise have been the case. Thus their blood was considered a never-failing antidote against stone, and shavings of the horn were as firmly believed to be a panacea for hysterics. We can therefore readily believe that the beast was made the object of the hardy mountaineer's most strenuous efforts. About its habitat similarly absurd details were firmly believed. Thus, one old author tells us gravely that old bucks, when they feel that death is near, are in the habit of repairing to the most solitary and loftiest pinnacles of rock, and there, hooking themselves by one of their horns to the topmost projection, twirl themselves round until the tip of the horn is worn away, when they drop down the yawning abyss and are dashed to pieces. That good old yarn which one is told to this day by the uneducated in all parts of the globe concerning other species of ibex, according to which the chief use to which the ibex habitually put its horns, is to break its fall when it throws itself over high precipices in its endeavour to evade the hunter, is an old friend that one constantly meets from the first day one dips into the literature of the ibex family.

In Tyrol the bouquetin became extinct towards the end of the last century, though isolated specimens have also there been seen much later; thus a fine male was spied by a

Tyrolese chamois hunter in the mountains near Nauders as
late as 1874. One district in Tyrol was once a famous ibex
preserve, probably the most celebrated that ever existed, for
it was the property of the Archbishops of Salzburg, powerful
temporal seigneurs, who, it would seem, if the accounts of
contemporaries do not belie them, were exceedingly keen
Nimrods. This preserve was in the glacier-mantled mountain range, really the main chain of the Central Alps, which
closes the valley of the Zillerthal towards the south. Here
—for these lines are penned at a window facing the mouth
of this very valley—there were in the year 1699 [1] still to be
found 115 male, 125 female, and 22 young ibex. At the
same "stock-taking" there were found, strange to say, only
464 chamois. To-day there is not a single specimen of the
former left, but there are as many thousand chamois as there
were then hundreds. For the *Stillup* and the *Floitten* glens,
which were their last refuges, are now part of the famous
chamois preserve of the Princes Auersperg, to which I have
already referred. The Salzburg Archbishops had their ibex
colony guarded most jealously by a small army of keepers,
who, one hears, were constantly engaged in a fierce war with
the poachers. It was this which caused, about 1730, the
then lord archbishop, John Ernest, who was a less ardent
sportsman than had been most of his predecessors, to issue
orders to relax the guard, giving as reason "that the great
number of lives that have been sacrificed in the fights be-

---

[1] The naturalist, V. Moll, gives the following particulars concerning the
head of ibex in these valleys, unfortunately without mentioning the source of
his information. In the year 1683 there were 48 bucks, 70 does, and 17 kids.
Also in 1694, 72 bucks, 83 does, and 24 kids. Between 1683 and 1694 there were
shot by the keepers 18 head, while 53 were found killed by snow avalanches
and stones. Between 1694 and 1700 there were caught and shot 13 bucks,
14 does, and 23 kids.

Kobell mentions that at the end of last century there were twelve bouquetin
in the Archbishop's park at Hellbrunn, near Salzburg (probably the last
descendants of the Zillerthal colony). They were all wantonly shot by the
French troops.

tween keepers and poachers would make a less relentless watch over the ibex a more God-fearing work." The consequences made themselves quickly felt, for by the year 1758 there were only thirty-one ibex left. The precise date when the last one was killed is unknown, but an octogenarian peasant whom I got to know while chamois shooting in these very mountains some twenty years ago, asserted that he remembered as a boy still seeing an occasional ibex while attending to his little herd of goats above timber-line regions in the *Floitten* glen.

The Carpathian Mountains are also said to have once been the home of ibex, as they still are that of the chamois, but I have never come across any documentary evidence concerning this fact.

If we now turn to the interesting creation of King Victor Emanuel in the Piedmont Alps, we first of all have to mention the efforts of the naturalist Zumstein, who about the year 1821, prevailed upon the Piedmont Government to pass stringent game laws for the special object of giving protection to a small herd which had found a refuge in the heart of the Graian Alps. But for these most timely endeavours of the scientist, it would in all probability have also proved to be the grave of the species. Thus Zumstein's exertions, followed thirty-five years later by Victor Emanuel's efforts, effectually rescued the ibex from sharing the fate of the dodo or of Steller's sea-cow. When Victor Emanuel visited, in 1877, for the last time, his beloved Alpine retreat, there were, notwithstanding the large bags—he often killed fifty bucks in the season—which he had been making during the last years of his life, from 500 to 1000 bouquetin in his unique preserve. Fifty-five keepers, whose rifles were said to shoot uncommonly straight, held ward and watch in those barren solitudes over their precious charges. So good was their marksmanship that the officers of law had but few opportunities to inflict the nine years' imprisonment, which was, and for all I know to the contrary, still is the punishment for killing one of the king's bouquetins.

Victor Emanuel, as also his son and successor, loved to take their holiday in the wilds of Aosta, in perfect freedom from all court ceremony and trammels of etiquette, and those who remember the burly *bonhomie* of the "peasant's friend," as Victor Emanuel was often called, will perhaps better understand than can a younger generation what that freedom meant. Fellow-potentates, were they ever so keen sportsmen, were never bidden to share the primitive hospitality of the Campo del Re, and two Austrian sportsmen, to whom I shall have to refer at length, are, so far as is known to me, the only strangers who were ever given a chance to slay this the rarest big game in the world. For since the discovery made by Mr. Littledale, that the aurochs exists in a perfectly wild and unprotected condition in the Caucasus, and is therefore to be obtained also by those who are not in the position to obtain the Czar's permission to shoot in the Bialowicza forest, the bouquetin is unquestionably deserving of that distinction. The steinbock, to give it for once also its German patronymic, is a sturdy-looking beast, the adult male weighing as much as 200 lbs., the doe less than half that number of pounds. Both sexes carry horns, those of the former being, however, more than double the length and girth of the latter. There are but few collections of these interesting trophies, for which, by the way, our sporting forefathers were wont to give in exchange their weight in silver, and that at a time when the latter's purchasing power was more like that of gold nowadays. The best collection is the one made by Victor Emanuel in his château-de-chasse, Sarre, near Aosta. It consisted in 1879, little more than a year after the great sportsman's death, of 232 pairs of horns of the male, and of 22 pairs of the female's horns. The largest

XVI

A FAMILY OF BOUQUETIN IN THEIR FREE STATE.
(From a sketch from life.)

of the former, according to Count Hoyos, one of the two fortunate Austrian *Jäger* already alluded to, measured 30⅓ inches along the curve, with a circumference of 9¾ inches at the base, while the largest doe's horns were just under 10 inches long, and under 5 inches in circumference. The distance between the tips of the former was particularly large, viz. 29¾ inches.[1] A pair of horns a trifle longer even, but not as large in the girth, is preserved in the museum of Berne, where many of my readers will no doubt have seen them. This trophy is that of a giant of his race, computed to have been twenty-five years old. It was obtained on the Swiss Piedmont frontier in 1809 by Alexis de Caillet, a famous Swiss chamois hunter, concerning whom a number of semi-apocryphal tales are told. In prehistoric times the ibex's horns reached much larger dimensions, to judge from the core of a bouquetin horn found near Windisch, which measures as much in circumference as do the largest modern horns including the horn-sheath. Another great ibex horn was pushed forth by the Rheinwald glacier a few years ago.[2]

Some most interesting notes respecting the habitat of the ibex were narrated to me by Count Hoyos's companion, Count Wilczek, of whom I have already had to speak.

Count Wilczek, who visited these mountains in 1874, and again in 1879, compares the bouquetin for elegance and nobleness of bearing to the red-deer, the most graceful game we know. Contrary to the general belief, the bouquetin shuns the company of the chamois, to which, as is probably

[1] Count Hoyos states that every one of the 232 ibex, and over 700 chamois, horns, have for some unknown reason been placed on false skulls moulded of papier-maché, an innovation of questionable utility, and one which one hardly expected from such a genuine sportsman as was Victor Emanuel.

[2] The two bucks shot by the two sportsmen on the occasion of their second visit to Aosta in 1879 weighed 106 and 85 lbs. respectively (I presume clean weight), and their horns (they were stated to be respectively twelve and six years old) measured 28⅝ and 18½ inches over the curve.

needless to point out, it bears no relationship whatever; for the former belongs to the antelope, the latter to the goat family. Count Wilczek not only participated in the royal ibex drives, of which more will be said anon, but he was also permitted to stalk this interesting game, which of course gave him many chances to observe it when undisturbed. Its eyesight, this sportsman maintains, is even sharper than that of the chamois, but its scenting powers are less keen. In surefootedness and knack of balancing, if not in agility, the bouquetin is superior to the smaller mountain game.[1] During one of the drives the sportsmen had a chance to watch first a chamois and then an ibex come down the same *couloir* or chimney-like fissure in the perpendicular face of a rock-wall, both animals being in full flight. The chamois, like hundreds of others he had observed under similar circumstances, jumped from side to side, "fluttering down," as one might describe this particular mode of descent. The bouquetin, on the other hand, seemed to come down by bold bounds, landing on projections minute and far apart. The whistle of alarm is common to both animals, but as the ground frequented by the ibex is far more barren and shelterless than is that with which the chamois stalker is familiar, the whistle of the larger beast is less often heard, for it generally has spied you miles off, and is gone before you have had a chance of getting within earshot of it. In some of its idiosyncrasies the ibex resembles

---

[1] Young semi-tame bouquetin at Schönbrunn, near Vienna, display a nimbleness which seems next to impossible for creatures without wings. Young bucks have been seen to leap with one bound to the top of a door standing ajar, and balance themselves on the sharp edge with their four hoofs close together. Walls 10 feet high, or four times as high as themselves, were insufficient to prevent escape. The way they surmounted them, was to select a corner where the walls met at an obtuse angle, and bounding from one wall to the other, their sharp hoofs finding momentary gripping space in spots where the mortar had fallen off. To do this they had to spin round in the air, but nevertheless when they reached the top at the second or third rebound they stood as firm as a rock.

the domestic goat more than is exactly dignified in the "king of the Alps." These defects are wanting in the chamois, making it really the more genuinely wild beast of the two. This strain of domesticity shows itself very markedly in half-bred ibex, and to a lesser degree in pure-bred animals which were captured when quite young.

Always a pugnacious animal, the rutting season brings out their innate combativeness to the full, and the Aosta keepers assert that one can hear at a great distance the sound of their horns clashing together in their fierce fights for supremacy, which seem to last for hours. According to Brehm they pair in November, while according to other authorities it occurs in December—a discrepancy which, however, can be explained by climatic variations at the period observations were made.

Male ibex not infrequently descend from their usual quarters close to glaciers, or even above them, and occasionally, strange to say, are so far led away as to form misalliances with humble domestic she-goats belonging to the herds of semi-wild beasts that are turned out high up on the Piedmont mountains during the summer, often without any caretaker at all. The offspring of such an ill-assorted union can again be crossed with true ibex, thus producing three-quarter breeds that resemble the latter in most details, though they are invariably distinguishable from the pure-bred stock by their darker coloured coat.

Victor Emanuel was fond of experimentalising in his gamepark, La Real Mandria, near Turin, with crossing members of a small colony of pure-bred ibex he kept there with semi-wild, as well as domestic, animals. The results, except for scientific purposes, were unsatisfactory, for the half and three-quarter breds appear to exhibit few of the good, but most of the bad qualities of both parents. These experiments came to a sudden end with the death of the

originator, and the contents of the gamepark, some fifteen
head of various hybrids, were in 1878 transferred to Welsch-
tobel in the Grisons Alps, where they were set at liberty.
There the worst qualities of these nondescripts soon developed themselves to such a degree, that some of the animals
had to be recaptured, or finally destroyed, for they turned
regular highwaymen, attacking inoffensive wayfarers and
shepherds in the most ferocious manner. Dr. Girtanner
tells us that in two years only nine out of the fifteen were
left alive. Three of the males distinguished themselves
particularly by their pugnacious conduct. One of them
attacked a man who, accompanied by his wife and child, was
passing over the Strella Pass. Rushing at the man, who was
quite unaware of the animal's near presence, he hoisted him
off the ground with his one horn—the other one was broken
half-way up—and threw him clean over his back. Before
the unfortunate fellow had time to regain his legs the furious
beast was upon him, butting him unmercifully, and striking
at him with his front feet. The frightened woman, unable
to help her husband, rushed off for help, and at last finding
a shepherd, the two returned after half an hour's absence,
only to find that the unequal fight was still going on. It
was only after the shepherd had with his knife inflicted a
serious wound in the ibex's neck that the latter trotted off,
and the man's injuries could be attended to.

Two fine half-bred bucks were kept about fifteen years
ago in a semi-tame state in Côire, and exhibited many of the
traits that gave the first-named animal such a notorious
reputation. In this respect another big half-breed buck, to
which the moat round the town of Berne was assigned as a
home, earned for itself a lasting evil name. Inoffensive wayfarers were attacked by him in the most audacious manner,
the sentries being his particular aversion. When this buck,
in consequence of the endless mischief he committed, was

turned loose in the mountains of Unterseen, one pure-bred doe and several half-bred females were given him as companions. He maltreated them all to such an extent that they fled from him, the former returning to her old home in the highest regions, the latter descending to the inhabited valleys. The domineering swain being left to himself pursued his evil courses, bursting in the doors of the goat stables and châlets, and even pursuing the frightened *Sennerinen* down the steps of the subterranean dairies whither the girls took refuge. To avoid further risks of this kind, the authorities, anxious to restock the mountains with ibex, appointed a noted chamois hunter as guardian over the colony, with instructions to keep them in the uninhabited Saxeten glen. Four powerful men conducted the buck with ropes to his new home, but such a strong and violent prisoner did he prove himself, that in the course of the journey the four strong men were often lying on the ground, dragged hither and thither by the ibex. The attempt to keep the buck in the glen proved an entire failure, and not only did he pursue his old ways, paying dreaded visits to the goats in neighbouring glens, but he almost killed his guardian by nearly butting him over a precipice. The complaints and claims for damages at last became so unpleasant that the authorities had to have him shot.

Several attempts have been made to reintroduce the ibex into mountain regions in which they formerly were at home. One was made in 1867 in the Upper Austrian *Höllen-Gebirg*, where a herd of twenty hybrids and one pure-bred doe were turned out. Some years afterwards one doe was shot by mistake, and the remains of four others were subsequently found. In 1875, on the occasion of a great drive in these mountains, six of the animals, amongst them four young ones, were seen, but since then they have disappeared; but from what cause is still a mystery. Another attempt was made

in 1876 by the well-known sportsman-naturalist Prince
Pless, in a neighbouring chain of mountains, viz. the Salzburg
Tännen-Gebirg.   In this instance twenty ibex, procured
direct from the King of Italy's preserve, were turned out, and
the experiment has proved more of a success than the former.
One of the chief reasons why the increase has not been
more rapid is the circumstance that the young of these imported ibex are born too early in the spring, and consequently

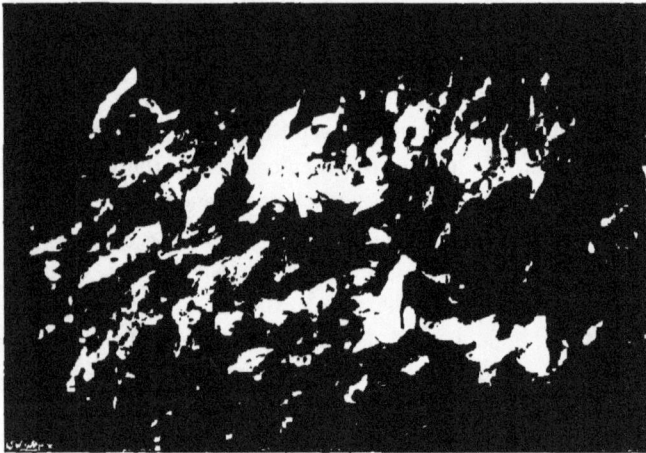

FIG. 16.—A band of Bouquetin (half-bred and three-quarter bred) in the
Salzburg Alps.
(Photographed from life by F. Grainer, Reichenhall, Bavaria.)

often succumb to the severity of the northern spring climate,
though, as has been said before, ibex as well as chamois once
inhabited these Salzburg mountains.

The instantaneous photograph of ibex here reproduced
was taken in their new home near Salzburg.

The chase of the bouquetin as conducted by Victor
Emanuel, and to a less ardent degree by his son, the present
king, did not partake of the hardships and dangers so inseparable from stalking, for these sportsmen confined them-

XVII.

THE LATE KING VICTOR EMANUEL BOUQUETIN-HUNTING IN THE MOUNTAINS
OF AOSTA. GETTING ACROSS AN AWKWARD PLACE.

selves almost exclusively to driving. Stone huts and lodges, primitive, it is true, for royal dwellings, but yet infinitely superior to caves, which in past times were the usual night-quarters of the hardy ibex stalker, gave shelter to the sportsmen and their few companions. Bridle-paths, passable for sure-footed mules and ponies, were constructed to the elevated scene of the day's *chasse*, and it is stated by good authorities that some 250 miles of these paths were made during the lifetime of Victor Emanuel. From 150 to 200 beaters, all picked mountaineers from Aosta and Cogne, circumvented the game by great detours, and finally forced it to pass certain well-known defiles, where the sportsmen lay in ambush behind screens of loosely heaped-up stones. Unlike the wary old buck chamois that frequent the uppermost fringe of vegetation, while the does inhabit the rocky barrens higher up on the mountains, the male ibex follows a contrary course, and is only found in the highest places, the females and young frequenting less elevated spots. With the latter, the older bucks only deign to associate during the mating season in November. For the reason stated, the king's ibex drives, which, of course, had for their object the bagging of old males, were confined to the highest ground, almost always at altitudes of over 10,000 feet. Great bags sometimes rewarded the efforts of beaters and keepers no less than the good marksmanship of their royal master. Thus the Rev. W. A. B. Coolidge, than whom few know the Piedmont Alps better, states that on one occasion he saw no less than twelve bouquetins and twenty-five chamois brought in as the spoils of the day.

For the burly, full-blooded royal sportsman the chase of the ibex was almost a matter of life and death, for the *Galantuomo's* full habit constantly caused his physicians the gravest anxiety; it was said by one of the latter that the bodily exercise he underwent in the two months—July and August—which he annually spent in his sportsman's paradise, added quite five years to his life. Be that as it may, sportsmen and naturalists owe a great debt to this royal *chasseur*. In the mountains over which he was master he was worshipped, his plain-spoken simple ways, his coarse home-spun shooting-dress, his unassuming *bonhomie* won him the love of his people to a degree not usually vouchsafed to royalty. Nothing pleased him more than to wander about *incognito*, chatting with every peasant he met, and some amusing stories were told of his adventures. Once, a peasant, seeing what he supposed to be one of the numerous staff of keepers, addressed to him a request to shoot a fox which was constantly raiding his hen-coop. "But what would the king say to that?" queried the *soi-disant* keeper. "Oh, he needn't know anything about it, and here are three lire to close your mouth," answered the peasant. The king forthwith pocketed the cash and shot the fox. Another time, when staying in strict *incognito* in the humble dwelling of the Courmayeur village priest, a peasant woman with some eggs in her basket came to offer them for sale. The king, standing in front of the cottage in his gray home-spun garb and battered Calabrese hat, was not recognised by the woman, who, after receiving her price for the eggs, said that as she had heard that the king was somewhere about, she would like to have a look at him. "He is standing before you," replied the former with a broad smile on his face. "Ah, you won't make me believe that," said the woman; "such a good and beautiful woman as is the queen would never go and marry such an ugly hairy man as you." [1]

The present King of Italy has, I believe, only shot in his ibex preserves two or three times since his accession eighteen years ago. The last of these occasions occurred, I believe,

---

[1] The Rev. Abbot Gorret, author of an interesting little work on the Alps of Aosta, relates these two incidents.

in August 1894. An account published in the Roman *Il Diritto* of 14th August 1894 may be worth quoting:—

"The king's headquarters for these ibex hunts is still the Campo del Re (the King's Camp), which is situated at a height of about 6600 feet, in the heart of the shooting, and is reached by means of an easy mule track, 6 feet wide, from the small town of Noasca, on the banks of the Orco, a tributary of the Po.

"This track, like all others in these mountains, was made by Victo Emanuel. As the difference in altitude between Noasca and Campo del Re is 3500 feet, the path zig-zags up the steep slopes in comparatively gentle gradients. The Campo consists of a small level grassy space not more than 50 by 50 yards in extent, and on it stand crowded together the king's shooting-lodge, stables, and the tents occupied by his suite and the keepers. The former is a very modest building of rough stone, containing five small rooms, hardly $7\frac{1}{2}$ feet high. The interior walls are all panelled with varnished larch wood, and while one of the rooms is used as a dining-room the rest are sleeping apartments. The roof consists of stone slabs, the only sort of covering which will withstand the fierce gales to which the building is often exposed. The members of the king's suite in attendance upon him on these occasions sleep, with the exception of two, who occupy rooms in the house, in tents erected immediately in front of the former.

"The king always rides his favourite horse, while the other sportsmen are mounted on mules, and, as tracks have been made (often at great expense) to the posts or stands occupied by the guns during the drives, there is practically very little climbing and hardship about this sport. The surroundings of the Campo are extremely wild and apparently inaccessible. Vegetation, excepting lichen and moss, there is none, so that the scenery has a barren and forbidding aspect, and the ice above, and towering rocks about one on all sides, increase this impression. The driving is done by some 300 beaters, all picked men, from the neighbouring valleys, who receive the princely pay of 10 frs. per day each. The runs or passes which the ibex take in their flight are of course known, for the nature of the ground, and the frequency of sheer precipices upon which even the surprisingly sure-footed ibex can find no foothold, forces it to take to the few existing passes in its gallant attempts to escape the ever-narrowing circle of beaters. The scene of the drives is invariably at considerable altitude, never less than 9000 feet, and as a rule over 10,000 feet; but of course the climbing is done by the beaters and keepers, and not by the guns. The details of the drives are arranged by Signor Valvassoni, upon whose shoulders rests the entire responsibility for success. This year six drives were made—the Bechi della Tribolazione, Deilvert, Treseta, Gioir, Montecastello, and Maon."

Bouquetin horns are highly valued trophies by Continental collectors, but many sham ones are about, Spanish and Caucasian heads being turned into bouquetin heads by skilful manipulation of the file and knife. Of late years, probably in consequence of a slightly relaxed watch upon the doings of poachers on the part of the present king's keepers (a staff of forty-five is, I believe, still kept up), genuine bouquetin heads are no longer quite so rare, but they still fetch very high prices.

What is, so far as I know, an unique instance of a malformed bouquetin head is shown in the accompanying sketch from a photograph which Dr. Girtanner kindly sent me recently, and concerning which he published some interesting details in the Swiss sporting paper *Diana*, which he has permitted me to make use of. This head was formerly in Dr. Girtanner's well-known collection, but it is now in the possession of an almost equally ardent Swiss collector, Colonel Challande.

Dr. Girtanner considers it is the head of a ten or twelve years' old male. The left horn is of perfectly normal shape, though rather less arched than usual, and having a length of 67 centimetres, or 26⅖ inches, with a circumference of 21 centimetres or 8¼ inches. The right horn, on the other hand, presents most abnormal features. Six centimetres, longer than the normal horn, the sharp curve sideways, which makes it such a remarkable head, begins at the base and causes the tip of the horn to reach a point some 8 inches in front of the animal's mouth, and only very slightly to the side of it. Thus seriously handicapped in its feeding, as well as in keeping its balance when fleeing along narrow ledges, it seems marvellous that the animal could have reached such mature age as is betrayed by the size of its horns.

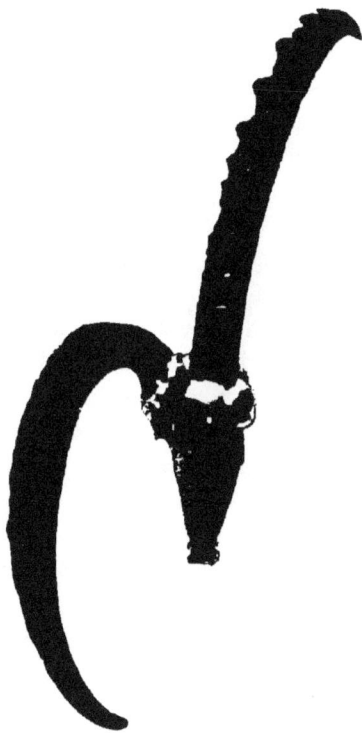

FIG. 17.—Very rare malformation of a Bouquetin horn.

The bone core of the malformed horn is considerably shorter than that of the other one, and according to Dr. Girtanner, there is no doubt that the process of malformation commenced when the animal was yet a kid. As the core is covered with a delicate periosteum, which is a mass

of blood-vessels, it becomes evident that the malformation
was not caused by any sudden violence, such as a blow from
a falling rock, but must have been brought about by some
persistent force, which bent the horn to one side at a period
of the animal's life when the core was still soft and yielding.
What force this could have been it is difficult to conjecture;
possibly the young kid got his horn jammed into a crevice of
a rock, where it may have remained fastened for some considerable time, the presence of the mother averting starvation. In
any event, it is a most curious instance, which in the case of
such a rare animal, is of all the more interest.

The Alpine ibex, it may be stated in conclusion, is a
distinct species, one of five to be found in the mountain
systems of Europe; three of these inhabit the snow-capped
peaks of the Caucasus, one the Spanish Alps, and the rarest
of all the Alps proper. Without examining into the chief
characteristics of these various ibex, a glance at the horns
they carry will not be without interest. The burrhel
(*Capra cylindricornis*) of the Caucasus has a smooth round horn
(resembling in this respect those of the burrhel of India)
which grow to an extreme length of 38½ inches, with an
extreme circumference of 12½ inches. The horns of the true
Caucasian ibex (*C. caucasica*) resemble much more those of
the bouquetin or Alpine representative; that is, they curve
back from the very start and are deeply notched, while
those of the first-mentioned kind turn out laterally before
they bend backwards, and have no indentations. The largest
known head of *C. caucasica* measures, according to Mr.
Rowland Ward, 40⅛ inches in length and 12⅝ inches in
circumference.

The third Caucasian species, *C. aegagrus*, is considerably
smaller in body than the two first-mentioned representatives,
and its horns are more of the common goat type, with a twist
and edged in front; extreme length 48¼ inches, circumference

8¾ inches. Throughout the Caucasus these three species are called indiscriminately *Tûr*, and the two first-mentioned kinds are often found in one and the same locality. ·

Of the Spanish ibex some good sportsmen, amongst them the late Sir Victor Brooke, contend that there are two species distinguished by the difference in size: those inhabiting the Pyrenees proper being much larger than those to be found in the Sierra Nevada and southern mountain systems; while others again maintain that no appreciable difference exists. Certain it is that heads obtained by the above-named authority in the Pyrenees exceed representative heads from the southern chains by many inches. The largest Spanish head, it may be mentioned, tapes 31 inches in length, 10 inches circumference, and 26½ inches sweep. As a good many Englishmen, particularly officers quartered at Gibraltar, penetrate into the otherwise very little known Sierras of Spain, the above dimensions, which are "record" ones, must be considered to be a good deal above the average. As showing that neither time, trouble, or money is spared by the English hunters when they are in quest of Spanish ibex, a competent authority states that, even to those men who are so comparatively close to the base of operations as is Gibraltar, each ibex killed by them stands them in,[1] at the lowest computation, £100.[2]

[1] Badminton, *Big Game*, vol. ii. p. 174.
[2] Since writing this chapter I learn that the Caucasian forests, in which Mr. Littledale found the aurochs in a wild and unprotected state, have now been placed by the Czar under the same strict protective supervision which saved the Bialowicza forest aurochs from extermination.

CHAPTER XV

To cross Europe from the Thames to the Neva, in order to
get a shot at a bear in the snows of Russia, or to travel a
couple of thousand miles to pick up a chamois on the
Tyrolese or Styrian peaks, or to have a crack at a stag in
the Hungarian primeval beech and oak forests, betrays a
devotion to the chase which most Englishmen will not only
understand, but show themselves possessed of, should a
chance present itself. Less intelligible to the uninitiated
will be the sport of capercaillie-shooting in the Continental
fashion. To hear of men travelling like distances, of their
seeking the depth of Alpine forests in the early spring, when
snow still mantles the slopes, of their rising in the middle
of the night to climb impending heights by the uncertain
light of a little oil lantern, of their chancing a broken leg
when scrambling in the dark through the forest, or a broken
neck when risking that *mauvais-pas* where the dim light
discloses an apparently fathomless gulf yawning at their side,
of their premeditatedly exposing themselves to all the ills
that flesh is heir to, by sitting under a dripping tree for an
hour, clammy with perspiration from the laborious ascent,
and drenched by the driving sleet, listening for the "call"
of their game and waiting, shivering with cold, for the first
streak of dawn, without the aid of which "ye game" would

remain invisible, of doing all this for the sake of taking a pot shot at a bird which in Scotland and Scandinavia is killed by the hundred and thousand, will appear to be an extraordinary expenditure, not to say waste, of time, trouble, and energy.

Very ancient as is the Continental manner of potting with rifle or gun the cock caper, as he sits on a branch of a tree busily engaged in warbling his guttural love-ditty, it is the outcome of natural conditions which must not be lost sight of when criticising the sport. For in the Alps the woods are dense, open moorlands are practically unknown, and the number of capercaillies and of black game to be found there is much too insignificant to permit the employment of the methods usual in Scotland. At the first blush both the manner of getting your shot, and the season of the year when you bag the cocks, seem unsportsmanlike, but it is really a species of *Jagd* which tests a man's love for sport as few others do, considering the insignificance of the reward which crowns success.

Let me make an attempt to describe the sport. The capercaillie, as well as the blackcock, with which the former shares to a certain extent the peculiar features which endow this sport with its chief charm, are shot on the Continent exclusively in the spring, during the latter part of the mating season. During this period the males of these two species exhibit the same bellicose chivalry and amorous excitement, which gives the skilled stalker the chance to approach, even in the densest forest, these otherwise extremely shy birds. Both birds, and I am speaking only of the males, for the hens are never shot, exhibit apparently absolute deafness and blindness during the paroxysms of excitement which seem to take possession of them when they emit their love-song. During the three or four seconds, which is the duration of the capercaillie's chief note, a shot can be fired a few yards

off without putting the cock to flight; but the instant it is
over, the extremely keen sight and hearing powers of the
bird come again into full play, and one has to remain perfectly immovable or the bird sees one from his high perch,
be the cover ever so dense and dawn of day as yet betokened by naught else than the faintest streak of pink on
the horizon.

The term "stalking" can very well be applied to the
mode of approach as practised on the Continent, and to be
better able to appreciate the difficulties that encompass this
sport the following details must be premised. The song or
call of the capercaillie consists at first of a preliminary series
of guttural sounds, which might be likened to the drawing
of a cork, and which are produced in some unknown manner
by the tongue or by the muscles of the larynx, for the beak
is at the time open. After sounding a number of these
preliminary *Schnalzer*, as the Germans term these guttural
smacks, the interval between each note becomes gradually
shorter and shorter, till finally they are blended into one
connected sound called the *Triller*. It terminates with a
loud clack, a welcome signal for the stalker, for it is immediately followed by the anxiously awaited *Schleifer* or
" whetter," during which the bird is insensible to sound or
sight. It is a perfectly different note from the first, but
equally difficult to describe. To give some sort of indication
as to its character, one might liken it to the whetting of a
long knife on the blade of a scythe, and it lasts usually only
two, and never over four seconds. How it is produced is still
unknown, though it has busied many scientific minds, and
numerous theories endeavouring to account for it can be
found in scores of books devoted to the sport, which have
appeared since the act of printing was discovered. That it
is produced by a violent muscular exertion is clearly shown
by putting one's hand on the trunk of the tree upon the

upper branches of which the bird is perched, for if the tree
is a small one, one can plainly feel the vibration produced
by it. When the cock makes this whetting sound his head
is thrust forward and upward, the neck feathers are ruffed
and display their peculiar shimmer, the wings are slightly
extended but droop, and the great tail-feathers are extended
fan-shape. Many authorities maintain that the blindness
and deafness of the capercaillie and blackcock during these
ecstatic moments are only apparent, and that the birds, as
numbers of experiments with semi-tame specimens have
shown, see and hear perfectly well, but simply do not take
heed of it. However this may be, it is certain that many a
bad shot has fired two and three times at the same bird
without disturbing him, always provided, of course, that the
former has remained perfectly motionless during the intervals
between each " whetter," and that the shots were fired at
the right moment.

The mating time of the capercaillie varies somewhat
according to the season; in an early spring it occurs sooner
than in a backward one, and in the Alps, where snowstorms
and frost in April are regular visitors, it is several weeks
later than in the hills of Bohemia and Central Europe, where
it begins in the latter half of March. In order to secure
perpetuation of the breed, the cocks should never be shot in
the first fortnight of the mating season. By that time the
various cocks in the preserve have been spotted by the
keepers, or, if one is shooting over unpreserved ground, one
has had time to do this spotting oneself. Unlike the blackcock, who, if not disturbed, invariably returns morning after
morning to the same *Balz-platz* or mating place, the
capercaillie, while keeping to one and the same district, is
less methodical, and the trees on which he perches on two
consecutive mornings may be 100 or more yards apart. It
is this peculiarity which obliges the stalker to reach the

neighbourhood of the mating place before the first sign of
day. There he sits down, puts out his lantern, and listens for
the first note, which a trained and acute ear can hear at a
distance of 500 or 600 yards.

If the cock proclaims his presence some distance off, the
little lantern, which, in the absence of bright moonlight, has
guided the stalker thus far, is relit, and by the aid of its
feeble rays the place where the cock is perched is approached
to within some 100 or 150 yards, when the light is again put
out, and the patience-trying watch for dawn is resumed. As
darkness gradually gives way to light, and one at last begins
to see the tops of the firs or pines more clearly silhouetted
against the sky, and the nebulous outline of the serrated
mountain chain opposite one becomes from minute to minute
more clearly defined, it is time to commence that supremely
exciting last approach—*Anspringen* the Continental sportsmen call it, from the series of leaps of which it consists.
Plainly one hears the cock's preliminary "cork-drawings,"
quite as plainly as one hears in that utter silence the beat
of one's heart; but there, had I not better let incidents and
events speak for themselves, and tell their own tale of what
to many a good sportsman is the keenest sport there is to
be had in the glens and forests of the Alps ?

" Will you shoot three or four capercaillie and some blackcock in the Scharnitz ?   I am unfortunately laid up with
rheumatism.   Eleven capercaillie are spotted (*verhört*)," ran
the telegram from the hospitable owner of a well-known preserve in North Tyrol.   Three or four capercaillie, and some
blackcock thrown in, is an offer which to many a Continental
sportsman sounds as attractive as would an invitation to
shoot half a dozen stags to a "dour" Scotchman pining in
dusty London.   From the Emperor of Austria or his heir,
who, by the way, shot fifty capercaillie last season in this
manner, down to the peasant youth who night after night

sacrifices sleep in his endeavours to spot the wily bird in the wild maze of his native forest, the *Auerhahn-balz* has keen votaries. No wonder, therefore, that forty-eight hours after the receipt of the aforementioned telegram, the express and a light country carriage had taken me to the little mountain-enclosed hamlet of Scharnitz, just awakening from its long winter's sleep.

As I descended at the door of the village inn, the well-known faces of my host's sturdy keepers greeted me. The inn was to be my headquarters, for the shooting lodge, situated in the heart of the chamois ground, where the dense forests, beloved by the capercaillie during the mating season, no longer thrive, is less suitable and too remote for this purpose. A very fine April had cleared the snow from the fields, and even the lower parts of the steep slopes of the great peaks, rising precipitously from the very back doors of the quaintly-gabled peasants' houses, had been free of it for a week or two. Now they were, however, mantled with fresh fallen snow, for I arrived in the midst of a snowstorm, that made the long drive in the open country carriage a somewhat marrow-chilling affair. What effect this sudden return of winter had upon oneself was not such an important question as the one I hastened to put to the keepers, " Will it prevent the capercaillie balz ? " To stalk a single bird in the depth of those vast upland forests in a driving snowstorm seemed as hopeless as to expect that even the hardiest bird would be warbling its love-carols with the mercury down to freezing-point, and a gale blowing so fiercely as to oblige me to tie my hat down with a handkerchief. " Oh, the capercaillie, don't mind it," came the answer, "but the hitch comes in when listening for the call; one can't hear it 10 yards off." Having had my share of snowstorms in the winters passed on the wind-swept uplands of the Rocky Mountains, where Alpine snowstorms could learn a trick or two, and still be

only considered a bit of a flurry, this quarter-fledged storm
would not have kept me indoors had it done its worst. As
it was, its fury was expended before I turned in, which I did
at an early hour, for it was a case of getting up at an hour
when men in town usually do the other thing. I was to be
called soon after midnight.

Heiss, the keeper who was to accompany me the first
morning to the trysting-place of a veteran cock, upon whom
he had had his eye from the very beginning of the mating
season, was pounding at my door most punctually; and, what
was more, he did not stop doing so till he heard me splashing
in my indiarubber travelling bath, for no doubt experience
had taught him that a drowsy man's murmured response
cannot always be depended on.

By the time some tea brewed by the attentive *Wirthin*,
who had not gone to bed, and a light breakfast had been
partaken of, the *Nachtwächter*, or village night-watchman,
was droning out in quaint rhymes, while pursuing his round
through the primitive village, the fact that it was one o'clock.
Considering that a disastrous fire had a short time before
destroyed the church, and with it the bells and the sole
public timepiece in the village, his services were decidedly of
use, as the inhabitants now depended upon him to rouse
them from their slumbers, which formerly the five o'clock
matin bell had done.

Leaving the village by the one road that leads to it, and
which soon enters timber, as it rises in zig-zags towards
the pass, across which I had driven the day before, we presently struck out into the woods, taking a short cut through
the forest towards a wooded height, close to the top of which
the capercaillie was holding his matutinal love-court. It was
a dismal morning; the clouds hung so low that it seemed as
if one could reach them with the *Bergstock*. Snow, if not
actually coming down, was, at any rate, in the air; and the

dim little oil lantern, swaying to and fro in the hands of
Heiss, who led the way, was a somewhat uncertain guide in
the intense darkness of the night. Before beginning the
actual ascent we passed a fenced-in field, in one corner of
which a small open fire was burning, over which a wretchedly-
clad old man was endeavouring to warm himself. It was one
of the half-dozen " deer scarers " whose duty it is to frighten
away the red-deer, which abound in the neighbouring forests,
from the few precious wheat-fields, which afford the Schar-
nitzers a precarious living. As the corn was just springing
up, these deer scarers, who are paid by the owner of the
preserve, had that night commenced their duties. So daring
do the deer get, that the sight of fire and the shouts of the
men often fail to have the desired effect, and the latter have
to fire blank shots to drive them away. To the fact that
the guard did not notice us as we passed, and that he presently fired a shot of this kind, the old capercaillie on whose
slaughter we were bent, owed his life that morning. But
I am anticipating. The ascent did not take us very long,
and when we reached our destination it was not yet three
o'clock. Our goal was a large fir tree, the like of which
there were hundreds and hundreds to our right, to our left,
behind us, and in front of us ; but a small freshly-cut blaze
on the trunk, on to which Heiss turned the light of his
lantern, proved that his bump of locality was not of a mean
order, for to be able to walk straight up to a given tree in
a wild waste of pathless and in most places dense forest,
without once hesitating or losing the direction during the
two hours' tramp on a pitch-dark night, was evidence of
masterly woodcraft, which reminded one of not unsimilar
feats performed by American red-skins.

" We are not far from the cock," whispered Heiss, as he
blew out the lantern ; for possibly the capercaillie might be
even closer than one liked, and be frightened away by a

gleam of light, mild as its power to penetrate the pitchy darkness seemed to be.

"The day before yesterday I sat here and listened to the cock for nearly two hours, but it won't be light quite so soon to-day," continued my companion, and I had no reason to contradict him; for, as yet, there wasn't the slightest sign of dawn, and his voice, though he was sitting quite close to me, seemed to come out of the darkness. I have passed more comfortable half-hours than the one that ensued, sitting under that dripping fir—for it had commenced to drizzle— and absorbing an astonishing amount of dampness from the soft bed of soaking moss which the darkness had kindly helped me to select as a seat. Dawn came very gradually, the outlines of trees became slowly more and more defined, and one began to see the rain-drops instead of only feeling them, when suddenly Heiss's gigantic paw gripped me like a vice by the arm, and the words, "Do you hear him?" were hissed into my ear. But, alas! a useless left ear, and an impaired right one, obliged me, as I foretold Heiss, to confess that I heard absolutely nothing, and that I wouldn't hear anything till I got close up to the bird, whose faint love-notes for the master-bird of the forest are so ludicrously low. From that moment Heiss's grip on my arm hardly relaxed for an instant. Far more excited than I was, his honour was at stake to get his *Herr* up to that cock; and, had I been a lay figure, I am sure he would have succeeded in planting me in good time, cocked gun in hand, opposite that bird. Fortunately Heiss and I were old acquaintances, and many a good chamois had I stalked with him at my side, or his contempt would have been untinged by pity at having to pilot me in this fashion to a point not more than 80 or 100 yards from the cock. Jumping when he jumped, standing still when he stood, a quarter of an hour saw us within that distance from the bird. There, at last, those well-known notes first became audible to me, and Heiss's iron grip could be shaken off to allow me to make the last *ansprung* by myself.

The two long or three short steps or leaps which one has time to make while the bird gives forth the "whetter" do not help to bring one quickly to the tree upon which the bird is perched, if the cock is not singing briskly, which he only does during the height of the mating season, and when deeming himself quite secure. On this morning, though it was the height, the icy-cold drizzle, no doubt, cooled the cock's ardour, for there were tantalisingly long intervals between the "whetters," during which the position one was in when that note terminated had to be retained, however uncomfortable it might be. Actually painful it becomes if one is obliged to kneel for ten minutes on a sharp stone, or has to keep the outstretched leg or arm in the same position for even three minutes. Never before has one discovered how difficult it is to balance oneself on one leg, or how quickly a 7 lb. gun held out at arm's length assumes the weight, first of hundredweights, then of tons, till finally the muscles of the arm refuse to stand the strain any longer, when, just at the last moment, the notes quicken again, and the longed-for signal strikes one's ear.

"Take your time, sir; it's too dark as yet to shoot," says Heiss, who is some paces behind me, during one of the "whetters"; and dark it certainly still seems. When the next "whetter" comes, I put up my gun to see whether a shot could be hazarded, but I cannot see the end of the barrels. The cock is still invisible; he seems to occupy the top of a fir of medium height, standing in the centre of several smaller trees. Perhaps it is just as well to wait five or ten minutes more, for, though it does not take much aiming to pot a bird the size of a turkey at 30 yards or less, it is just as well to have sufficient light to make sure that the dark lump one is shooting at is really the bird, and

19

not one of those shapes of interlaced branches which in the
uncertain light of early dawn are only too often taken for
the cock. Few sportsmen who have shot capercaillie have
not on some occasion or other been misled, though it need
not necessarily spoil the sport, so long as the shot is fired
during a "whetter."   A very few minutes more and that
capercaillie would have had some No. 3 whistling round him,
for I was getting ready to make the last approach to a spot
where I felt sure he would be visible, when bang went a loud
report.   Coming from the field at the base of the hill, the
echo went rolling and thundering from mountain to mountain.
With a whirr of wings, and just one instant's view of him
against the horizon, the capercaillie betook himself to other
regions.   Poor Heiss was more inconsolable than I was, for
these men take inordinate pride in the success of their master
or his guest, and he knew that next morning another keeper
would be my pilot.   With strides it was difficult to keep up
with, Heiss rushed off in the direction the cock had taken,
stopping from time to time, and straining his ears for renewed
love-notes.   But it was quite useless, and, though we kept
up the search till full daylight, when it would have been
almost impossible to approach the wary bird, it had quickly
taken itself off to safer regions.   Work in the fields, and
among the ruins of the fire in the village, was already in full
swing by the time we got back to the inn, Heiss the more
crestfallen of the two, for to return with a clean gun from
the *Auerhahn-balz*, however good the excuses may be, does
not redound to the skill of the keeper.

The next morning David, the head-keeper, was my cice-
rone, and, as we had not so far to go, the start was a trifle
later.   Our goal was an eminence in plain sight of the
village, and, the weather having cleared, the stars were
shining brightly when we turned out, and an hour's walk
—there was no climbing to speak of—brought us to a fine

beech wood, with some firs interspersed here and there. The manœuvres of the previous morning were again repeated, and the cock's notes heard by my companion a quarter of an hour before they became audible to me. This time there was no " scare " shot, as the men had been ordered to discontinue shooting, and, with pleasant-spoken and keen David first at my side, then behind me, I got within 40 yards of as fine an old cock as I have ever had the luck to bring down. With the flash of the 12-bore, the heavy bird came crashing down through the branches, striking the ground with a thud.

It was quite an old fellow, the feathers on the underside of the fan of his tail being almost black, younger cocks having them more or less tipped with white. It was twenty minutes to four when I shot, the light being still far too dim to use the rifle, which, if one has the chance, it is thought more sportsmanlike to use. The arm ordinarily carried for the *Auerhahn-balz* is the combination rifle-gun which one frequently sees in Germany and Austria.

Our next morning's stalk took us to a particularly fine bit of forest high up on the flanks of a great peak, where two cocks had been spotted in close proximity to each other. It was a lovely night for our walk, through what one might almost call primeval forest. When the lantern was finally put out on reaching a knoll which commanded a large stretch of wooded slope, dawn unfolded a superb panorama before one's eyes. We overlooked a great basin surrounded by wildly serrated, absolutely verdureless peaks of the boldest shape. Always of an ashy hue, these formidable mountains assumed, in the gray of early dawn, a yet more ghostly tint, while the utter silence of sleeping nature only added to the impressiveness of the picture. With the increasing light, the details of the mountains became gradually visible, and well-known spots, which failure or success in chamois-stalking in past years had impressed upon one's memory, were, of course, those looked for and recognised first. That *arête* yonder where an October snowstorm had once made a certain stalk very nearly the last I was to enjoy ; that chimney where a band of chamois above had peppered me with stones of decidedly unpleasant size, as the animals clambered out of sight and range of the sportsman crouching under the insufficient shelter of a projecting ledge; that great precipice where the trophy that was to reward an arduous stalk came to grief as the beast tumbled over the brink to be dashed to pieces at the bottom, these and other well-remembered and boldly-outlined localities became dimly visible.   But David has already heard the cock, and is dragging one away back into the dusky forest of giant trees.   And now his ear has caught the notes of the second cock, and as only one is to be shot in that neighbourhood, so as not to thin them out unduly, his ear strives to decide which of the two birds is the old one—the cock which, as he says, has sung to his knowledge in that locality for the last three years.   But to thus distinguish a five or six-year-old cock from a two or three-year-old one is mere guesswork, and, as it happens, the veteran's life is saved that morning at the expense of his rival's, who turns out to be a young bird of fine plumage. He comes flopping down from a fairly high fir, on the very top of which he had been greeting dawn.   I got a good view of him against the gray sky, and so far as shooting was concerned, it was only a matter of pulling the trigger. As it happened I timed my shot well, for the other cock, not more than 300 yards off, was cheerfully continuing his love ditties, and, after getting the direction from David, I stalked up to his tree.   It was a low fir, and the cock was perched on one of the upper branches.   Circling round the tree, so as to approach him from the back, and always waiting for the " whetter " before I moved, I managed to get to the base of the tree, put my hand on the trunk, and assure myself of the vibration I have previously alluded to. Not often is one able to get so close to a "singing" capercaillie. After watching him for some time, I flung a pine cone at him, and though it hit him it had no instantaneous effect. He flew off, however, a second or two later, when the note was finished; but, as I made a slight movement with my arm, it may have been that and not the missile which caused him to do so.

The next morning similar good luck rewarded an early turn-out and a sharpish climb to the top of a ridge of most precipitous formation overlooking Scharnitz. It was, in fact, so steep that one wondered, when daylight disclosed one's position on the top, how on earth one had got up by the light of that miserable lantern; but, as a matter of fact, a light illuminating only a very confined circle is on such occasions better than a very bright one—a good guide, knowing every step and every crevice, being, of course, a *sine quâ non*.

Where the mountain-side we were on was not absolutely a precipice, small ledges gave a scanty holding-ground to scattering groves of larch trees of medium size, and as the whole slope faced the south, it was a favourite *Balz-platz*. Two cocks were here also delighting, in close proximity to each other, their respective circles of hens, and many a fierce battle had probably been fought on that elevated cock-pit to decide the mastership of the mountain-side. On this occasion the stalk was not of the easiest, for rolling stones and the precipitous nature of the ground threatened to make it almost impossible to get near the bird in the dark with the necessary noiselessness. However, by taking things slowly, and looking well ahead for a safe spot whereon to land on making the two leaps or strides, I managed to succeed. As it was quite impossible to approach the cock so as to bring him in outline against the sky, I had to shoot at a dark spot only dimly visible against the sombre background of the mountain-side, without being able to make sure first that the line of fire was free from intervening branches. This nearly lost me the cock, for, as it appeared, his body was protected by a number of twigs, which broke the force of the shot so considerably that the bird, instead of coming down with a thud, fluttered to the ground in a slanting direction, which, as we were standing on an incline as steep as a church spire, caused him to land at an invisible spot below us on the slope. The way David darted down that precipice after the wounded bird was a thing to see and admire, and though, of course, he was almost at once lost to my view in the gloom, the avalanche of stones that rattled after him proved his speed and the steepness of the angle. He reached the bird none too soon, for it was already on its legs running off, and no doubt would have shared the fate of most winged capercaillie who elude the sportsman, only to fall victims to the nearest fox. It was a fine three-year-old cock, and he must have been ensconced in a bower of branches, for eight or nine twigs lay under the tree, as we found when it got lighter. The second cock, undisturbed by the shot and the noise of David's pursuit, was singing quite complacently a short distance off, but his approach, in consequence of the advanced hour and the difficult nature of the ground, was not so easy. The incidents of these three stalks will give the reader some idea of capercaillie shooting; only actual experience can really prove its attraction.

Blackcock-shooting in the Alps is harder sport than capercaillie-shooting, which it resembles in many respects, for their *Balz-plätze* are higher up on the mountains. In fact one has generally to ascend some 3000 or 4000 feet, right up to timber-line, near which are to be found the isolated trees which generally mark the trysting-place. At the base of these, the love-sick cocks dance and strut about and fight in the diverting manner which has been so often described. In one respect the sport is different from capercaillie-shooting; for while the capercaillie, in consequence of having no fixed *Balz-platz*, has to be searched for by the sportsman, the blackcock frequents day after day one and the same trysting-place, near which the sportsman has to be secreted before the cocks arrive, which they do at the first streak of dawn. The mating season, which occurs at the same season of the year as the capercaillie's, is subject to the same slight variations according to the earliness or lateness of spring, the last week of April and the first week of May marking in ordinary years its height. There are said to be really two kinds of blackcocks, those that frequent the moors and hills of Germany and Scandinavia, with which the Scotch bird is probably identical, and the true Alpine blackcock which frequents only higher mountains. The latter is a somewhat larger bird, with much finer plumage. Never having shot them anywhere else but in the Alps, I can compare only dead birds, and certainly the mountain cock's characteristic tail feathers are much finer than those of the Scandinavian or Scotch birds.

To get to the *Balz-platz* is the only hard part of the sport, for in the regions I am referring to, snow, often to a considerable depth, still mantles the slopes, particularly those facing the north. And what is the worst, it is then of that rotten consistency which makes climbing steep slopes covered with a couple or three feet of it, one of the most tiring jobs I know. The spell of warm weather, coupled with a week of the hot *Frohn* wind, which, down below in the valley, has ushered in spring, has up here near timberline, first made it soft and slushy at the top, while the night's frost has coated it with a thin crust of ice. This, too thin to bear one's full weight, gives way under one in the most tantalising manner, and in spite of the round snow-hoops, one sinks down in the soft underlying mass to or beyond the knee. Every step up the interminable slope is a sore trial, and a couple of hours of this kind of work puts one literally in a lather. So much so, that on more than one occasion I can remember that my heavy frieze coat was wet through with perspiration about the shoulders. As I had to sit for an hour or two exposed to the icy wind of dawn, the coat froze on my body to board-like stiffness.

Desperately cold work is this sitting in a hastily constructed screen of pine boughs, or behind a handy *Latchen* bush, waiting for the first gray of morning to light up those cold-looking, ghost-like peaks around one, and extremely foolish does the whole proceeding seem. But the first rush of wings that tells one a cock has come to the tryst, though it is still too dark to see the bird, dispels all faint-hearted regrets. From that moment ears and eyes are on the *qui vive*. Now another rush of wings, then a low cluck, cluck, followed by sharp angry clucking as the two cocks meet in the first joust of the morning. Presently one discerns the birds against the white background of the snow. What strange manœuvres, what ridiculous poses! Now approaching each other with outstretched necks and trailing wings, creeping towards each other in a ludicrously would-be-stealthy manner, then jumping into the air a foot or two, clucking and gobbling most wrathfully, and then clinching in a rough-and-tumble beak-to-beak fight, which ends in the discomfiture of the weaker, who speedily betakes himself to other pastures, leaving the victor master of the field, and of the three or four hens that have been watching the combat in close proximity. Soon it is light enough to shoot, and if you have luck you can bring down two cocks with the one shot.

A very much rarer bird than either the capercaillie or the blackcock is the *Rackelhahn*, concerning the identity of which much has been written and argued. This bird (*Tetrao medius*) is supposed by the best authorities to be a cross of the two first-named species, and in the rare instances of hybrids mating, young *Rackelhahne* are the offspring. In the Alps they are very rare, and the bagging of one is a memorable event. In size this bird is a medium between its parents, and its habits during the mating season partake of the same duality. The cock bird chiefly affects the *Balzplätze* of the smaller blackcock, where it easily beats off its weaker rivals—a trait to which other species are not strangers.

CHAPTER XVI

LOOKING back to the Sixties and the beginning of the
Seventies, when one was still a firm believer in the superiority of muzzle-loading rifles over any breechloader then
made, one remembers what an unpleasantly conspicuous *rôle*
miss-fires used to play. In the Alps, more than anywhere
else, they were the bugbear of the stalker, and what was
the worst no precaution could prevent these mishaps. One
would not like to say how many good heads were lost, how
many arduous stalks were successless, how many long days
over the roughest chamois ground were abortive, simply in
consequence of miss-fires. Sleeping in damp hay, stalking
across mountain slopes, where one had to traverse patches
of *Latchen*, from which one emerged in a dripping condition, were incidents of Alpine sport which brought them
about. But, on the other hand, what capital shooting, of
course, only at ranges which to-day would be considered
pop-gun distances, could not be made with those selfsame
old muzzle-loaders. Without the slightest desire to put
myself forward as anything more than a moderately good
rifle shot, I can honestly say that in those days, when the
rifle chose to go off, I rarely missed, and my average (not
taking "finishing shots" into account) was for whole seasons

but little above the number of shots fired. Of my two favourite muzzle-loading rifles, one was a double barrel, the other an old-fashioned single barrel made by Leithner, a once famous Ischl riflemaker, who for years made the Emperor of Austria's weapons—the latter invariably shoots to this day with a single barrel. Hanging on my gun-rack alongside of some Express rifles by Holland and others, it is an odd-looking fire-iron. But in its day it somehow did better work at ordinary ranges than one has since got out of the beautifully finished, far better balanced, and far more service-able modern rifles. One reason of this is, I think, the fact, that one used to aim far more carefully with the muzzle-loader, than one does with an arm with which one can fire ten or more shots within the time it took to reload the former.

I remember well when, now close upon a quarter of a century ago, I was for the first time invited by the late Duke of Coburg to take part at the chamois drives in the Hinter-Riss. I arrived at the rendezvous with my old-fashioned single barrel, and soon saw that the other guests, chiefly Prussians, were all armed with Lefaucheux, or other breech-loaders, by Continental makers. A smile of conscious superiority mantled some of the faces when they saw the long-barrelled, ill-balanced, short-stocked old muzzle-loader I was carrying. To stand their mild chaff was, however, easier than they perhaps realised, for as a rule North Germans do not impress one by their exterior or by their speech as fitted to pose as your dare-devil chamois hunters, so that I was not uneasy as to the result in the end.

It was even better than I anticipated, and long before the fortnight's shoot was over, that venerable muzzle-loader was looked at with admiring deference, and handled with awe, for in the first week it had rolled over six good bucks with seven shots—all easy ones, though one buck took two

bullets to finish him—and no miss. While the joint bag of
those three Prussians was—well, perhaps I had better not
disclose the secret, but simply content myself by saying that
the rapidity with which those three men scared chamois was
something that did more credit to the quality they had
previously insisted upon as by far the most useful in rifles,
viz. quickness of fire, than to their accuracy.

But on that occasion I saw shooting of a very different
character by a breechloading rifle in the hands of my host.
It was a double Henry, and the like of it for accuracy I have
yet to discover. It caused me to change my opinion about
breechloading rifles, and the old friends were henceforth
relegated to idleness. But not without pangs of regret on
many a subsequent occasion, when hasty shooting and that
instinctive reliance on the rapidity of fire was the cause of
more or less shameful misses, which, I felt sure, would not
have been misses had I had that awkward old blunderbuss
in my hand, and had taken aim with that "make-sure"
feeling which is at the bottom of good shooting at reasonable
distances.

The men that participate at chamois drives are often
execrable shots, and considering that, with the sole exception
of very cold weather, causing the sportsman to shake and
tremble with cold, there is no legitimate excuse for missing
such easy shots as are the rule, one feels surprised at their
being not more ashamed of it than they are. But in nine
out of ten cases it is the old story : hasty shooting in consequence of having a breechloader in their hands. In
chamois-stalking the long-range shooting qualities of the
new arm becomes a frequent cause of misses, for the novice
only too often will insist on opening fire at 200 yards or more
when another ten or fifteen minutes' "creeping-up" would
bring him to a point 60 or 70 yards nearer, from where
the shot would have been more of a certainty. At all

distances over 200 yards the chamois is a small mark, and to hit it in a vital spot, if the animal does not stand broadside on, takes steady shooting and fine sights, even if the rifle be the truest shooting-iron ever turned out.

Another thing that has struck me more than once is the carelessness of sportsmen, who, though they have come great distances, and have taken a lot of trouble to participate at a chamois shoot, have nevertheless only the haziest notions of the shooting qualities of their rifles. Not long ago a Britisher came out from England to shoot chamois in a Tyrolese preserve. He brought a brand new small-bore rifle which he had never fired. Thus equipped he went after the shyest game in Europe! The same thing I have noticed in the case of English sportsmen visiting the Rockies, taking out rifles and ammunition galore. As representatives of their country they by no means always do credit to it as shots, even if the mishap which I know happened to one British outfit, of having their cases filled with the wrong cartridges, is not of frequent occurrence. But it is high time for me to come to the practical bearing of these remarks : What rifle is the best for chamois and deer stalking in the Alps ? To answer this question properly, a distinction must be drawn between the two. For chamois-stalking, which, so far as the actual shooting is concerned, resembles Highland deer-stalking, the rifle that is the best for the one will also be the best for the other. For deer - stalking in the Alps, particularly in Hungary, a more powerful rifle is called for, and a ·500 Express will not be found too heavy an arm. For those giants take a lot of lead to grass them, and as it is very often impossible in those dense woods to place the bullet where it should be put, you want something that will produce the most copious flow of blood. No end of good stags are annually lost in Hungary on account of the great difficulty in tracking wounded animals. Moreover, the range of nine out of ten shots is not over a hundred or at the most 150 yards, for the simple reason that you rarely can see farther in an Hungarian forest.

As for the best rifle for chamois-stalking I would prefer, in offering advice, to strictly confine myself to the outcome of my own personal experience. Did the latter embrace also the new small-bores, such as the Austrian and the Roumanian pattern of the Mannlicher rifle, I daresay I would also have become a convert to their advantages, as so many others whom I know as good judges, have become. As it is, I have for some years past stuck to ·400 and ·450 single Expresses. They are built as light as possible, rather under than over 7 lbs. The one shoots the ordinary hollow Express bullet, the other a solid one. The former I use when stalking, the other at chamois drives, where there is plenty of assistance in the shape of keepers, and generally also a bloodhound to track cripples. On such occasions it is therefore unnecessary to risk inflicting, as one now and again cannot help doing, such ghastly wounds as are caused by Express bullets at short range, when placed back of the ribs.

Formerly I used also for chamois a double barrel ·500 Express, which I carried on many of my expeditions to the Rocky Mountains, the one barrel shooting solid, the other hollow bullets, but this arm I discarded on account of its weight, for as years go by every extra ounce more and more tells its tale at the end of a long day on the rocks. That the new small-bores, with their splendid trajectories, have a great future before them, and that doubtlessly a man starting for his first chamois stalk could not possibly do better than commence with a Roumanian Mannlicher, restocked by an English gunmaker to suit his reach, are facts beyond dispute. Sir Edmund Loder, one of the best game rifle shots in Great Britain, who, as a prominent member of the English Eight, takes an absorbing scientific interest in all matters concerning rifles, and to whose opinion I would therefore give the greatest weight, used the latter rifle exclusively last season in the two months he spent in his Styrian chamois preserve, and with results that satisfied him. He quotes to me, as I am writing these lines, the opinion of another first-rate game rifle shot just returned from Central Asia, who writes: " The Mannlicher turned out not only a trump, but an ace of trumps. It is simply deadly. I don't believe that one animal in five moved its own length after being hit, and it doubled up yak just as easily as ravine deer. Given a good light, distance is no object; I never latterly attempted to get within 250 yards; there was no use."[1] Of course the tip of the Mannlicher bullet must, for sporting purposes, be filed off, to expose the lead. But great care must be taken not to take too much off, as there is danger of the lead cone being driven through the steel and nickel mantle.

I must still touch upon one important advantage possessed by the small-bores which use the new explosives, viz. their comparatively noiseless report. This is a vast advantage in ground where towering rocks throw the sound great distances. Last year I had a practical illustration of this circumstance, which may be worth repeating. Sir Edmund Loder, who was using his Roumanian Mannlicher, was stalking chamois in a side ravine in the S—— shoot in Styria, while I was stalking (with my Express) in the side gorge that branched from the main valley right opposite the one in which he was giving the chamois a taste of his long-range shooting. While his shots were just faintly audible to me, and failed to disturb in the very slightest a buck I had at the moment under close scrutiny, my shot, that soon afterwards went roaring and rumbling through the glen, had its echo thrown with such

[1] After writing above I see in the March number of Baily's that Mr. Fremantle, in the concluding remarks of his most interesting series of "Notes on the Rifle," quotes in very similar terms Mr. St. George Littledale's high commendation of the Austrian ·256 Mannlicher.

force into the opposite ravine, that some chamois my friend
was watching at once moved off, though the air-line distance
must have been quite two miles. On other occasions, Sir
Edmund told me that chamois, not more than 1000 yards
from the spot where he fired his Mannlicher, were so little
disturbed by the report, that after raising their heads and
looking about for a few minutes, they went on feeding, and
never moved from the spot.

Another advantage is the smokelessness of these new
explosives, particularly in damp weather when one is posted
(at drives) in sheltered ravines where black powder smoke
hangs about an unconscionable time.

On the other hand, to be fair to both weapons, these
small-bores are in my humble opinion not such "sporting-
feeling" rifles. They are neither so well balanced nor so
handy for quick snapshots as one's old friend the Express,
and whenever I have handled a Mannlicher, it has seemed
to me to be essentially a military rifle, the breech arrangement giving it a great resemblance to the old-fashioned
Prussian *Zündnadel* rifle that seems out of place in other
hands than those of a stiff *Soldat* with the hideous spiked
Pickelhaube on his head! But these are, of course, very
stupid prejudices, and were one's fingers not so accustomed
to the old-fashioned hammer, and one's shooting not so
dependent upon the beautiful balance and ready "come-up"
of the Express, I am very sure one could not do better than
take to the new arms as speedily as possible.

For fine shooting at long range a peep-sight has, in the
opinion of those who do not habitually use the Lyman sight,
decided advantages. A little invention of mine, by which the
speedy and accurate adjustment of this peep-sight is attained,
may be worth a word or two of description. It consists of a
disc the size of a threepenny bit, in the centre of which is
the peep-hole. The disc is on a stem which moves on a

hinge, and when not needed the whole sight disappears by lying flat in a recess cut in the metal of the stock behind the hammers. A spring, released by a little knob the size of No. 3 shot, sends the sight into position ready for instantaneous use, while, when not needed, nothing but the tiny knob is visible. Messrs. Holland and Holland have put this sight on some of my Expresses, but, of course, it can only be put on hammer rifles not having the "top-snap" action.

A few more hints and I have finished this disquisition upon matters concerning which my counsel will, I fear, be considered somewhat behind the times. One bit of advice is to always carry the rifle oneself when one has once reached the ground inhabited by the game one seeks. For when stalking in anything like a decent preserve quick shooting is often necessary, for now and again one comes upon game in the most unexpected places. Topping the most insignificant ridge, or turning the corner of a mountain-shoulder, may suddenly bring one right on to it, for the *mise-en-scène* in the Alps is very different from that of Highland stalking, where one generally sees one's stag half an hour or more before one fires, and there is plenty of time for the gillie to take the rifle out of its case and hand it to one. In the Alps it rains much less, so that the rifle-case is only a useless encumbrance, preventing one from carrying it in the only way in which the shortest experience in the Alps will show you the rifle should be carried, viz. by a sling over the left shoulder, leaving both one's arms and hands free to assist in climbing, or to hold the *Bergstock* or the telescope.

Not very long ago the columns of the *Field* contained a correspondence regarding the first shot out of a clean barrel. It brought out some highly interesting though divergent opinions concerning the vexed question whether the second bullet (out of a foul barrel) will strike higher or lower than the first one out of the clean barrel. This divergence

clearly shows that the variation depends upon powder,
weight of the bullet, and the rifling. In nine cases out of
ten, while chamois or deer stalking in the Alps, one fires
one's first shot under far more favourable circumstances than
one's second at the same beast. It behoves one therefore to
make quite sure of how one has to hold the *clean* barrel so as
to hit the spot aimed at. Second shots are almost invariably
hurried ones, at game moving away at a rapid pace, and
while nothing gives one more confidence than a hit with the
.first shot, the reverse is the case when it goes wide of its
mark. In the correspondence alluded to it was suggested
that more uniform shooting can be attained, if before starting
out a blow-off is fired. This may be a very good suggestion
for the rifle-shot practising at the butts, but, as is perhaps
hardly necessary for me to mention, it is one that the sportsman cannot carry out in the Alps, except in very isolated
cases.

As to other accoutrement of a sportsman bent on
chamois-stalking, the colour of one's dress should be a medium
gray or green, so as to match the tint of the rock as much
as possible. If the national dress is to have the preference
over knickerbockers, long stockings that can be turned up
over the bare knees are advisable. Chamois-leather shorts
are of course the best for really rough rock work, and if they
are made to order, by all means select skins dyed gray and not
black. For a pair of shorts for a tall man, two buck skins
are needed.

Boots should be thick-soled stalking boots of the stoutest
make, and be large enough to allow thick stockings and a
felt sole, and the nails should be put in by the Tyrolese or
Styrian cobbler nearest to the scene of one's sport. The
native flange nails put in close together, so as to form a continuous ridge round the "treading" surface, are infinitely
better than the usual English hob-nails, and I for one give

them the preference to the Alpine Club nails, which I have found fail to give one the same firm grip, and are more liable to get loose and come out.

Crampons are a source of danger till one has got used to them, for they are apt to trip up the tyro, and they are only needed for winter sport. Then they are absolutely necessary. There are thousands of men in the mountains in Tyrol, Salzburg, and Styria who do not get them off their feet for months at a time, except when they go to bed, and many a

Fig. 18.—How *Steigeisen* or Crampons are fastened to the boot.

church in the byeways of the Alps is filled every Sunday in winter with congregations, every member of which, female as well as male, have crampons on. They should be made to fit the boot in the manner I have shown in Fig. 18, by having the cross-pieces turned up to grip the sole. The shoddy ready-made *Steigeisen* that are to be bought in tourist outfitting places are as a rule to be avoided. Remember that your life may depend upon the forging of a single spike, for often only one of the six " bite " the rock or ice, and if that one should break, there will be one more victim of shoddy goods. Most Alpine village blacksmiths can make reliable crampons.

The *Bergstock* to be of practical use, and not for mere adornment, in the way brand new ice-axes and formidable coils of rope are nowadays often carried by drawing-room climbers, should be a substantial iron-shod stick, at least 6 feet long, made of well-seasoned hazel. It should bear one's full weight without more than slightly bending. Bamboo *Alpenstöcke* have lately come into fashion on account of their extreme lightness. For pottering about on easy ground, or for going up to your stand at a drive, such toys are well enough, anything almost will do for that, but for real chamois-stalking in difficult ground, these bamboo sticks are no good, for they cannot be reversed without damaging them to an extent which soon makes them useless. This reversing of the stick, so as to avoid the iron-shod end chinking against rock when approaching game, is constantly practised, and one can see by glance at a man's *Alpenstock* whether he is a practised stalker, for in that case the top of the stick will show the use to which it has been put.

The *Rücksack* is too important a part of the sportsman's kit for the Alps not to receive a few words of commendation in this place. How this useful game-bag is worn can be seen by the illustration on Plate IX. It is made of stout home-spun linen of dark green colour, and can be waterproofed, or a regular waterproof stuff can be used. Two leather straps form loops through which the arms are slung, and in consequence the weight of the contents of the bag is distributed between the shoulders and the small of the back—the best possible apportionment—and the arms and muscles have perfectly free play. The bag weighs, if made of homespun linen, about a pound ; when empty it can be shoved into one's pocket, and yet its folds are so capacious that it will easily hold a chamois, or a roebuck, or fifteen brace of grouse, or 60 or 70 lbs. of fish. For Norway, the Rocky Mountains, or rough shooting of any kind, it is without question the most practical game-bag existing, while for mountaineering its usefulness is too well known and generally acknowledged to require further notice. An elaborated and therefore heavier kind of *Rücksack*, of English make, can now be bought at the stores and other places in town.

The question which is the most useful for the tyro: a telescope or a pair of field-glasses, cannot be answered off-hand. When once he has learnt where to look for chamois, the former is of course by far the best, but till he has had some experience the larger field and easier handling of the latter have decided advantages. The man who has learnt deer-stalking in the Highlands should, of course, come with the best telescope he can lay his hands on, giving some attention to its lightness, the new-fashioned drawn steel being superior to aluminium, which does not stand rough wear.

Concerning ammunition the following might be added. The Austrian as well as the Roumanian Mannlicher rifles can be obtained, of course, in Austria, where both arms are manufactured, as also the ammunition. But as the latter is also made in Germany it happens that not all so-called Mannlicher cartridges fit the genuine Mannlicher rifles, it is advisable to be very careful that the right sort is obtained. One sportsman tells me that he was satisfied with the cartridges he obtained from the firm of G.-Roth in Vienna, while some he obtained from another firm would not go into the chamber. It is, therefore, evident that not all Mannlicher ammunition is of the same size. If an Express is to be used a small supply of the ammunition for it had best be brought into the, country in one's pockets. The sale of powder is in Austria a government monopoly, hence any loaded cartridges of foreign make are liable to be stopped and retained at the

boundary. But to enable foreign ammunition to be obtained
in the empire, the Government has started a place in Vienna
called *K. K. Pulver Verschleiss,* Nr. 7 Petersplatz, where
English powders of all the new makes, and also ordinary
Express ammunition, can be obtained. Special kinds, if
ordered beforehand, can, I believe, be obtained through this
agency, but through none other. A *Waffen-pass,* as already
stated, should be procured beforehand so as to avoid all bother
in entering Austria with one or two rifles, but it does not
enable one to bring in any larger quantity of loaded cartridges, which, if discovered, are liable to be confiscated as
competing with the Government monopoly.

In conclusion, a few hints to sportsmen attending drives
may not be unacceptable. On being shown to your post see
that you have rocks or *Latchen* bushes behind you, and be
careful to avoid showing yourself at any time against the
sky-line. Always face the point most to your right where
game can come, for it is easy to shoot to the left, but not so
in the contrary direction. When once the drive has commenced keep as quiet as possible. Find out from the keeper
your "limit of fire," and if possible see for yourself where
your neighbours are posted. Nothing is more annoying than
to find, when the drive is over, that by shooting at long
ranges you intercepted and shot game which was bound to
come to your neighbour, and really was his. An oversight
on my part to make myself acquainted with this detail once
caused me some embarrassment on the occasion of a formal
court-chasse. I was posted about 100 yards from the
base of a perpendicularly rising wall of rock. A small
ledge ran transversely down the face of the cliff somewhat to
my left. Four good bucks came at intervals one after
another down this giddy path. Each halted for a few
moments, as is their way, at a point where the ledge broadened
out a bit, presenting long but by no means impossible shots

to me. I had not been informed that at the point where the ledge touched the bottom an English sportsman of exalted rank was posted, the ledge in question being one of the principal passes. Not knowing this, I shot at and got all four, and only at the conclusion of the drive learnt that I had killed my neighbour's game, to whom they must have come had I not shot so much farther than was expected of me. The consternation of the dumfounded officials when they discovered the result of their neglect to inform me, as they should have done, where my neighbour was posted, was lamentable to behold till the amiable prince good-naturedly made light of their awkward oversight.

As a last word: do not leave your post till you are certain that the drive is over, both on account of the danger to yourself, as well as for sport's sake, for the wary old bucks dash out often at the last moment when the beaters are right upon them.

CHAPTER XVII

OPPORTUNITIES, it is said, make the man, but do they not, one might ask, first make the boy ? The opportunities which, in the case of the writer, united to make the boy the father of the man who has here attempted to describe the pleasures of sport in the upland regions of the Alps, were of a nature such as could hardly fail to leave a lasting impression. Two adjoining estates, one my father's, the other my grandfather's, embracing several ranges of high hills—if mountains be too grand a term for eminences not exceeding 6000 feet—covered with fine forests, which were the home of red - deer and chamois; numerous trout streams and three or four mountain tarns high up close to timber-line; a large lake,[1] some 7 miles long, acknowledged to be the gem of the *Salzkammergut*, that picturesque lake country of the Austrian Alps, whereon in summer to boat and swim, in winter to skate and toboggan, and, overlooking this mountain-framed sheet of water, from precipitously rising ground, a rambling château, the halls and corridors of which were hung with ancient as well as modern trophies of the chase—this, in brief outline, was the home of my childhood. Old-fashioned wainscotted rooms, devoted to

---

[1] The St. Wolfgang lake, from which my grandfather's estate received its name.

the appurtenances of the chase, racks filled with rifles and guns, and fishing-tackle of all sorts and shapes, showed that the owners of these hills and lakes were keen lovers of country sports. Stalwart keepers in the shapely mountaineer's dress, the sons of a soil which, as Ruskin truly says, produces strong men with sound lungs, as well as buxom lasses with amply rounded waists, were also among the surroundings which helped to lure the youngster from the narrow path of learning and taught him to climb, to track the deer, to stalk the chamois, to rob the eagle's eyrie of its prize, and to become generally versed in woodcraft.

In the days to which I refer, this beautiful mountain country was still in its pristine condition, undefiled by railways, unspoilt by the hordes of tourists who have now long robbed it of its olden charms. No puffing tourist steamers darted restlessly hither and thither on those mountain-bowered lakes. Undesecrated by their shrill unmelodious whistle was as yet the echo, given back fourfold in some places where perpendicular cliffs towered straight up from the profound depth of dark green water. While in other spots a narrow beach of silvery sand was all that intervened between the water and the silent pine and fir forests, or occasional groves of fine old beeches and sycamores.

As one strolled along the shore of those mirror-like expanses of water, where the dip of the wooded flanks of snow-flecked peaks left sufficient room between water and rock, the only craft that occasionally furrowed their untroubled surface was the primitive "one-tree" of the native. Hollowed out of a single trunk of massive girth, they are of precisely the same shape and make as were the dug-outs that thousands of years ago assisted communication between the lacustrine settlements which dotted in prehistoric days the shores of many Alpine lakes. Then, as now, they were propelled by oars of the same rude shape, while withy bands have for tens of centuries acted as rowlocks.[1]   As one watched one of these quaint craft, with a man of old-world type standing in the stern, approach the shelving beach, even a child's imagination could easily wander back to the ages when skin-clad lake-dwellers would return in much the same fashion from their day's hunt to their rude huts, built for protection's sake on piles as far out in the lake as the depth of water allowed.

With no companion of my own age, for my brother was five years younger, and free as yet from the dreaded super-vision by tutors, the mountains and the lakes became my favourite playground almost as soon as I could scramble up a hillside or swim 50 yards.   At an age when boys as a rule have not yet escaped from their nursery governesses, I was spending my days roaming about the upland forests, or push-ing out into the middle of one or the other of the remote lochs high up on the mountains, standing on a somewhat unsteady raft made of a few logs tied together.

What more entrancing game than playing " lake-dweller " could boyish ingenuity devise ?   Driftwood piled in the shape of a rude hut on the extreme point of some sandy spit jutting far out into such a mountain tarn that lay hidden away in the seclusion of timber-line, a water-logged " one-tree," or a raft of the primitive construction already alluded to, a chamois skin as a cloak, with a corresponding absence of most of the garments of civilisation, made up the *mis-en-scène.*   The utter solitude of those upland regions, uninvaded save perhaps by deer coming down to drink, and the solemn stillness, broken only occasionally by the cry of a golden eagle circling overhead, made the boy's play as life-like as it well could be.

Playing " chamois poacher " was another favourite game, which brought the boy in a similar manner in close contact

[1] The man propelling the " one-tree " stands in the stern and pushes a broad-bladed oar in gondolier fashion through the water.

with wild Nature, and taught him, at the age of ten or eleven, self-confidence, which otherwise would have been wanting until a more advanced age.

At the outset, the solitude of my surroundings, which I soon learnt to love so much, was not quite as great as I imagined, for instead of being miles and miles from any human being, as I fondly imagined, watchful keepers were shadowing my steps. When, as happened once or twice, I came upon them unawares, they would, of course, betray beguiling surprise at meeting their young master in such out-of-the-way places. After a few months of this unsuspected supervision, the authorities at home became satisfied of my capacity to get out of any scrape I was likely to get into, and I was made free of the mountains, to roam henceforth un-watched whither I pleased.

My ninth birthday was a memorable one, for on it the present of the first real gun—none of your makeshift toys, but one in which real gunpowder and shot were used—made me the happiest boy the sun shone on that day all the world over. Now all those long-hatched conspiracies against the lives of certain roebucks, whose haunts were as well known to me as were the turns and twists of the cloistered corridors in my rambling home, could be put into execution, and need no longer remain projects of which one thought during the livelong day and dreamt of at night. But those roebucks were after all not to die at sunrise of the day on which the shooting season opened, for a stupid hare, which I started from her form during a preliminary stroll with the gun the preceding afternoon, was vile and cunning enough to place the legs of a keeper between the muzzle and herself, just as I pulled the trigger. The results were, fortunately, not very serious, so far as the keeper was concerned, but were more so to the youthful sportsman. One of the least painful con-sequences of this little mishap was the decision at which my father arrived, that I should have a lesson or two in shooting. He began by teaching me how to "follow" a stone wrapped in paper which he threw up in the air. Unfortunately, I "followed" one of the first he tried me with to such good purpose that I shot his hat off his head and scared my mother, who was looking on, almost to death.

This gave the roebucks a fresh lease of life, for my father, while leaving me the gun and permitting me to fire blank charges, strictly forbade the use of shot, and I knew it was decidedly advisable to follow the governor's command to the very letter. It was well that the little gun was by a good maker, for even at that age familiarity with gunpowder had bred the proverbial contempt for its dangerous powers. From the day when, as an urchin of seven, I turned the mater's silver thimble into a mortar, with a touch-hole drilled into the bottom, and tried the strength of the glass panes in the nursery bookcase by shooting a tight-fitting bread pill of the requisite staleness against them—the propelling charge being a layer of powder grains I had picked up, one by one, on the floor of the gun-room—from that day, villainous saltpetre and I were on the most familiar terms.

I suppose I should not have been a boy had I not pondered muchly and deeply how the governor's most distressing ban upon shot could be evaded. An accidental occurrence came to my assistance. Sending me one day to the head-keeper with a message to have certain cartridges loaded, each with six *Pfosten*—a very large size of buckshot—an innocently put question addressed to my respected parent, whether these large buckshot were the same as shot, was answered in the negative. *Pfosten* not the same as shot! What immense possibilities did not that incautious reply open to the young scapegrace? And curious results I attribute to that innocent "No"; the one about which there can be least doubt being that, however able to hold his own with the rifle, a

worse duffer with the shot gun than that boy turned out to
be, it would be hard to find. But I must not forestall events.
My little muzzle-loader had a very small bore, and not many
hours had elapsed after that " No " had passed my unsuspicious
parent's lips when I could have been seen retiring stealthily
to the remotest part of the home park, a number of the largest
obtainable *Pfosten* in one pocket, and a roll of my mother's best
lint rags filling to bursting strain the other trousers pocket,
while the gun, from which even at bedtime it was difficult to
part me, was of course the most important of all. The place
to which I sought refuge was my private shooting-range,
where I was in the habit of practising with my cross-bow on
" self-marking" targets, consisting of panes of glass purloined
from the greenhouses. With no stinting hand was the
charge of powder measured out, buckshot carefully wrapped in
linen rag till, in shape like a bullet, it could be shoved down
the barrel and securely rammed home, as I had seen the
governor do hundreds of times when loading his rifles. The
experiment proved a grand success ; at the very first try the
shivered target told its tale of good marksmanship, while a
boy lying on his back with a copious flow of claret streaming
from nose and forehead had taught to him a never-to-be-
forgotten lesson concerning the proper proportion of powder
and lead ! On what trifles do not life's destinies often turn ?
Had I missed that pane of glass some 10 or 12 inches
square, the recoil which grassed me so unexpectedly, was
quite severe enough to have disgusted me for some years
with rifle shooting, and probably I should never have taken
it up again with the same zest. As it was, the hole in the
forehead knocked by the hammer of the overloaded gun,
received far less attention than did the one in the board
behind the shattered pane of glass. From that moment
my vocation in life became clear to me, and morning,
noon, and night, I was either practising at the target

with the new "rifle," or experimentalising with loads, or
devising improvements in the manner of wrapping up the
bullets.   The latter was destined to lead to my father's
discovery of how I was evading his interdict.   Very private
reasons make me remember the occasion very distinctly.
Unconscious cerebration, duplication of inventive ideas, bad
luck, good luck, or whatever you like to call it, led me
to discover what a great sportsman in another country [1]
had found out a decade or two previously, that time in
loading was saved and greater accuracy secured if one
sewed up the bullet in a patch of leather.   This discovery
led in my case to the further one that the tips of the
governor's driving gloves, which were of very thick leather,
made admirable patches.   After that, raids upon dressing-
room and hall-table drawers became more and more frequent,
until one fine day my father, wanting a pair of his gloves, found
that his entire stock was thus cruelly mutilated.   Never shall I
forget my consternation as I stood by and watched him push
his hand into pair after pair only to find each one minus the
ten finger tips!

Excellent indeed must have been the make of that much-
tried little weapon.   As I withdraw it from its third of a
century's retirement, and examine the barrel worn thin by
constant use during three years of my early boyhood, and
test the main spring, now, alas! so weak that it no longer
retains the hammer at full cock, I can only wonder at my
being alive to write these lines.

Not many months afterwards my first deer fell victim to
a rag-patched bullet, for as a consequence of that untoward
discovery, as well as from sheer exhaustion of the stock of
finger tips, I had to return to my more primitive methods.

---

[1] The sportsman alluded to was Lord Lovat.   When my father shot with
him in Scotland in the Forties the former was using balls tied up in kid
leather patches.

From that day, shooting with the shot gun was to me a dead art, and the rifle the only arm I cared to handle. Before I attained the full dignity of owning a real rifle, which I did before I was twelve, I had a little adventure to which I also look back with some amusement. My father's woods being extensive, there was a staff of foresters as well as keepers, and the former were under the management of an *Oberförster* or chief forester. This man, a Swiss by birth, was an ill-tempered martinet, and though learned in the management of forests, was by instinct anything but a sportsman. As he considered that I had too much liberty, and consequently placed difficulties wherever he could in my way, there was no love lost between us. There was, however, one possession of his for which I heartily envied him, viz. a beautiful little Swiss rifle, nicely inlaid with silver, which was highly prized by its owner, as his former employer, Prince Lamberg, who was a noted sportsman, had given it to him. According to the latter it was a rifle of almost miraculous accuracy, although no living person had, so far as I could learn, ever seen him fire it off, much less bag a buck or score a bull's eye. Another possession of which the world held this disagreeable old man equally unworthy, was the *Frau Oberförsterin*, an extremely good-natured smiling old body, ever intent on smoothing out the frowns her crabbed husband managed to produce on the faces of every one with whom he came into contact. Whenever the *Oberförster's* back was turned, and I knew he was safely away in the forests, I loved to visit the buxom goodwife, not so much on account of the charms of her jams made after a particular Swiss recipe, as on account of that beautiful little Swiss rifle, which to have a chance of trying became the dearest wish in life. An opportunity to do so presented itself before very long, when business compelled the owner to visit a distant part of the estate which would oblige him to stay away overnight. To get the good old dame to consent to my borrowing the precious arm "just for an hour or two" by dint of all kinds of promises on my part, was finally managed, though she spoke with awe and trembling of the consequences if her lord and master ever discovered the liberty taken with his treasure. An obstacle which the old lady at first hoped would frustrate my intention to try the rifle, viz. the fact that her spouse had as usual locked up the bullets and bullet-mould belonging to the rifle, was overcome as soon as detected, by my previous discovery of two bullets secreted in the small recessed chamber which is to be found in the stock of old-fashioned Swiss and Tyrolese rifles. Victoriously and in the highest spirits I carried off my prize. The next question was what to do with those two precious bullets so as to test in the best manner the shooting qualities of the rifle. One thing was certain, that to do so conscientiously, at least one of the two balls must be expended upon a trial at the target. If that turned out satisfactorily the second might then be used for a shot at a deer or other game worthy of the arm. The trial shot, though I had to make a guess at the powder. charge, was a perfect success, and I had the afternoon left for finding a billet for the remaining ball. Roebucks seemed hardly worthy of the honour, as my mind was still full of a good stag I had spied not far from one of the higher tarns when I paid that spot my last lake-dweller's visit. But it was too far off to return that same day, and I passed my word of honour to the *Oberförster's* goodwife that she should have her treasure back before bedtime. After much pondering I decided that the surest place to find roe or red-deer was after all near some clearings half-way up the slope of the mountain range on the opposite side of the main lake. In my diminutive "one-tree" I had soon ferried myself across, and a keener young stalker than the boy who made those woods unsafe during the rest of that afternoon it would have been hard to find. But luck was against me; one time the wind, by suddenly shifting, spoilt a carefully-laid plot; another time a dry branch cracking under my weight, caused a couple of roe to give me the go-by, their white targets bobbing up and down as they made off through the forest. Very clearly do I remember my supreme disgust when dusk brought home to me my failure and the futility of continuing the stalk in the gloam.

Very dejectedly I was returning to my "one-tree" drawn up on the sandy beach, when just as I was crossing a little stretch of grass that intervened between the shore and myself, I descried a large mountain hare quietly feeding about 75 or 80 yards off. Getting quickly behind some bushes I had the sight of my rifle on her a second later. But the light was very bad, and for a second I wavered whether it was worth chancing the shot. It was too tempting, however, and by moving a little on one side I managed to get my quarry for a second against lighter background. So it was, after all, not such a difficult feat to send the ball through the hare's back. And now comes the event that has left such a lasting impression on my mind. Unfortunately the ball only paralysed but did not kill the hare, and when I got up to her she was writhing about the ground, uttering plaintive squeals, the like of which I had never before heard. I had absolutely nothing with me to despatch the wretched beast, not even the oar of the "one-tree" could be removed from the boat, since it was fastened to the hull by an iron chain which my father had insisted should be put on to avoid a repetition of a somewhat awkward scrape into which I had got one stormy afternoon in consequence of my oar falling overboard and drifting away, while I was intent upon taking up some lines for lake-trout. I was naturally highly distressed by the sight of the unfortunate hare's sufferings, and after casting about for a few

21

minutes, I at last determined to kill her by a blow on the
head with the butt end of my rifle. How it happened I
never realised, all I know is that by the last kick which the
hare was destined to give, she wriggled her body a little to
one side, and instead of my bringing the butt of the rifle
down straight on her head I gave a slanting blow. It hit
the head all right, but lo! crack went the stock just below
the lock, and as I looked down I saw that I held but the
barrel in my hands! Never, never shall I forget the distress
of that moment, and indelibly fixed in my memory is that
dismal row over the dark and silent lake, and of that hapless
home-coming with the broken treasure! My parents were
unfortunately away, so I had nobody to assist me in breaking
the dire news to the person upon whom I knew the blame
would fall heaviest. As I entered the lamp-lit room where
the thrifty old lady was doing some needle-work, and she saw
my tear-stained face and guilty mien, her ever-smiling
countenance underwent for once a change that only made
my delinquency appear yet more unpardonable. I forget
now how the matter was patched up between the three
persons concerned, but the incident was a lesson to me in
the treatment of rifles, a lesson which at least on one
occasion in after-life was of use, for my warning shout
to a Western hunter about to do the very same thing to a
wounded jack-rabbit, using for that purpose a Sharp's rifle
which he thought was not loaded, caused the rifle to be held
more upright, so that when the jar of the blow discharged
the cartridge which after all was in the chamber, the ball
went through the man's wide-brimmed hat instead of through
his head or body.

In the decade following the Revolution of '48—the period
which I am desirous of recalling to the reader's mind—the
head of game in most Austrian forests had not yet recovered
from the exterminating raids of the armed peasantry to which

they had been exposed during the Revolution. Ruinous to landed interests as was this great uprising, and clean as was the sweep it made of the feudal institutions which up to then had been in force, the sportsman was undoubtedly the heaviest sufferer of all, for the new constitution which the lower classes had wrung from a weak and completely demoralised Government, now recognised rights on the part of the newly-created peasant proprietors which from time immemorial had been the exclusive prerogative of the seigneur or lord of the manor. Previous to 1843 none but the latter could exercise the rights of the chase, and the farmer or peasant, living in feudal dependence, and subject to the law as administered by his lord, could not even fence his field or raise his hand to ward off the deer or wild boar from nightly incursions into his crops. Now with one clean sweep the tiller and the lord of the soil were placed on a footing of equality before the law. Thus, to give but one instance of the radical change it wrought, every peasant owning 200 *Joch* (about 280 acres) could now shoot all the game he found on his land. Revelling in this new-found liberty to wreak vengeance upon their lord's detested deer, excesses of the grossest kinds were committed. In the unsettled state of the country which prevailed for several years after 1848, the authorities who had not yet fairly recovered from the abject fright the late events had given them, either refused altogether or took steps only very half-heartedly to suppress poaching, which had sprung up to an unheard-of degree all over the country. In consequence, one had, in this respect, to rely more or less upon the efforts of one's own keepers, and consequently poaching affrays, often of a murderous kind, were frequent.

My father's estate marched on one side for many miles with one of the Emperor's best preserves, but on the other sides it had bad neighbours, and many a battle-royal, fought out high up on the mountain-sides, testified to the faithfulness of our keepers, who thus in their own way resented the change in the condition of things.

To the boy who grew up among such surroundings it was but natural that this sort of internecine warfare, waged high up in the isolation of pine-woods or on moraine-flanked peaks, should have exercised supreme attractions. To the charm of roaming about in the wild desolation of timber-line in quest of mountain game, already sufficiently glorified by the romance of the country, was added another and no less potent attraction, in the shape of possible adventures with well-armed and determined poachers.

Poaching in those days was no tame affair, for fellows who bravely risk their lives in the pursuit of the wild game of the Alps, not so much for the sake of pecuniary gain as to indulge their innate love for sport, cannot be likened to the Bill Sykes who sneaks about a "warm corner" in Norfolk, or to Tom Stubbs who lurks behind Yorkshire hedges. Encounters between them and their sworn enemies, the keepers, were generally affairs of life and death, if the surprise was not so complete as to render defence an impossibility. Circumstances, as well as tradition, had instilled into both a bitter hatred towards each other, so that little mercy was shown by either side. If they did not shoot each other down, the rifles were reversed and used by brawny arms as clubs, in which case even such hard skulls as are to be found among these hardy mountaineers had to succumb.

Hardest of all skulls, brawniest of all limbs, were those of my favourite among the keepers, the bold Hiesel, who, as a local saying went, "loved to jump in where the devil had enough with one sniff." He was one of a family of keepers, and two of his brothers had been killed by poachers; his hatred of *Wilderers* was therefore of a deadly character.

Very clear does that picturesque figure stand out in

my memory among a sufficiently large crowd of similar
types with which my life in the byeways of the Alps has
brought me into contact. Lithe, and yet immensely strong,
unsophisticated Hiesel was the beau-ideal of mountain-bred
forceful vigour. His frieze jacket, with green weather-stained
facings, displayed a vast breadth of shoulders; his short
chamois-leather breeches reaching down to the brown and
scarred knees, left the latter bare as if in unconscious con-
firmation of the vicissitudes of a life the greater part of
which was passed in the solitude of rocks and snow. Notwithstanding immensely heavy iron-shod shoes, his tread was
springy and light, and his weather-beaten green Tyrolese hat
adorned with the never-absent blackcock's feather, sat jauntily
on crisply curling hair. Not an ounce of fat could be
detected about that spare athletic frame, and a look into
those keen eyes told one plainly enough that mind as well
as body was fit to cope with the dangers and privations of
his life. As a rule, young, unmarried men make by far the
keenest keepers, for it is but natural that the responsibilities
of married life, or worse, the cares of a family, take the edge
off a man's spirit and willingness to risk his life in the
performance of his duties. Hiesel made in this respect an
exception, for a buxom lass of bonny mien had not long
before been installed as mistress of the châlet-like keeper's
lodge of sun-browned timber, standing solitarily on a forest-
girt clearing well up on the mountain-side.

Each of the districts into which the forested part of the
estate was divided, had two keepers, who, living in the same
lodge, took turns of twenty-four hours each to watch those
parts of the boundaries most exposed to unwelcome intrusion.
From points of vantage on some prominent crag whence they
could oversee hill and corrie they would keep guard and
would relieve each other at appointed times, while the head-
keeper, by unexpected visits, assured himself that the men

were at their posts. In Hiesel's case this latter precaution was entirely unnecessary, for to him the word *Wilderer* had much the same effect as " Rats " has on a prize terrier. Twice he had brought down from the uplands, poachers bound with their hands to their backs, whom he had managed to surprise while gralloching deer, covering them with his rifle before they had time to make use of their own weapons, which were leaning against trees at their side. And though he never willingly told any of his adventures, it was well known that on more than one occasion poachers' bullets had whistled past him rather closer than was pleasant. On another occasion, again, he had been beaten well-nigh to death by several poachers who had waylaid him. His body was one mass of wounds, for not only had these fiends broken their rifles over his body, but while he was lying stunned on the ground they had jumped about on him with their crampons. The inch-long spikes had broken his jaw and nose, and lacerated his face in the most shocking manner. It happened in a remote glen in the latter part of the winter ; and there he lay for a night and the best part of two days till the search parties, by following his tracks in the snow, came upon him. The lass who nursed him back to life, which, in spite of his iron constitution, hung for some time on a thread, became ultimately the sunny-faced mistress of the keeper's lodge. Was it a wonder, therefore, that in after years those smiling eyes should often be dimmed with tears when her stalwart Hiesel failed to return from his round at the expected hour ?

To the youngster eager to learn woodcraft, burning to become proficient in the art of stalking the chamois or tracking the antlered " royal," this man was, of course, a hero the like of whom would never be seen again. To follow his lead, to creep as noiselessly as he did through the thick and tangled *Latchen*, to bare my feet and learn to suffer the pain of moving about on sharp stones with the least possible noise, to become inured to cold and snow and to other little hardships inseparable from sport in the high Alps, and finally to see Nature and to watch the habits of game when the mantle of winter hangs like a shroud over all—these were lessons it was a dear pleasure to learn.

But what unhappy memories does not that word "lessons" recall to me? Be it spring, summer, autumn, or winter, books and tutors were alike intolerable, for did they not mean imprisonment in beastly rooms? How cruel to have to bend over the one and listen to the other's dronings, while the blackcock was merrily singing his spring love-ditty and cutting his merry capers at his well-known trysting-places high up on the mountain-side; or in summer the chamois were standing about in the breeze on the knife-back ridges and beetling crags, or in autumn the antlered master of the forest was sending forth his challenging roar, or in winter the gallant little roebuck was stalking through the silent snow-laden pine-woods.

And those tutors! It still makes me smile to think of those grave, spectacled professors, decades younger in years than in looks, who one after another tried their hand at taming the young savage. Their erudition was no doubt great, but greater was their lack of knowledge about everything that interested their pupil. Of rifles, shooting, stalking, of boats and fish, they knew absolutely nothing, and although they could tell the component parts of gunpowder, they exhibited the strangest ignorance as to the various uses to which a boy can put that compound. What was less easily forgiven them by their pupil was their unwillingness to participate in his pleasures, and the coldness with which they received his invitations to ascend favourite peaks, sleep in haylofts, or to drift about on the deep green water of some pet loch on a raft, which I grant may have been of somewhat unsafe construction.

The first tutor I ever had, I happened to meet some
quarter of a century later, when he confessed to me the
despair evoked in his mind by my love for the mountains and
sport. The pleasant chat that ensued recalled to me an
early miss I achieved as a nine-year-old urchin, with that
famous single barrel to which I have so often referred. On
the morning the tutor was to arrive, I had gone out on a
hare-stalking expedition to some fields where I hoped to get
a pot shot. The desired chance presently offered itself in the
shape of a hare asleep in her form. Whether in my excitement I had forgotten the shot when loading, or whether the
gun was too heavy for little arms, I know not, but, to my
intense disgust, I missed my quarry.

Try wherever I would on that unfortunate forenoon no
other hare was kind enough to make a target of herself, and
so, finally, I had to return home with a full heart and an
empty *Rücksack*. When I reached home, hours late, I found
my mother talking to this pioneer of bear-leaders, a meek-
looking, grave-faced personage, to whom stooping shoulders,
spectacles, and somewhat long hair gave an unmistakably
professorial air. There was also, I remember, on that morning
a decidedly perplexed look on his face, but whether it was
caused by my mother's German, which at that time was not
of the most faultless nature, or whether it was called forth
by some puzzling instructions embodying her English ideas of
the freedom which she desired should be meted out to me, I
knew not until this subsequent meeting with my old dominie.
The following was his explanation of that puzzled look.
" That first interview," he explained, " was one full of surprises for me. After your mother telling me in her quaint
German that she did not wish you turned into a book-worm,
and other instructions evincing similar fears, to have you
rush into the room, tears in your eyes, the highest distress
depicted on your face, in your hands a gun taller than your-

self, and to see you fling yourself on your knees hiding your
face in your mother's lap, exclaiming, 'Oh, mother, mother,
punish me as hard as you can, for I have missed a sitting
hare at twenty paces!' was, I think, enough to make me
look a trifle puzzled." And perhaps it was.

The last tutor I had before I was sent to a public school
in England was Dr. Stockmann, whose severity did not belie
his suggestive name. He had but recently retired from
the tutorship he had held for many years in the family of
the Duke of Würtemberg, whose son, the present Duke of
Teck, he had educated up to the time he entered the Austrian
army, which, as will be remembered, he only left on his
marriage with Princess Mary of Cambridge. Dr. Stockmann
had one quality that gained him my boyish respect. He
was a good pedestrian and very fond of mountain walks.
Unfortunately the object for which our long mountain
rambles were solely undertaken was one far too tame for
the urchin who had tasted the keen pleasure of the chase,
and to whom the chamois and the deer seemed far worthier
quarry than flowers, for botany, be it said, was the doctor's
hobby, and if he entirely failed to make of me an enthusiastic herbalist, it was verily not his fault. Indefatigable
the good doctor proved himself, and to get certain botanical
specimens exactly at the right time, no climb was too hard,
no weather too bad, no road too long. Thus I remember
that in the three years I was under his charge, we ascended
a certain mountain no fewer than twenty-seven times!

Revisiting after the lapse of decades the scenes of a happy
childhood is usually a pleasant event, but it can be a
melancholy one too. Thrown into chancery soon after the
events I have attempted to narrate, the estates passed not
long afterwards into other hands. The iron horse, land
speculators, and builders invaded the country from all sides,
and soon the whole district from Salzburg to Ischl, in the

centre of which lies St. Wolfgang, was undergoing the desecration so hateful to the true lover of Nature, which is dragging down to the same miserable dead level the choicest nooks in the Alps, turning them into tourist-ridden, hotel-cursed gathering-places for droves of over-dressed, chattering sightseers. Railways and steamboats, filled to overflowing during the season, now skirt or traverse the quiet lakes, the tranquil surfaces of which had formerly been lightly furrowed by the quaint old dug-outs. Their shores are lined with rows of hideous gimcrack villa-like châlets, full of ugly excrescences in the shape of useless balconies. To cap all, some speculative connoisseur of mountain-top views discovered that the *Schafberg*, on the flanks of which I had stalked my first chamois, and where my little gun drew first blood, was really the Rigi of Austria. So that for some years now, I believe, an abominable mountain railway puffs up its slopes, while an agglomeration of staring hotel buildings occupies the top. At the foot of the mountain, the quiet little village nestling round a bay of the lake, has blossomed forth into a fashionable watering-place, in the hotels of which waiters in greasy swallow-tails have long replaced the pretty country lasses that used to tend to the wants of the few travellers who found their way to this once delightfully secluded mountain retreat. Staring advertisements of the usual hideous order are affixed on all prominent rocks and landmarks, while splashes of red, blue, and green paint betray the inane activity of the path-marking *Wegmarkirer*. And what is perhaps the saddest reflection of all, is that not only has Nature's wild beauty been thus irredeemably defaced, but the population has been correspondingly demoralised. What was once a sterling, self-respecting and independent race of mountain people, has degenerated into a band of waiters and touts who have learnt to despise the honest labour of their forefathers.

Even in the Alps times are indeed changing apace! And
with sorrow in one's heart one asks what the next half
century has in store for those byeways that have hitherto
escaped such fate, if the last one has worked such deplorable
changes in so many spots.

APPENDIX

THE two printed works named respectively *Weisskunig*, or the *Wise King*, and *Theuerdank*, or, to use the original spelling, *Tewrdanckh*, originated about the years 1512 and 1517, the latter being the date of the first edition of the second-named work. Both were planned by Maximilian, as there is ample evidence to show; the former was put to paper by his private secretary—secret secretary being the literal translation of his title—Marx Treizsauerwein, and is adorned with 237 wood engravings by the famous pupil of Dürer, Hans Burgkmair, and the less known Leonhard Beck. It is a prose work, partly a chronicle, partly a romance in three parts; dealing first with the life of Frederick III., then with that of his son, Emperor Maximilian I., the author, up to the termination of his wars with Venice.

Weisskunig remained in MS. form for more than 250 years, for it was not until the providential recovery of 236 of the 237 original wood-blocks in the old Schloss at Gratz, that the first edition of the work was printed in 1775. In 1779 a small edition of the woodcuts was published (with a title-page in French) in London by S. Edwards. The manuscript itself seems to have been lost or mislaid in the confusion which ensued after the untimely death of the great sportsman author, for we know that it was discovered by a lucky chance in the year 1665 in Castle Ambras, near Innsbruck, by Petrus Lambecius, who forthwith took his find to the Emperor in Vienna, whither, alas! so much

of Ambras's unrivalled antiquities have followed in the course of
the last two centuries.

Theuerdank, on the other hand, is in verse, but the hard and
forced metre of the original edition was a good deal improved
in a later edition (1553). It treats in an allegorical manner with
the adventures of the warlike and renowned hero and knight
Tewrdanckh. It was put to paper by another secret secretary
of the Emperor, the Very Reverend Provost Melchior Pfinzing.
The wood engravings, 117 in number, which adorn this highly
interesting black-letter volume, are by Schäuffelin, Hans Burgkmair the elder, and Leonhard Beck. They also represent adventures of various kind that occurred to Maximilian in his numerous
wars, and while hunting or travelling on terra firma and on the
sea. Three allegorical personages, *Fürwittig*, *Unfallo*, and *Neidhart*,
surround the adventure-loving knight Theuerdank, as Maximilian calls himself, and in various guises tempt him to risk all
kinds of dangerous enterprises and perilous deeds, from which
his good spirit saves him, at the last moment, in a more or less
wonderful manner.

In 1884 the Holbein Society of London published a facsimile
reprint of *Theuerdank*, but the woodcuts, reproduced by a photographic process, are not as good as might be, while the explanatory
text fails to do justice to this unique work.

Both *Weisskunig* and *Theuerdank* are little known in England;
how little is shown by the fact that a recent writer of a series of
articles on old hunting prints, ascribes a reprint of one of the
illustrations in *Weisskunig*, of which he gives a reproduction in
one of his articles (*Badminton Magazine*, August 1895), to Hans
Burgkmair. A glance at Alwin Schultz's monograph, which·
prefaces the well-known last reprint of *Weisskunig*, published
in Vienna in 1888, would have shown him that the woodcut in
question is by a less famous artist, Leonhard Beck.

NOTE 2

TABLE SHOWING DETAILS OF THREE BEST RED-DEER HEADS IN EIGHT ANNUAL EXHIBITIONS HELD IN BUDA-PESTH

Name of Shooter.	No. of points.	Weight in lbs. avoirdupois.	Length along curve.	Circumference of burr.	Circumference above burr.	Circumference above middle tine.	Circumference below crown.
1888.		lbs.	in.	in.	in.	in.	in.
Prince Philip Coburg .	12	21·01	40·94	*12·21*	*10·63*	7·09	8·27
Count F. Nadasdy .	18	18·26	41·73	10·24	9·25	7·09	8·07
Count G. Erdödy .	20	17·05	45·27	9·84	8·07	7·28	7·48
1889.							
Prince Victor Ratibor .	16	20·68	46·46	11·02	9·45	8·07	6·89
F. Pausinger .	14	20·24	43·70	10·43	8·27	7·09	7·28
Count Mittrovszky	16	19·91	46·06	11·81	9·25	6·89	7·28
1890.							
Prince Philip Coburg .	16	18·92	42·91	10·04	8·66	7·48	8·27
Count R. Erdödy .	18	19·14	43·70	10·04	8·46	7·09	9·64
Count Erwin Schönborn	20	18·81	42·13	10·24	9·25	6·69	7·87
1891.							
Count F. Nadasdy .	16	17·60	42·13	11·61	10·24	7·09	7·68
Count M. Esterhazy .	8	17·38	44·09	11·41	9·84	7·68	7·68
Count Bela Szechenyi .	14	16·17	44·49	10·63	9·45	6·49	8·07
1892.							
Count Tassilo Festetics.	20	15·73	44·49	9·05	7·87	*9·05*	*12·21*
Prince Philip Coburg .	14	18·85	42·13	9·64	9·05	7·09	7·87
Count Bela Szechenyi .	12	20·46	45·27	10·04	6·49	6·69	7·48
1893.							
Count Bela Szechenyi .	20	22·55	46·06	10·63	9·05	6·69	8·46
Prince Philip Coburg .	16	20·57	47·84	11·21	9·25	7·87	7·87
Count Tassilo Festetics.	20	17·60	43·31	10·04	8·07	7·28	8·27
1894.							
Count G. Andrassy .	16	*23·36*	*53·54*	10·04	8·47	7·28	7·28
Count F. Nadasdy .	20	20·79	46·46	9·84	7·87	7·09	7·87
Jeno Kund . .	14	18·37	44·09	11·41	10·24	7·28	6·89
1895.							
Count B. Keglevich .	14	20·06	42·91	9·64	8·66	7·68	7·28
G. Jankovich .	16	16·06	42·91	9·84	8·27	6·69	7·09
Prince Philip Coburg .	14	15·95	43·31	10·43	8·66	7·09	7·28

The last but one dimension was taken in the years 1888, 1889, and 1891, not above but below middle tine.

The following letters upon the influence of food, climate, and shelter upon red-deer appeared in the *Field* under the dates given.

In the *Field* of 26th January 1895 a correspondent signing himself "Rika" wrote :—

The correspondence between "Nevis," "Wyvis," Mr. Gordon Cameron, and "Carn Dearg," in recent numbers of the *Field*, has greatly interested me, as owner of a pretty good deer forest myself, and I may be permitted perhaps to give an opinion on this much-ventilated subject.

In Germany and Austria sportsmen have a good deal of experience in these matters, especially since people have found out that one really good head is worth twenty bad ones ; and, I believe, some of your correspondents might profit by their experience.

I can testify to the correctness of every word written by "Carn Dearg," but not so to all the other opinions given.

The breeding of deer is governed by much the same influences as that of cattle or other animals. To put it briefly, these are : (1) Introduction of fresh blood (no interbreeding) ; (2) hereditary influence ; (3) food (of the greatest importance during the period of antler-shedding) ; (4) climate. Of course proprietors will be able to get on the best side of all four conditions, and nobody can change a climate ; but if all four are against a man, it will be quite impossible to secure first-rate horns.

(1) Fresh blood and the intermixture of different stocks is the most important point of all. So one ought not to have more wire fencing than necessary, and let the deer roam as freely as possible during the rutting time. If possible, the importation of stags from Germany, Austria, or still better, Hungary or Poland, will do a great deal of good. Even bringing stags from a distant part of the county will be useful.

(2) As Mr. Cameron says very truly, antlers are inherited. One should therefore have good stags and hinds, and keep the best for breeding purposes ; mercilessly shooting every weakly hind and every stag (the younger the better) that has a tendency to bad form. This precaution alone has vastly improved many Continental shootings.

(3) As to food, the chief thing is not to overstock, and not to keep more deer than can easily find food in summer ; the fewer the better ; and giving extra food in winter is a necessity. This is not spoiling

nature ; for sportsmen have already interfered with her by artificially increasing the natural stock all over the country, and they are bound to make amends.

Mr. Cameron need have no fear of the deer getting tame by being fed in winter, provided they are not tame already. My own deer are as wild as the hardest sportsman and keenest mountaineer could wish ; and I feed them regularly in winter and give them salt all the year round. The most beneficial influence is exercised by food on growth of antlers in the time of shedding and shortly after, and this is the time of year which generally yields the least natural food. On this point proprietors should be very careful. One need not go in for Mr. Cameron's £1500. Give them hay (inferior quality will do), horse-chestnuts (a first-rate food for growing antlers), oat straw, or anything like that. A very good thing, and cheap, are young leafy branches of oak, willow, and some other trees, cut at the end of May or beginning of June and dried like hay, tied in bundles, and kept in an open shed until wanted. Deer like that very much. Of course feeding adds to cost ; but how many there are who pay enormous rents with pleasure, and a very little more would feed too, as the owner might give a part of the large sum he gets for the animals that make him rich. This, I would suggest, should be the rule in short leases, for feeding must be attended to regularly ; and to neglect this for one year might spoil the improvements of three or four previous ones.

In the *Field* of 9th February 1895 I wrote as follows :—

I quite agree with what "Rika" says of the importance of fresh blood being infused, of assisting nature's selection of the fittest by weeding out poor representatives of both sexes, and of providing not only a sufficiency of food, but of selecting the latter with some regard to the end in view by providing bone-producing nutriment. "Rika" proceeds to say that he agrees with every word written by your correspondent "Carn Dearg." In the main I do so too, except when the latter states (*Field*, Jan. 5) that "heads are inherited, and no combination of climate, food, and shelter will ever turn a bad head into a good one." Taking these words in the sense in which I suppose they are meant to be taken, I am at issue with this dictum. Heads, in one sense, of course as regards their character, are inherited, but not the weight ; or in other words, the length as well as the massiveness of the antlers varies in the same stag from year to year, and these are directly influenced by the food the animal eats during the develop-

22

ment of the new antlers, and the climatic conditions during this period, as well as during the preceding winter and spring. Privation causes not only emaciation of the body, but also, as experience shows, a very sensible reduction of the horn-producing power. Incidents out of number could be cited to prove the beneficial effect of proper food and shelter, particularly during spring. Quite incontrovertibly can this be shown in the case of a series of shed antlers belonging to one and the same stag. Under ordinary circumstances, these horns will resemble each other in their modelling so closely that, had one 1000 pairs of shed antlers collected in one hall, 997 sets belonging to 997 different stags and three sets coming from one and the same stag in consecutive and similarly conditioned years, the man who would fail to pick out the three latter would be lacking the eye of the specialist versed in antler lore. In the weight of these three pairs of antlers, on the other hand, there would be no such similarity if the three respective heads were not grown under similar conditions of food and climate. Nor would the increasing number of tines be a sure indication of the sequence in which the heads were grown. "Setting back," usually only occurring in the case of old stags, can, it is well known, be artificially brought about also in young stags by exposing the deer to hard weather and giving them inferior food. And this brings one to a matter to which too little attention is paid by English sportsmen, i.e. the weight of antlers. In Austria-Hungary and Germany, where antler lore has many attentive students, the weight of antlers is the most important point of merit in ranking heads—and quite rightly too, for no other point of merit, measurement, or quality can be so accurately ascertained. A case which I recently mentioned in a contemporary illustrated the importance of consulting the scales in deciding the respective ranks of different first-class heads, each of which has some special merit of its own. Take half-a-dozen first-class heads of red-deer or wapiti, each on a par with the rest in general dimensions, but each having about it a special point of superiority over the other five, such as length, or width, or number of tines, or massiveness, and select as a jury to decide which of the six heads is to be called the best head of the lot, three perfectly unprejudiced sportsmen ; I am sure that those three experts will be at variance within five minutes if it has not been previously arranged that the scales are to decide between the pretensions of the six competing heads. Given a regularly proportioned head, does not its weight give the only true index to the volume of the annually recurrent growth, the extent of which really constitutes the "merit" of the trophy ?

It is only of late years that English sportsmen have begun to evince that keenness concerning the size and quality of their antlers which has manifested itself for centuries in the countries I have named. If one who knows Scotland only from a traveller's point of view may be permitted to express an opinion upon the question under notice, it would seem that the first thing to do is to promulgate among those concerned the principal laws of nature that govern the growth of antlers. This general knowledge once established, unanimous action will follow almost as a matter of course, and Scottish deer-stalkers will look back to the "days of theories" as we do upon those bygone ages when filings from the stag's horn were taken medicinally against fits, and the blood was drunk to ensure fleetness of foot.

There are two details in the management of Scottish deer forests which for many years have puzzled those acquainted with Continental sport. They are details in which the latter consider they see the two chief causes of the inferiority of Scottish antlers and the lightness of Scottish deer. The first is that, owing to the stalking season in Scotland commencing so early in the year, most of the good stags are shot before the rutting season has commenced, thus cutting short the career of the "muckle hart" before he has covered a single hind that season. The second and quite as important reason is the shortness of the deer forest leases. To Continental sportsmen there is something somewhat too commercial in letting well-stocked deer forests for one season to the highest bidder, irrespective of the latter's character as a sportsman. On the Continent, no owner of a good, or even moderately good, deer preserve would dream of letting it to any one about whose sporting proclivities he had not made the closest inquiries ; indeed, it is rare that anything like a good forest will be let to a stranger at all. To me it seems very certain that, so long as this system of short leases is in vogue, the yearly tenant will ever try to get his money's worth and secure the best heads he can get. If sportsmen are really anxious to bring about an improvement they will have to resort to more radical remedies—remedies that strike at the root of the two evils which experience in other lands points out to them. And why should they not benefit by the experience of those across the Channel, whose forests are stocked with deer running up to 40 stone, and antlers that have the making of six of the puny heads carried by the Scottish stags of the present day ? It is quite true that the present condition of most of the deer forests in Scotland is different from what on the Continent would be described as good deer country ; but money and

care could overcome many of the defects, such as want of shelter,
want of food in time of snow (not necessarily by hand-feeding), and
provide at no extravagant outlay horn-producing food, such as horse-
chestnuts, during those critical weeks in spring when stags, much
exhausted by the privations of a long winter, most need good and
proper food. Surely, as long as the present enthusiasm for the fine
and manly sport of deer-stalking endures, ensuring to the owner of
a forest producing big heads ample pecuniary reward, there should
be every inducement to bring about every possible improvement in
the most prized trophies that the sportsman knows.

If the correspondent who signs himself "Horse-chestnut," who
asks aghast where the necessary quantity of horse-chestnuts could
possibly be obtained, will address his inquiries to proper quarters, he
will find that a five pound note will buy enough of this food to put
different antlers on at least half-a-dozen of his stags.

If food and climate have nothing to do with the size of the antlers
or with the weight of deer (as I understand some of your correspondents argue), how can the great heads set up by stags in English parks,
as well as their enormous weight in comparison with that of Scotch
deer, be explained ? I have in my possession numerous photographs
of the chief heads grown in Warnham Court Park, in Sussex. One
set of photographs represents the heads of a celebrated stag which set
up the following antlers: in 1889, antlers with twenty-nine points ;
in 1889, thirty-four points ; in 1890, thirty-four points ; in 1891,
thirty-seven points ; in 1892, forty-seven points (they weighed
17 lbs.) ; and in 1893, forty-five points (weighing 16½ lbs.).
He was killed the same year as a fourteen-year-old stag. While
Mr. Whitaker, in his *Deer Parks of England*, mentions that a stag in
this park weighed 44 stone. The same influence can be shown
negatively by the experiment of introducing a Stoke Park stag into
Scotland, made, I believe, two years ago by an English sportsman
who leases an extensive forest in Scotland. Not only did the deer
fall off at once in condition, but he set back two points the first year.

In conclusion, I may mention that the opinions I have expressed
are shared by several sportsmen of the first rank, who have the
advantage of being as intimately acquainted with some of the best
deer forests of Scotland as they are with the pick of preserves on the
Continent. Without the moral support of their opinions I should not
have ventured to express my own.

In the *Field* of 16th March 1895 I published the following letter :—

Sir—Various engagements prevented me from replying earlier to the several correspondents who either addressed questions to me or with whose reasoning, with all due deference to their superior local knowledge, I make so bold as to differ.

As various details are touched by these correspondents, I shall make what poor attempt I can to arrange my replies under the several heads, and take first the influence of climate, food, and shelter upon the growth of antlers.

I must at once acknowledge that Mr. Allan Gordon Cameron's researches in palæontology, so forcibly illustrated in many of his interesting previous contributions, such as " The Value of Antlers in the Classification of Deer," and his "Notes from an Island Forest," are of such an exhaustive and erudite nature that it would be "riding for a fall" with a vengeance on the part of one lacking this deep reading to argue with Mr. Cameron upon what, after all, are and must remain theories. It is all very well, to give only one instance, for him to explain the origin of the annual recurrence of the casting of antlers in the way he does in the first-named of the two articles : " Accident led to injury of the soft hairy skin, thence to a stripping of the bone, which left it bare and brittle, and thence to irregular fracture, which gradually merged into periodical casting." This theorising, if Mr. Cameron will pardon my using this term, cannot, I think, lead as quickly to the discovery of a remedy for the evil which we are considering as would one single fact adduced by actual practical experience, and it is in this spirit that I ask you to grant me space to narrate the following observations I and others have made ; and the only indulgence which I claim is that my remarks be not misconstrued. This I think your correspondent "Horse-chestnut" did when he derides as "ludicrous in the extreme" an assertion which he fathers upon me, without the slightest reason. The statement to which I allude, and which I repeat I never made nor intended to make, is that "artificial feeding or infusion of foreign blood could cause the Highland deer ever to approach those on the Continent, as regards size, weight, and beam." What I said was that "Scotch sportsmen might benefit by the experience of those across the Channel." If the subject of this correspondence be worth discussing at all, can it not be done in a temperate spirit ?

And now to my facts. While enjoying the hospitality of their

owners, I have lately had the chance of making extended personal
observations in three of the most interesting British deer parks,
viz. those of Lord Powerscourt and of Sir Douglas Brooke. Long-
continued experiments made in the latter's parks which were commenced by the present baronet's famous father, Sir Victor Brooke,
and are now carried on by the former, illustrate the influence of
alimentation and shelter upon the growth of antlers. The two deer
parks, both of large size, belonging to Sir D. Brooke, in Fermanagh, are
about three miles apart. The one, called the Home Park, is on a limestone formation ; the other, called Largie Park, is on sandstone, which
overlies the limestone. The former park has dense underbrush and
good timber ; the latter occupies a bare hillside, with but little cover.
The artificial feeding is in both parks the same, consisting of hay and
oats in winter, and is continued in both to the middle of May. The
red-deer in both parks sprung from the same stock, and in all other
respects, except as to the limestone formation and the superior shelter
in the Home Park, there is nothing to explain why the deer in the
latter park should have such much finer heads, both in regard to
number of tines as well as to weight of horn, than those hailing from
Largie Park, but three miles off. In the latter no stag has ever grown
a head of more than fourteen points, so Sir Douglas Brooke informs
me, nor have the shed antlers grown there been found ever to weigh
more than 7 lbs. ; while, in the Home Park, the lime-impregnated
grass or the shelter, or both combined, produce stags that usually carry
heads up to eighteen, and in several instances, to twenty and more
points, being in weight as many pounds heavier than the Largie Park
heads as the live weight of the whole deer is stones heavier than that
of the Largie animals, extreme cases, such as that of a certain stag
killed in the Home Park on 1st September, and which weighed 33 stone
1 lb. as he fell, being, of course, not taken into consideration. With
no noticeable fluctuation, the weight of the deer in the more favoured
park is from one-fourth to one-fifth greater than that of the Largie
Park stags ; and, what is very important, these observations cover not
a brief season or two, but are the observations of just thirty years,
the first red-deer having been brought to Colebrooke by Sir Victor
(so I was informed) in 1865. But even more convincing proof is
afforded by the following experiment. A three-year-old stag was
brought from Largie to the Home Park, and put with the deer there.
He at once improved, and as a four-year-old he had antlers with fourteen points, weighing 4½ lbs. ; as a five-year-old he had also antlers of
fourteen points, but their weight had increased to 6 lbs. ; when six, he

carried seventeen points, and the weight of the castings was 7½ lbs. ; at seven, he bore a head of nineteen points, which weighed 8 lbs. ; while this year seventeen tines graced his massive, finely-proportioned antlers, as I myself saw last week.

It is not often that such carefully kept records covering a long period assist investigation, and still more rarely do such observations confirm so conclusively what from a common-sense point of view may be said to be a law of Nature which most sportsmen with practical experience see no reason to doubt. Both of the above-named gentlemen, whose observations have added so much to our knowledge of the British red-deer's habits, concur, I believe, with what I have said, and, to quote another of acknowledged experience, the following passage in Sir Samuel Baker's *Wild Beasts and their Ways*, vol. ii. p. 190, is worth repeating here, though it is probably well known to many. When speaking of Highland deer, Sir Samuel says: "The deer exhibits in its horns the ratio of its vigour. If the animal has been well matured and protected from its birth, never unduly exposed to privations, but sheltered and well fed through every season, it will develop antlers superior in length and solidity, and it will increase in weight."

One more instance proving this influence may be cited. The red-deer that produce the heads bearing the greatest number of tines in the United Kingdom—nay, one might almost say in the world, for I know of no other instance of modern heads with forty-five and forty-seven points—are those kept in Warnham Court Park in Sussex. These extraordinary antlers, of which the heaviest castings (1892) weighed no less than 17 lbs., are very remarkable growths. As I have recently been given a chance of inspecting them personally, I hope to give a more detailed description of them at some future occasion. As to the cause of their great size, the owner (Mr. Lucas) has been good enough to place at my disposal the following summary of his extended observations. He attributes the size to the rich nature of the grass in the park. He says: "The pasture in our park is naturally good, but, in addition, half of it is well 'dressed' with bone manure every two years alternately, and it is cut for hay. I have invariably found that the horns of the deer come much heavier after the park has been dressed with a mixture of bone dust and nitrate of lime, not so much so when it has been done with other artificial or ordinary farmyard manure, so I conclude that the bone dust, etc., absorbed by the grass is imparted to the deer in the form of extra good feed, and tells especially upon the horns. I also believe in a constant change of

blood from other deer parks, and killing all puny-looking stags with
poor heads when young."

I feel it in my bones that many a critic will impatiently exclaim,
" Ah, but all this relates to the inmates of deer parks, and not to the
Highland deer, the antlers of which are the subject under discussion."
True enough ; but where does the difference (so far as goes the value
of all these observations) come in, say, between a park, consisting,
for instance, as Lord Powerscourt's does, of 1000 acres of as rough
ground as can be found anywhere in the United Kingdom—so rough
that I felt I could conscientiously recommend the owner to start
a chamois preserve in his Wicklow Mountain enclosure—and, on
the other hand, a modern Scotch deer forest of the average size ?
That the one is perhaps ten or twenty times as large as the other does
not alter the fact that both are more or less enclosed and equally
exposed to the evils of inbreeding if the same be not artificially
remedied.   But even to such cavillers good evidence in support of
my argument can, I claim, be adduced by citing the good results which
have followed the importation of Scotch red-deer into New Zealand.
There is ample evidence before one to show that better climatic conditions, and presumably better food, in that colony are instrumental
in turning out heads that are much superior to those of the parent
stock brought direct from Scotch moors not more than forty years or
so ago.   These New Zealand heads show, I believe, frequently
eighteen and twenty points, a girth of from 6 to 7 inches, and a curve
length of from 36 to 38 inches.

No race under the sun is so devoted to animals, takes such loving
pains to improve breeds, and possesses to the same extent the wherewithal to carry its national foible to a high pitch of excellence as is
the English race.   Is it not singular that probably the one and only
exception that occurs relates to the very beast which is acknowledged
to afford the most prized sport obtainable in Europe—i.e. the red-deer?
For ten rich men in the United Kingdom able to carry on experiments in the improvement of deer, there is perhaps one on the Continent, and yet how much more freely does that one devotee spend his
means in the advancement of antler lore ! If his deer forest is in
Styria or in Tyrol, he will import—and with very good results, as I
know—Hungarian stags ; if he is a Magyar magnate, he will purchase
a few wapiti, and watch what effect an infusion of that foreign blood
will have ; if he is a Silesian " Grossgrundbesitzer," stags from
Bohemia or from the Carpathians will be tried ; while the sportsmen
of Northern Europe are not behind their experimentalising Austrian

brother Nimrods, though handicapped by inferior ground and a less favourable climate.

Mr. Cameron asks me several specific questions which require specific replies. The most important of the former is his query whether I have personal experience to support the assertion that the antlers of wild deer vary from year to year, and are directly influenced by the food the animal eats during the development of its new antlers. If Mr. Cameron includes among wild deer animals that were born in a wild state, and placed into enclosures as adults, I can reply affirmatively. The following two experiments that I saw carried out, and a third of which I was reminded only the other day by Lord Powerscourt, who possesses a very intimate acquaintance with Continental deer, may interest my questioner. The one was carried out by that master sportsman, the late Duke of Saxe-Coburg, in his Thuringian forest, where deer, as a rule, carry somewhat poor heads. The subject upon whom the experiment was tried was a stag caught in a wild state as a three-year-old, and placed in a large enclosure constructed in the very forest where he was taken, and where he was probably born. Upon him the duke tried, in different years, the effect of various food, and, as he finally grew quite tame, he was given his liberty, but usually would come at a fast trot when called by the duke, who would reward him with his favourite chestnuts. In the years in which (during the growth of his horns) he received no other attention or food than the rest of the deer did, his antlers were of the ordinary size. In those seasons, on the other hand, when he was kept up and received stimulating food (horse-chestnuts, maize, etc.) during the critical period alluded to, his head would be very much finer; in fact, when I last saw him, his antlers were magnificent, as his picture from a photograph given me by his fond master amply proves. I have, unfortunately, mislaid some notes I made at the time, showing the accurate weight of the shed antlers for a series of years. The difference was very considerable; if I remember rightly, the "stimulated" antlers were almost twice as heavy as the ordinary ones.

Twenty years or more previous to this my father carried out a similar experiment on much the same lines, and having the same results, with a stag caught as a two-year-old in his forests in Upper Austria, though in this instance the stag never got sufficiently tame to give him his liberty, and the increase or curtailing of stimulating food was done while he was in captivity. A number of castings of this stag make an interesting series, which is in my possession.

The third case, the one of which I was reminded, is perhaps not

quite so much to the point, for it was not an experiment in the sense
the others were, and it simply showed what good rich food will produce
in the way of antlers.   Most middle - aged travellers who visited
Vienna in the days of old will remember the superbly antlered red-
deer in the Prater grounds, on the banks of the Danube, near Vienna,
now long done away with.   As well as I remember the facts of the
case, these deer were chiefly fed on horse-chestnuts—the cheapest food
in that neighbourhood—and twenty-two and twenty-four pointers of
great massiveness were the result.   Lord Powerscourt, amongst the
many treasures of keen interest to the sportsman that fill Powerscourt,
possesses a set of early photographs of these giants of the Prater, and
he confirmed my hazier impressions as to the extraordinary size of
their antlers.

Mr. Cameron says " that these Continental experiences are obviously
out of court in this discussion, for the simple reason that Continental
sportsmen possess exactly what British deer-stalkers lack—the right
material to work upon ; in other words, a race of deer with an
inherited tendency to throw large antlers."   In another part of one
of his letters he insists, and with good right, that at one time the
German and Scotch deer roamed together over what was then one
Continent ; or, in other words, they were members of one and the
same family.   How, I should like to ask, do these two assertions,
together with the acknowledged deterioration of Scotch deer when
compared with German stags, fit in with the theory which he so
strenuously defends, that heads are entirely inherited, and that no
combination of climate, shelter, and food will turn a bad head into a
good one ?

The consternation with which " Horse-chestnut" regards my suggestion of feeding the stags during spring with this useful food is
rather amusing ; but he makes out the expense much worse than it
really is, and his argument that, because he can feed half-a-dozen deer
for a £5 note, it would cost him £500 to feed 600 deer, is, as I shall
show, very much at fault.   If he will take the trouble to refer to my
letter in the *Field* of 9th February, he will see that I distinctly stated
that £5 will purchase " enough of that food to put different antlers on
at least half-a-dozen of his *stags*."   Now, if ever " Horse-chestnut"
has watched a herd of deer being winter-fed, he surely must have
noticed that at any food appealing particularly to the taste of deer, as
horse-chestnuts do, and supplied only in limited quantities, only the
big stags get a look in, quite aside of the circumstance that the larger
stags at that time of the year keep a good deal together and apart

from the herd, so that as a matter of fact it is very easy to manage the distribution of this delicacy in the right quarter. In a herd of 600 deer there would not be more than fifty stags worth feeding for heads, and the cost would therefore be a trifle over £40 and not £500 !

To judge by the expressions used by one or two correspondents when referring to the importation of Continental deer into Scotland for freshening-up purposes, they seem severely predisposed against any such experiment being made. Their minds appear to have been made up there and then that such experiment would be folly ; but as they omit to give any grounds, good or bad, for such conclusion, one naturally cannot attach much weight to opinions that apparently arise only from an indistinctive dislike to anything foreign.

I do not by any means wish to be understood that I recommend a wholesale importation of Austrian or Hungarian deer, for, so far as I know, no such experiment has ever been made in Scotland, and the conditions, if not the climate, differ a good deal ; but I certainly think it would be worth while making a trial and letting the result tell its own tale. Contrary to commercial commodities, of which the British-made goods are always the best, I think the stag "Made in Germany" has continued to possess qualities which might with advantage be reimparted to his sea-bound Scotch brother, with whom he once roamed the same forest, and did battle for the mastership of the same herd.

In the *Field* of 30th March 1895 " Rika " writes :—

SIR—Judicious sportsmen who take scales and measuring-tape must see that even in Scotland a great deal can be done towards improvements, and in time even Mr. Gordon Cameron, who holds that Scottish antlers are by fate predestined to be small, and that there is no use trying against it, will be convinced. In parts of Germany a similar state of things prevailed some time ago until a few owners practically proved that quite unhoped-for results might be obtained by a little care and judicious treatment. Exact dates, weight, measurements, etc., I could obtain for Mr. Cameron if he wishes.

Now a few remarks in detail. Does not " Carn Dearg's " observation, that an early and mild spring improves horns, tend to corroborate my impressions as to the influence of good food pre-eminently in time of antler-shedding ? "Horse-chestnut" will find that the preservation of young plantations can be secured by the orthodox method of fencing until the trees are strong enough to withstand the nibbling of deer, and that chestnuts can be shipped to Leith or Glasgow

in any quantity, and at a low figure. I shall be glad to get him
addresses and prices if desired. I wrote of artificial feeding, not hand-
feeding, and the former, if done with care and knowledge of the habits
of deer, need not make them tamer than they are already. I myself
only feed them in winter, as stated in my former note, and give hay,
for their natural food is good and rich enough, winter excepted, and
contains enough horn-producing ingredients. The other kinds of
food I suggested were found useful by friends of mine in different
localities. Salt is only given in summer. Example of results: Stag,
clean weight, $43\frac{1}{4}$ stone; antler, $17\frac{1}{4}$ lbs.; length along curve, $45\frac{1}{2}$
inches; beam, 49 inches.

NOTE 4

To those who desire to try the Continental way of cooking
roe venison (it answers also for chamois) the following recipe
may be of use. The cleaned game, whether red, fallow, or roe-
deer, is hung for at least two days after it is shot before it is
skinned, the inside of the carcase being repeatedly wiped with
clean dry cloths; water or dampness being detrimental to it.
Then, after skinning it, it should be jointed; if it is a roebuck
the back should be left entire, though the shape of the haunches
will suffer, for the back is considered the best piece. The game
can then hang another couple of days, if the larder or cellar has
good ventilation and the weather is not too hot. It is then put
into a pickle made of half a pint of claret (*vin ordinaire*), one
pint of wine vinegar, and two pints of water, five crushed juniper
berries and five whole juniper berries, a few cloves, some thyme,
parsley, black peppercorns, a celery root, a few carrots, and an
onion (cut up), also a few slices of lemon. Boil this pickle for
half an hour, allow it to get quite cool, when it is ready to pour
over the venison in the pickling-tub. The meat should be
turned every four or five days, and if the venison is to be kept
long the pickle should be reboiled, to prevent it getting high.
When the venison is to be cooked, some of the vegetables are
to be taken from the pickle and placed with the meat in the
roasting-pan. The joint should be wiped and the thin film of
skin removed and the whole well larded. An hour before the
joint is done a pint of sour cream (not thick) should be poured
over the joint, which should be well basted till ready to serve.

Then take all the gravy and vegetables from the roasting-pan, pass through a sieve and pour over the meat prior to its being served. Should there be insufficient cream, a little gravy stock and flour may be added to what cream you have got.

Another recipe I received years ago from a great authority, viz. the former chef of the noted gourmet Marshal Canrobert. It differs from the one I have given as regards the strength of the pickle; only three-quarters of a pint of vinegar being used to four pints of water.

NOTE 5

For more than a century the gestation of the roe was one of the most hotly disputed problems of Natural History. The point in dispute centred itself upon the question whether the rut occurs in July or in November. At both these seasons the roebuck shows in a marked manner sexual impulses. Those who maintained that the November rut was the true one, seemed to have the strongest possible evidence on their side, for even their adversaries had to confess, that with the appliances then at the command of science, no trace of the ovum could be discovered in does killed before the middle of December. During the first half of the century many scientific men busied themselves with this problem, and then only did the true circumstances of the case become apparent. Among those who did most in clearing up the mystery may be mentioned Dr. Ziegler and Dr. Bischoff, Professor of Physiology at Heidelberg. At a Congress of Naturalists and Physiologists held at Bremen in 1843, where the recent discoveries were fully discussed by those eminently fitted for this duty, it was finally shown with scientific positiveness, that the true rut of the roe takes place in July and beginning of August, and that the ovum does not reach the uterus for several months, and that the first development of the embryo does not commence before the middle of December, but remains dormant for four and a half months. What the false November rut has to do with this highly singular physiological retardation was not shown; possibly it may have a quickening influence. Parturition occurs in forty weeks from the date of impregnation, one, or two, rarely three calves being the issue.

INDEX

Printed by R. & R. CLARK, LIMITED, Edinburgh.

OPINIONS OF THE ENGLISH PRESS

ON

MR. W. A. BAILLIE-GROHMAN'S

SEVERAL WORKS:

'*Tyrol and the Tyrolese,*' '*Gaddings with a Primitive People,*'
and '*Camps in the Rockies.*'

" We have read nothing of the kind that has struck us so much as this book of Mr. Grohman's. He has a bright, easy style. We can recommend the book as singularly readable from the first chapter to the last."—*The Saturday Review.*

" Mr. G. is so familiar with his subject, and he writes so well that it would be almost impossible for him to be anything but interesting."—*The British Quarterly Review.*

" Mr. G. is, above all, a sportsman. His style is always bright and picturesque, and the book is eminently readable."—*Westminster Review.*

" Mr. G. tells a story well, and writes like one who knows, not with the flimsy flippancy and off-handed judgment of the ordinary tourist."—*The New Quarterly Magazine.*

" His natural history notes seem to us admirable. The book deserves little but praise."—*The Academy.*

" A delightful book. Very few sportsmen, we fear, can write so delightfully as he can, for he is not only a sportsman with a considerable literary gift, but he has a keen sense of humour and a very happy way of expressing and communicating that sense on paper."—*The St. James's Gazette.*

" A prize ! A most fascinating book, which I could not lay down at meal times or at bedtime until I had unfortunately finished it. Full of most vivid pictures and good amusing and characteristic stories."—*Truth.*

" A book of rare interest and charm . . . such as the public seldom has the opportunity of reading, and indeed as a necessarily rare combination of circumstances can alone produce. A book of quite unusual charm."—*The Spectator.*

" The pictures could hardly be better chosen or better drawn. The writer has not only a thorough knowledge of the world he describes, but the power, too, which is very commonly wanting in the authors of such books, of knowing what to take and what to leave. A pleasanter or more entertaining book we have not seen for a long time. The book is thoroughly fresh and interesting."—*The Examiner.*

" This is a work of which it is hardly possible to speak in too flattering terms."—*Land and Water.*

" Turn where he may in this well-written volume the reader is sure to find entertainment. Mr. G. has written a capital book."—*Pall Mall Gazette.*

" A most delightful volume."—*Graphic.*

" A most interesting volume. Everything is vivid and forcible and fresh."—*The Field.*

"A perfect book of its kind. The charm is irresistible. A very bright, agreeable and interesting volume... which can be cordially recommended."— *Illustrated London News.*

"It is not often that a book has equal claims to the attention of the scientist and general reader."—*Scotsman.*

Of Mr. W. A. Baillie-Grohman's

CAMPS IN THE ROCKIES

The American literary journals express the following opinions:

"Among the legions of books on the Far West, we have found none so fresh, so full of the truth of its Alpine woods and peaks, and giving withal so fair and representative a view of frontier life, as Baillie-Grohman's 'Camps in the Rockies.'"—*The Nation.*

"His close observation and accurate statement of fact, given with a frankness and modesty free from all attempts at fine writing, carry the readers with him."—*New York Evening Post.*

"There has been no more entertaining and honest book written on the Far West than this of Mr. Baillie-Grohman's."—*Literary World.*

"An exceedingly bright book, as good reading as anything we have seen on our frontier life."—*Boston Advertiser.*

"It is, without any qualifying adjective, the best book of the kind we have ever seen."—*Boston Times.*

"One of the most delightful as well as truthful descriptions of Western out-door life that we have ever read."—*Inter-Ocean.*

"His narrative is an admirable book—full of delightful descriptions and accurate information."—*Philadelphia Press.*

"It is an honest book, too ; a record of interesting adventures, robust and full of good humour and good stories."—*New York World.*

"There is a freshness and a charm about his narration of scenes and circumstances that is very delightful. It is a very entertaining book, and on the whole very true to nature."—*Forest and Stream, New York.*

"It rarely happens that any work of this kind is at once so plain, honest, and truthful as this."—*The Post, Boston.*

"The book is one of the best that has appeared on such subjects."—*The Spirit of the Times, New York.*

"It is seldom one meets with a volume more replete with entertainment and information."—*Herald.*

"The best book of frontier life and sport."—*Philadelphia Bulletin.*

"One of the best books on Western travel and adventure that have yet appeared."—*Providence Journal.*

"One of the most delightful books conceivable."—*C. Ch. Standard.*

"Some of the stories are better than anything in Bret Harte's pages."— *Intelligencer.*

"The most noteworthy book of its kind."—*Chicago Advance.*

*** *Copies of* 'CAMPS IN THE ROCKIES' *may be obtained through any Bookseller, or from*

A. & C. BLACK, SOHO SQUARE, LONDON.

NEW NOVELS.

A. & C. BLACK, SOHO SQUARE, LONDON.

In One Volume, Fcap. 4to, containing 22 Page Illustrations, and 11 Diagrams
in the Text. Bound in Buckram, gilt top. Price 21s.

ARTISTIC AND SCIENTIFIC

TAXIDERMY AND MODELLING

A MANUAL OF INSTRUCTION IN THE METHODS OF PRESERVING
AND REPRODUCING THE CORRECT FORM OF ALL
NATURAL OBJECTS

INCLUDING A CHAPTER ON THE

MODELLING OF FOLIAGE

BY

MONTAGU BROWNE, F.G.S., F.Z.S., ETC.

CURATOR OF THE LEICESTER CORPORATION MUSEUM AND ART GALLERY
AUTHOR OF 'PRACTICAL TAXIDERMY,' 'THE VERTEBRATE ANIMALS
OF LEICESTERSHIRE AND RUTLAND,' ETC.

With 22 Full-page Illustrations and 11 Diagrams in Text

A. & C. BLACK, SOHO SQUARE, LONDON, W.

www.ingramcontent.com/pod-product-compliance
Lightning Source LLC
Chambersburg PA
CBHW032338280326
41935CB00008B/378